PAULA
MICHAEL
& BOB

everything you know is wrong

PAULA MICHAEL & BOB

everything you know is wrong

GERRY AGAR

MICHAEL O'MARA BOOKS LIMITED

First published in Great Britain in 2003 by
Michael O'Mara Books Limited
9 Lion Yard, Tremadoc Road
London SW4 7NQ

A CIP catalogue record for this book is available from the British Library.

ISBN 1-84317-024-8

3 5 7 9 10 8 6 4 2

Designed and typeset by Design 23

Colour plates sections designed by www.glensaville.com

Printed and bound in England by The Bath Press, Bath

'The unexamined life is not worth living.'
SOCRATES

It is to you, David Fennell, that I dedicate this book. The unsung hero who has worked tirelessly with me, without complaint, on every word, sentence, paragraph, of this book. Thank you for the light you have brought into my life, the peace into my heart and the harmony into our home. An incredible father to our two children, and loving stepfather, who has turned hurt into hope, mistrust into joy. You are indeed an amazing man, loved by all your friends, cherished by all your brothers and the pride and joy of your parents: but I think you'll agree you're going to have to work on your memory (Where are the bloody keys?).

author's acknowledgements

Tom, Sophie, Millie Loveday, Louis – my beloved children, thanks for all your patience.

Katerina, Aiden, Claudia, Alexander, Harry – my very special godchildren.

Michael O'Mara – my Wizard of Oz. Thank you for granting my wish and sending this book home.

To the denizens of the Principality of O'Mara – Rhian McKay, Helen Cumberbatch, Glen Saville, Ron Callow at Design 23, Judith Palmer – May the great Oz grant you the massive pay increases, large bowls of ice-cream and three months' holiday a year that you all deserve.

Gabrielle Mander and Karen Dolan – my new e-mail pen pals and editors most extraordinaire.

Among the many unmentioned friends and family who offered or would have helped at a moment's notice, the following were asked and came through with great generosity, giving time, emotional or material support without a second thought and without whom you would not be reading this now:

Mary Anne, Helen, Donna, Ken and Rosie, Simon and Amanda – whose daily vigil of unconditional love and support kept me going in the darkest moments.

Michael and Felicity Fennell – For all your love, support, kindness, help, generosity, forgiveness, understanding and for the inspired nurture of six sons; your eldest went home to God, but five remain, giving five very lucky girls, myself included, the very best of men.

Andrew and Christine Fennell – May your boat forever float and your tax account forever bloat.

Sue Morris – Aunt Zoo, thank you for staying involved
Becky Morris – for support and encouragement
Mary Rafter – you are loved
Liz Maxwell – keep up the good fight, sister
Sandra Buchanan – who knocked on the door until I awoke. I am forever indebted
Mia – my Polish mother, who put my heart back together
Suzi Streeter – for working tirelessly to mend bridges far and beyond the call of duty
Nick Agar – without whom I would not have taken this journey
Alice Maclaine – a spoonful of sugar…
Nigel Curtis – we have all been together before and no doubt it was just as fulfilling

CONTENTS

INTRODUCTION

The heroes of the day are the personalities who parade their professional and private lives across our TVs, newspapers and magazines. For a decade there was something indefinable about Paula Yates that caught the public imagination and held our attention even when she walked to the shops. In person her magnetism was palpable, her personality dazzling and her intellect unparalleled. When she met Michael Hutchence they were caught in the spotlight, and we were gripped by the plot turns of their volatile romance.

A fatal chemistry took them to the very extremes of human experience. While they seemed to inhabit a world of glamour, their insecurities were not so very different from the challenges facing every one of us. At first it seemed that the trappings of success would protect them from discomfort, instead it magnified their pain. It seems so easy to pop a harmless little pill, take a little drink and find all the problems melt away for a few blissful hours. But pill by pill, drop by drop, this solution became the problem in a vicious circle of ever-increasing complication and dosage. The symptoms of addiction escalated and they both descended into their own personal hells. But so might any one of us, in the same circumstances, from the same beginnings…yet their ends were as inevitable as the many alternative choices they might have made. Help is just a phone call away, in the right friend, the right counsellor or the right support group.

This is a story writ large, that plays out every day, in every town, in every country. The pressures of our technological, shiftless world seem to drive an ever-increasing number into the welcoming jaws of alcohol and chemical dependence. While we might feel helpless in the clutches of our chosen addictions, an industry of professionals reach out, only streets away, to help us beat the odds. There are no quick fixes – recovery is a lifetime's endeavour – but the effort is repaid tenfold. Paula and Michael did not find their way home, but perhaps they have not died in vain, if this book communicates where the easy road can lead if we don't heed the call.

GERRY AGAR,
AUGUST 2003

1 friends reunited

IN SEPTEMBER 1992 TOM, my first-born, was to start school. He was enrolled at Newton Prep, a school in Battersea, southwest London, which prided itself on an elite and gifted intake. But it was not with pride that I made the journey to deliver my angelic little three-year-old to his first ever day at school and his first ever day away from me.

As I took in the coloured bricks and tissue-paper-montage of my son's new classroom, I was pleasantly surprised to see another mother whom I recognized immediately: Paula Yates, with two of her children, Peaches and Pixie. As she bent to give Peaches a hug she pulled a theatrical, but nonetheless heartfelt, face that perfectly expressed the comic pathos of the room, and glanced in my direction. We had barely seen or spoken to one another in over ten years, so I wasn't particularly surprised when she detached almost instantly from our momentary connection and returned to the hugging of little arms around her neck.

Paula Yates and I first met in 1981, while I was on a night out with Jim Henson of *The Muppets* fame, for whose Henson Enterprises I then worked. I had seen her on previous occasions on the gig circuit but it would hardly have been cool to sidle up to this ultra-hip peroxide blonde and announce how I really enjoyed her column in *Record Mirror* with my croissants and cappuccino every week.

But it was against the backdrop of a far more sophisticated and mainstream scene that we first struck up conversation. The venue was a large house in Kensington, belonging to one of Jim's stockbroker friends.

I had slipped off to the sumptuous loo, I dare say to examine the excessive gloss and glitter on my face for any imperfections; this was, after all, the eighties. A lithe figure slipped through the door and joined me at the altar of Narcissus. I recognized her at once.

Paula immediately launched into conversation while, with a pastel pink painted nail, she checked her unfeasibly long black lashes. 'Last week one of these things fell in my boyfriend's coffee, while he was reading the paper,' she giggled, without turning towards me. 'I wondered where it went, and I was on my hands and knees, looking for it under the table, when he took a gulp and got the damn thing stuck half-way down his throat.' Her wry, surreal sense of humour was delivered in her eccentric voice, a curious mix of private-school elocution and lazy glottal stops, which was almost hypnotic. She introduced herself and we shook hands. Her grasp was firm.

On the afternoon that Tom started school I wasn't alone in my eagerness to be on time for collection, as some ten other mothers simultaneously screeched to a halt, left their cars and fell in step like latter-day suffragettes. As we lined up outside the classroom door, a breathless Paula, clutching Pixie in her arms, ran into the hallway. She joined us with an entirely ordinary air of hassle, that frenetic bustling associated with being a modern mum. I shot her a sideways glance and glimpsed her breathing in the smell of her little child's hair.

Paula was wearing ripped jeans, a coat two sizes too small for her, no make-up and she had tousled white hair. She looked natural, healthy and unpretentious. Had it not been for her white blonde hair, sparkling eyes and eccentric wardrobe, she would not have stood out even slightly from the rest of the mothers, and motherhood definitely suited her. She hardly looked a day older than when we had first met. That night she had looked stunning in a tulle frock with her enviable seventeen-inch waist. Even in those anything-goes days it took courage to wear such a flamboyant dress. It was like something Vivien Leigh would have worn in *Gone With The Wind*, though not quite floor-length. Paula was always more Vivienne Westwood than Malcolm McLaren. She bought her dresses in Oxford charity shops, in the days when her escorts were Classics scholars, and she was attending May Balls and debutante parties when not being seduced with Shelley and Byron. Those frocks became her trademark look later on.

She had always been more natural, much prettier and more petite in person than she appeared in the photos in glossy magazines. Her unusually china-blue eyes sparkled with mischief while managing to emanate a reassuring warmth, and her childlike openness had made me feel instantly protective towards her when we first met. I was flattered, too, when she admired my frock and complimented me on my figure. Looking at her own body, she had commented rather disconcertingly that her small breasts made fried eggs look sexy! We were still looking at her boobs when with a last glance in the mirror she asked, 'Are they all right?' 'Yes,' I replied. 'No,' she giggled at her deliberate ambiguity, 'my eyelashes!'

I smiled at the memory as I turned my attention to Peaches. From early childhood, Peaches was a walking Pears soap advertisement, with her red cherub lips and translucent skin. She was without doubt her mother's daughter and always made a glamorous entrance at school. This afternoon she instructed her mother to wait while she finished telling an audience of two teachers and a few children about her recent trip to Barbados. Paula watched her daughter drawing so much attention to herself with bashful pride, and waited with the rest of us for Peaches to finish her story.

'God, she looks like a precocious little tyke, doesn't she?' one of the mothers stage-whispered to another, as they turned to leave the gathering. The two women, typical of the parents who sent their children to private London prep schools, wearing sensible blue moccasins and blinkers, continued to confer in lowered tones. On the way back to the car park, they made little effort to hide their criticism. 'What, the daughter or the mother...?' came the catty reply. 'I know! She looks different in the flesh, without an army of make-up artists to paint her up, doesn't she?' 'Obviously doesn't look after herself. But then I suppose you would get like that, living with Bob Geldof, wouldn't you?' the friend replied. 'Yes, but you'd think she'd at least brush her hair before coming out.' 'I'm surprised it hasn't fallen out, with all that peroxide,' the first retorted.

Paula was doomed because she stood out and could not help it. Like her three-year-old daughter, Paula's talents and her effervescent and original personality were irrepressible – they were the reason that she was so unusually good on TV. But there would always be detractors, those who felt threatened or jealous, just as there would always be the fawners and flatterers. She could sometimes appear arrogant and reckless, but some would call that unselfconscious. That freedom of spirit was one of her most endearing and attractive features. In that autumn of 1992, I reflected that much had changed in the decade since I had last seen Paula. I had moved in 1983 to Clapham, which was now attracting the yuppies who pronounced it 'Claarm'. With their country casuals, Barbours and Volvos, they found my eccentric wardrobe a little hard to take, but their disapproval never really bothered me, as I was hardly angling for an invitation to the Christmas cocktail party – I was re-evaluating my life.

My marriage had broken up the previous year and my ex-husband was living in North London with his new girlfriend. To say that ours was not a civilized divorce would be grossly to understate the animosity that persisted between us at the time.

We separated in 1991 after four years, but I am proud of what we achieved in our short time together and I would not change a moment of it, not even the break-up. But life was very different now. There was no longer the security of a fat salary every month, and no more abundant help with raising a young family. I was on my own and I had everything to do. Miserable and hopeless, towards the end of my marriage I had decided to analyze what I perceived to be the problems in our relationship. A close girlfriend of mine introduced me to a highly successful PR executive. He was a kind man, surprisingly open about his own challenges and he recommended a therapist who specialized in addictions and co-dependency. He warned me that she was Sergeant-Major-tough, but I really wasn't prepared for her uncompromising directness in examining my problems and ignoring any mention of my husband's part in the

breakdown of our marriage. She insisted I attend Al-Anon groups –
Alcoholics Anonymous for the families of alcoholics and others addicted
to co-dependency. She focused exclusively on my problems – my *care-
taking* (looking after others to the exclusion of one's own needs) and my
co-dependency (the tendency of an unaddicted individual to care-take an
addict).

I stopped being outraged at the suggestion that there was anything
wrong with me and began to face the long list of issues that were emerging
in my sessions. Slowly I unravelled the mess within me 'one day at a time'
(a motto of the AA meetings) and I listened, with a knotting in my
stomach, to stories from other members in the group that mirrored mine.
When Tom started school, I began to suspect that my need to work was
conflicting with the children's need for my more regular attention,
particularly in the aftermath of the acrimonious divorce. So I took the
plunge and left my job in PR at McCloud & Company, working for
interior designer Kevin McCloud. In doing so, I had to trust that my ex-
husband would ensure the security of his erstwhile family. We were broke,
but the kids seemed happier and I was able to collect Tom every day,
enjoying the brief social exchanges that occurred each afternoon outside
the school.

Paula's life had changed, too, in the intervening years. The last time I
had seen her was at a party in a dingy basement flat in Primrose Hill, long
before it became a fashionable place to live. It was a typically crushed
house party, thumping out some percussive thrash through tired speakers.
As my punk boyfriend Steve and I made our way through the ruck of
young men, high on dope and poppers, I spotted Paula sitting on a low-
slung sofa, arms draped around a particularly sullen individual in the punk
mould (no pun intended).

As usual, the air was thick with the cloying sweetness of marijuana, and
I spotted the drug dealers in the crowd. Paula remembered me, and I was
flattered and relieved that among the mad throng there was a kindred
spirit. In complete contrast to the majority of partygoers, Paula remained
sober and politely refused a spliff, as well as the lude (Quaalude) my
boyfriend offered her, convinced as he was that she wouldn't turn it down,
given her punk-rock status. By this time she was co-presenting the cult TV
music show, *The Tube*, with Jools Holland. Paula stayed longer at this party
than at the smart function where we had first met – perhaps the mix of
raw London music talent was more her scene. She was with her boyfriend,
Bob Geldof, around whom she wrapped herself for most of the evening.

Actually, although I had never seen Paula partake of drink or drugs, she
wasn't entirely without vice. She was, I observed whenever our paths
crossed, an Olympic flirt. Paula flirted with everyone, male and female.
She was just playing and somehow everyone knew that, so no one took it

seriously. Had anyone responded to her provocative gestures, I think she would have squealed and been horribly embarrassed. It was far more likely that she intended to make others feel special than to test the water. But to me her position was always clear, albeit occluded behind an out-pouring of artful teasing familiarity – she was deeply in love with Bob and very open about her desire to be Mrs Geldof at the earliest opportunity. She even admitted to practising her new signature and leaving it about the house in the hope that Bob would be inspired to seize the moment with a romantic proposal.

———— ◆ ————

Paula rarely missed a lunchtime pick-up from Newton Prep. On the other hand, the sight of Bob at the school was a notable rarity. When the demands of her busy media career prevented Paula from attending, their devoted nanny, Anita, would cover the school run.

It was a few weeks after term started that Paula recognized me. We had politely acknowledged one another over the past few days and I imagined that our previous encounters had been forgotten in more than a decade of her incessant social functioning. Then things clicked into place and recognition lit Paula's face as we queued for the midday collection. 'I *thought* it was you, but I wasn't sure. Still as glamorous as ever,' she flattered. 'I didn't think you'd remember me, it's been yonks,' I replied. 'Yeah…a couple of world wars have probably been and gone… have they?' She patted the floor beside her, encouraging me to join her at the knee-level of all the other mums. 'Sorry I didn't click before, but I'm blind as a bat without my glasses,' she said, adding mischievously, 'I sat on them.' The doors of the classroom sprang open and Paula disappeared into a room of excited children with an enthusiastic shriek, gathering up Peaches into her arms. Looking back at me, she smiled, 'See you soon… got to dash,' and departed hurriedly, carrying Peaches out.

We continued to meet at school line-ups, plays and fundraisers. It was always a treat to see her and we got along quite spontaneously. Our chats were brief and light, with the natural guardedness of the early stages of friendship. We already shared common ground in poking harmless fun at the institutional starch around us, but I guessed she might be quietly wary of people's intentions. I was wary of getting too close – after all, I was beginning to accept that it was through my choice of glamorous and complex friends and partners that I found myself in uncomfortable situations.

Although the parents came to regard the Geldofs as part of the classroom furniture, the children drew regular praise. They stood out, not just for their extravagant wardrobes but for the star quality stamped clearly across their foreheads. Pixie, the youngest, was still in a pushchair and she attended the school later, but even then it was clear to see that she had inherited her parents' captivating qualities; even before she could speak she seemed to be telling the world, '*I'm different*'.

It was obvious that the children did not just arrive special – gallons of love had been poured into these remarkably bright and talented little individuals. Paula would burst with pride when anyone praised her girls; she was a mother besotted with her children and still very much in love with her husband.

The Geldofs had it all. Beyond the house in Chelsea, a country retreat, and the other trappings of money hard-earned and well-managed, they had a blissful marriage, three beautiful and unusual girls, with equally unusual names – Fifi Trixibelle, Peaches Honeyblossom and Little Pixie. They also had a nanny, Anita Debney, who was the kind of home help most people can only dream about. Bob had a knighthood for services to humanity, and, although he couldn't use his title, as he was an Irish national, they were nonetheless unofficially known as Sir Robert and Lady Geldof. She wrote magazine articles, had published several books and appeared daily on breakfast TV. Paula and Bob had accomplished so much and their potential remained unlimited.

The sight of well-known faces at Newton Prep kept the other parents' tongues wagging for only a few weeks. Everyone got used to the sight of pop star Simon Le Bon and his wife Yasmin, the fashion model; film star Britt Ekland; author Tessa Dahl; actor John Standing, and various MPs and lesser-known faces that people would point out to me. But somehow people didn't treat Paula and Bob with the same familiarity. There was something dauntingly unapproachable about this particular couple, not as far as Paula was concerned, but certainly about Bob. When Bob was not on his cell phone, which was rare, he maintained a rather intimidating aloofness. He never remembered that Paula had introduced us in those early punk days. She always excused him by saying that he lived for the bigger picture, small details didn't interest him. I thought he was one of the rudest men I had ever met, while she remained forever polite. Paula seemed carelessly oblivious to her surroundings. She had an unpredictable and bizarrely flamboyant wardrobe, sometimes with bare feet and at other times looking as if she was about to appear in a comic opera about Ascot, and she was always on the move, in a hurry.

While Bob's erratic manners could be deflected with quips and cheek, I found myself increasingly open with Paula. I never expected our acquaintance to extend outside 'these prison walls' as she called the school, so I was somewhat taken aback when, having not seen her for a week or so, she bounded up and gushed, 'Hi, how are you? I'm sooo sorry I haven't been in touch, but I've been away…'

For a moment, as she wrapped her arms around me in a glad-to-see-you embrace, I wondered if she had left her glasses at home again and muddled me up with someone else, but the only other people Paula talked to at the school were Yasmin and Simon Le Bon.

As we sat together on the steps outside the nursery department I began to realize how pleased I was to see her, even though my enthusiasm was a little more tempered than hers. We really did not have a history long or deep enough to warrant such a greeting but, more to the point, there had never been a suggestion, or hint even, that I expected her to get in touch. Paula's hand, with huge purple-stoned rings on three fingers, fumbled for a piece of paper and she scribbled down her number for me. As we parted she was insistent: 'Please call, I'll be at home all day. You will call me, won't you? Come over for a coffee.'

Strange and unlikely as it may have seemed, Paula wanted to get to know me again. Should I call her? So much of my life had changed. I no longer ran with the jet set. But here was this dazzling creature, beloved of the press and queen of all she surveyed, adamant that we become friends. I did eventually phone and she insisted that I come over that afternoon. As I replaced the receiver I sat in my kitchen giggling to myself. She had obviously expected me to know where she lived for she had given me no address, and I didn't have a clue.

Paula's home in Redburn Street in London's Chelsea was immaculate. Her children were polite, ate carrots and didn't watch TV, and she was disarmingly unassuming. We sat in the opulence of her sitting room with its voluptuous plum curtains, red and blue tartan carpet, deep red walls, a gallery of family pictures, and shelves lined with Enid Blyton books and fairy lights. Through the long afternoon of reminiscing and laughter, we got to know each other beyond our schoolyard banter to the childhood, life-story phase of the relationship. What unfolded was a series of incredible parallels in our lives. It was like a meeting of long lost sisters.

At the time, Bob and Paula were the toast of media town. Against thirty rival bids, they had won a £10-million contract for Channel 4's new morning show with their proposal, *The Big Breakfast*. Though Planet 24, the production company Bob owned, would produce the show, the press focused exclusively on the couple who had masterminded the format and who would also present it. It launched on 28 September 1992 in three converted cottages by a canal in Bow, East London, and was well under way by the time Paula and I reconnected.

'When I formatted *The Big Breakfast* with Bob,' she told me, 'I thought the team realized that when I wrote "in my bed" I meant "in my bedroom". I wanted my interviewees to be brought to me, where I could reach over for my notes, yawn a little, ask a few poignant, earth-shattering questions and go back to sleep. It was all a little bit of a shock to find out

I would have to get up at four o'clock in the morning!' But she loved the idea that it would be set in a house; in fact much of the pilot show was shot in their house, and Paula contributed many of the innovative ideas that made *The Big Breakfast* format work so well. When Bob and Paula discussed new slots for the show, the ease and rapidity with which she reeled off suggestions was incredibly impressive. But until I got to know her better, I had no idea quite how much Paula did, or quite how accomplished and clever she was. I knew about *The Tube* – at the time her name was still synonymous with this off-beat music show. In 1982 *The Tube* had launched Paula straight off Bob's arm and right into big-time celebrity. Mick Jagger called it 'the best Rock review ever' and acts queued to appear on it – everyone who was anyone, or wanted to be. It was zeitgeist TV, one of those sleeper hits that bubbles up from the underground to achieve cult status, without ever quite losing its integrity. Paula and her co-host Jools Holland were the funkiest presenters of the time and there was nothing else on TV to match the chemistry between them, until the *X-Files* came along.

Then there was Paula's coffee-table book, *Rock Stars In Their Underpants,* for which she had taken all the pictures herself, never having held a camera before – Andy Warhol had described it as 'the greatest piece of art in the last decade' and requested a signed copy which he 'would treasure for ever'.

Paula appeared in a string of commercials, appearing as herself for Ford and for Paul Masson non-alcoholic wine, alongside Oliver Reed. She was a natural choice for magazine covers, with her perfect androgynous looks, white hair and intense eyes; what's more, they could write something interesting about her too, or she could write it herself, which was more than could be said for most cover girls. Besides this, Paula had had several other books published, and was working on more. She said that she sometimes got up at 3am to write before she left for the studio. There were regular magazine articles and columns, photo shoots, and all manner of other engagements that she managed to fit around the dedicated care of her children.

But she swore that, left to her own devices, she would have been blissfully content to stay at home. In fact, it was Bob who had always encouraged her to have a career. It was curious that she pushed the fluffy side of herself so prominently. Contrary to the image she portrayed as a social butterfly, and 'It' girl about town, always out at this première and that opening, she was a voracious reader who preferred an early night in with a book. Paula was quite ambivalent about her television career. Though it appeared that she courted controversy and loved the limelight, it became quite clear that she only did it for the money.

She had a great wit and a razor-sharp intellect. It would seem Paula had initially inspired Bob's *Band Aid* campaign. In October 1984, she and Bob were sitting together watching the news, when Michael Buerk's report on Ethiopia filled the screen, with its harrowing images of skeletal bodies and mothers trying desperately to feed their babies from wasted breasts. The scenes of women watching helplessly as their babies died in the dust rocked her to the core. Neither of us was surprised to find out that we both went to our children's bedrooms straight after the news to check that they were all right.

The day after the report Paula stuck a notice on her fridge and asked everyone who came to the house to donate £5 to the victims of the famine. Bob decided to help the cause by calling in favours from all his friends to record a song and donate the proceeds to famine relief. The record 'Do They Know It's Christmas?' generated far more than the £70,000 they were hoping for. Eight million pounds were donated to Ethiopia, and until the death of Diana, Princess of Wales, when Elton John's 'Candle in the Wind 97' was released, it was the biggest selling record of all time.

Stuck to the fridge now was a picture of Michael Hutchence. I wondered why Paula had chosen this particular smouldering, dishevelled young rock star to occupy such a valuable space. Other pictures of her with pop personalities were dotted around the house. None was framed – the frames were reserved for family pictures – but a single row of tiny twinkling multi-coloured lights surrounded the photo of Michael Hutchence.

The crush had developed after she interviewed Hutchence, the lead singer of Australian band INXS, for *The Tube* in 1985. When Paula had been told about his imminent appearance on the show she was not impressed – INXS was a band she knew little about and she called them the 'Rolling Stone Wannabes' to emphasize her point. Her protests were ignored and when she finally met the shy Australian in the studio bar, her attitude changed. She went weak at the knees. 'He made me feel quite feeble,' she told me later.

———— ◆ ————

Through the autumn of 1992, Paula and I became closer. We had enormous fun together, with our complementary eccentricities and shared sense of humour. I was the straight guy to her off-the-wallness, but there was something more to the friendship that both of us realized but never articulated. It became clear that we provided an outlet for frustrations for one another that perhaps had no other form of release.

I was waiting in a coffee shop on the King's Road in London, the famous street that had been the scene first of the Swinging 60s and then the 70s Punk Rock revolution. Now the *avant-garde* stores had been replaced by the insipid uniformity of middle England's retail chains. Paula was already thirty minutes late, but punctuality was not one of her strong points and a total no-show was a distinct possibility. She had let me down once before and the frustration stayed with me, not least because I really relished our snatched hours together. On this occasion, and to my relief, I spotted the familiar blonde bob, just visible weaving through the bargain hunters of the 1993 January sales. Typically, she was underdressed for that time of the year, and all eyes turned to follow her flamboyant entrance.

She had a magnetic effect on the general public, but was apparently oblivious to the craning necks and hushed tones. 'Sorreee, I'm crap at timekeeping, but this time I really do have an alibi.' I could tell by the tone of her voice and her gleeful smile that my patience was to be rewarded with Paula's best entertainment, peppered as always with gross exaggeration and probably all-out fabrication. She was livelier than ever before. She was frequently light and joyful, but was often quietly reflective, and there was sometimes a tone of depression in her conversation. 'I've been fucking two men called Colin!' she exclaimed. 'Blimey, one Colin would be bad enough,' I replied, encouraging her to delve further into her imagination. Her stories always opened with an outrageous or barely credible announcement and part of the sport for me was wondering what real events had inspired the tale.

'Ever since I came back from Faversham I've been stalked by a disgusting hack. He was waiting for me outside the studio for hours,' Paula replied. 'A ludicrous story is being touted around the illustrious desks of Fleet Street about two brothers called Colin, who I am supposed to have slept with.' 'Who's going to believe a story like that?' I asked sympathetically. 'In this business, slander is a stubborn stain. But if it wasn't for Bob's total moratorium on me speaking to the press, I would be tempted to announce the imminent arrival of a sprog named Colin, after the fathers, whether it's a boy or girl.' 'Golden rule number one,' she continued, 'the Geldofs do not reward the press by replying to their lies. Anyway, even if I had tried I wouldn't have got a word in edgeways. It's like the Spanish Inquisition when they accost you. "Did you sleep with all your brothers and sisters and the dog? If you deny it, we'll pull out all your fingernails and if you sign away all your rights to a fair trial, we might consider a painless execution,"' she mimicked. 'I eventually escaped from his lunatic questions, but not before he shouted after me, "Are you pregnant?" Have you heard of anything more farcical? It's like something out of the *National Inquirer. ALIENS CLONED MY BABY*. I mean, who in their right minds would fuck someone called Colin anyway?' Paula grimaced.

We laughed, partly at the story and partly at her creativity. It was the kind of game you play when the outside world is banished for the moment. Bob's attitude to treat the tabloid tittle-tattle like tomorrow's fish and chip paper was laudable, but it was clear that, although Paula could laugh at the press intrusions, they also got to her. During the course of the conversation it became clear, too, that for all her artful humour, she was disturbed by other issues lurking just below the surface of her well-practised cover-up routine.

Half-jokingly, she told me she was having a midlife crisis. 'It's the earliest midlife crisis I've ever heard of. You're only thirty-four!' I said. 'Maybe', she replied, 'but it's out to pasture the moment you've blown out thirty candles in this business, and believe me, if you don't watch it, everyone's forgotten your name by the time you're forty.' 'Not if you keep screwing Colins in front of the tabloids. Come on, Paula, I think you're being a little melodramatic,' I chided. 'You look great and it's rubbish about the papers. Most of the time they're extremely flattering; I saw a piece recently where they described you as a British intellectual Marilyn Monroe.' 'And they put her out to pasture for good well before *her* fortieth, didn't they?' she countered.

Paula was very proud of *The Big Breakfast* but neither she nor Bob was entirely happy with the format of her slot. 'I need to get back to my writing,' she told me. I knew she was capable of a far more heavyweight role; lounging semi-naked across a bed, with gold pomegranates stapled to the headboard, was far more suited to someone a good ten years younger. Judging how far to go and how honest to be, I took the opportunity to launch into what I hoped would be an inspiring appraisal of her career prospects.

I told her that she was still absolutely *dazzling,* but I suggested that she revel in her age, changing with it and *enjoying* the changes. She was not the only one growing older, her fan base was moving at the same rate – all those ageing *Tube* fanatics were settling down with their ambient music and young families, but to them she would always have the edge she traded on. If she could only transcend this self-defeating mood, she could turn herself into an icon of the times. Who knows? She could find herself presenting the political commentary show, *Newsnight,* by the time she was forty-five, and have a bloody good time getting there too.

'Do you think you could replay all that for Bob? He refuses to see me as a grown woman at all,' she replied. Though her tone was light, there was a weariness when she talked about Bob and their marriage. From what she was saying, he led an entirely separate life to the rest of his family. There was a standing joke on *The Big Breakfast* that he could not get up in the morning and was seldom available for his own programme, which went out live. When he did conduct an interview, it was always pre-recorded. Paula confirmed that he rarely rose before midday, when she had sometimes already been up for nine hours. She liked to write in the peace of the early morning and knew the milkman by name.

In the afternoon, Bob would haunt the coffee shops on the King's Road, networking on his mobile. *The Big Breakfast* was not an instant success and Planet 24 was a young company. As the front man he had plenty of deals to do and was always trying to revive the success he had found with his music in the 80s. His last successful single with the Boomtown Rats had been in 1982. Since then he had recorded several albums, none of which raised more than a respectful ripple from the music press. The upshot was that the couple saw little of each other and Bob guarded his freedom jealously.

As Paula told it, Bob was in charge, the king of his domain, while Paula played the demure wife, meeting all his and the children's needs. I don't think I can recollect one time that I saw them walk side-by-side. Bob was always charging ahead while Paula walked a good few feet behind him with the girls. Every night, Paula said, she would collapse exhausted in front of the TV and fall straight to sleep. She had to be in bed by eight for her early start; Bob would be getting ready to go out networking at a gig or party. A scenario not so very far removed from those of the evenings of a billion couples across the developed world, but Paula was starting to wonder how she had arrived here. It was not in her nature willingly to let her life slide quietly down the back of the sofa with the remote control.

When I suggested that perhaps she and Bob should seek counselling, she said: 'You must be joking, a bunch of Indian squaws on heat couldn't drag him to therapy – he despises all that.' Paula looked wistfully away, then announced briskly: 'I'd better get back... I promised the girls.' She always ended our conversations with this line. Her children were her refuge and in her own unique way she always put them first.

She pulled out her purse from the wicker basket covered in colourful plastic flowers that she carried everywhere and went to pay the bill. Paula was always concerned about my continuing struggles with money, offering on a few occasions to help out, which I always declined. 'You're so brave,' she would say. 'I'm not sure I could cope.'

For the next three or four months, conversations like this cropped up with increasing regularity but the course of the argument remained just as circular. She was stuck in a loop, aware of the problems, resigned to their continuing and averse to the solutions. 'When you left your ex did you get very lonely?' Paula asked me one day. 'It was lonely,' I said. 'I was so unhappy I became rather neurotic and I lost most of the friends we had shared together. Still, at least I know the few that stuck by me are true.' It was then that Paula said, 'It's just that I'm terrified of being alone...'

On 19 February 1993, I held a party for my daughter Sophie's third birthday. Paula arrived with her two younger daughters, Peaches and Pixie. The girls looked wonderful in their matching Victorian rose-patterned frilly dresses, but Paula looked very sad. Bob was away at the time, so I put her mood down to the fact that she was probably missing him.

A mutual friend had the longest chat with Paula. At one point she wrapped her arms around my sad friend's shoulders while Paula's head drooped towards the floor. Later another friend commented on Paula's detachment from her surroundings and said that she had immediately recognized the signs of depression. Back at my house after the party, Paula told me that she thought she was going mad. She had been having a recurring dream that always left her drained the next day, and she was beginning to feel frightened about going to bed. But she needed her sleep because of her early morning start.

She dreamed she was stuck in a box as the lid closed over the top, trapping her inside with no air. Paula was convinced that the nightmare was connected with her childhood and I listened aghast as she told me that her father often kept her in a cardboard orange box at his feet, sometimes well into the night, as he played his Wurlitzer organ. She lived in fear of that box and was only grateful that, in reality, it had not had a lid on it. When Paula had regained some composure, I told her of my own strange and lonely upbringing in my grandparents' cold Dickensian house.

Paula nodded in sympathy. Tears were running down her face. It was the first time I had seen her cry and it took all my strength to hold my own emotions in check when she went on to tell me that in her dreams she would feel a rising tide of panic until she awoke with a start, dripping with sweat. Petrified and unable to fathom the source of her anxiety, Paula decided to see her doctor. He gave her two options: Prozac or therapy. She had a strong aversion to prescribed drugs, particularly anti-depressants, having spent years with her father almost permanently dependent on lithium. So, she told me, she had embarked on a course of therapy.

2 daddy dearest

AT 4AM ON GOOD FRIDAY, 9 April 1993, Paula's father Jess Yates died of a stroke, aged seventy-four. His live-in girlfriend Serena was at the hospital with him when he died.

It was at a school ballet demonstration that I first realized something had happened. Paula looked really upset; Bob had his arm round her as they watched the dancers and was constantly attentive to his wife, an unusually public display of affection for him. Paula later told me the news, and said of her father: 'I hope he knew I really loved him.' Since an early age she had harboured ambivalent feelings towards him. 'I hated my father and then we made up,' she said solemnly. 'As a child I obsessed about my beautifully fragrant mother, and fantasized about some glamorous man being my real father. I just didn't know how ill my father was at the time – how could a small child understand? – but I did later.'

Over several conversations, Paula told me about her parents and her eccentric childhood as she tried to make sense of her grief. Jess had begun his career in show business working as a successful film producer, Paula proudly recalled. He had been involved with the early James Bond films and produced several biblical epics with Victor Mature in the lead roles. When he was thirty-five years old he met and fell in love with Paula's mother when he was asked to judge a beauty contest in which the nineteen-year-old Elaine Smith was competing. Elaine, who adopted the stage name Heller Toren, had been one of the legendary Bluebell girls with the characteristic six-foot stature of the troupe. She had vibrant red hair and was startlingly intelligent. She was everything Jess Yates yearned for in a woman.

It was a typical celebrity marriage, doomed before the confetti fully fluttered to the ground. If Heller dreamed that marriage to Jess would bring an entrée to a wider stage and celluloid stardom she was to be disappointed. Jess gave up show business shortly after the wedding. He set off with his bride – and his manic depression – to run a vast hotel he had bought in a village near Llandudno in North Wales.

At twenty years old, Heller grappled most unsuccessfully with her new job as manageress, chief barmaid and bottle-washer. Neglectful and seriously depressed, Jess left his struggling spouse to run the show, while he, inspired by lithium, congratulated himself on his latest career move by 'playing Wagner till four o'clock in the morning on his treasured Wurlitzer organ'.

Paula's arrival did nothing to lighten her father's darkness, nor draw the couple closer together. With her mother frequently absent in pursuit of film stardom and finding herself alone with her doped-up father, the little girl withdrew to the cottage in the grounds. Paula's haven was littered with copies of *Life* (for which Jess had been a photographer), issues of *Vogue* from the 1930s and the *Saturday Evening Post* from the 40s and 50s. She found solace in the anodyne images of American dream families; these were the fantasies to which she escaped, images of what she imagined life must be like in every other family but her own.

Paula's withdrawal from reality intensified at five when she was teased and bullied at the local school. Jess Yates's lithium dose was increased and Paula's mother was increasingly absent. Jess reacted by obsessing over his daughter's safety and wellbeing, for fear of losing the last member of his dwindling family and in a distorted attempt to replace the motherly love she had lost. Thus Paula was installed, for safety, in the orange box next to the pedals of his organ. There she would sit patiently for hours, grateful that no one at school could see her. It was only when her mother returned that the orange box went into storage. Paula would 'keep vigil outside Heller's bedroom door, to ensure she would not slip away again'.

Paula wrote 'I hate Daddy' over and over on pieces of paper and then destroyed the evidence. Pining for her adored mother's return, she refused to eat. At the age of eight she was a practising anorexic, finally becoming so ill that she was hospitalized. To Paula's delight and relief her admittance brought her mother tearing back from London. Heller's maternal instincts eventually triumphed over her desire to be an actress and she returned to Wales to look after her daughter who, in her absence, had steadily become weirder and weirder. Reunited with her mother, Paula was in seventh heaven.

By 1970, things had taken a turn for the better. Jess's illness had become more manageable as he became an executive and star with Yorkshire Television, producing and presenting shows like *Junior Showtime* and the legendary *Stars on Sunday*. This ground-breaking show was built around the nation's favourite hymns, sung by the stars of the title and linked by Jess 'the Bishop' Yates at the organ, reading viewers' requests in a sanctimonious tone.

This on-screen persona couldn't have been further from the truth, as he was, as they say, very 'popular with the ladies'. It was the perceived hypocrisy of his role that led to his tabloid downfall some years later when the *News of the World* broke the scandal that Jess Yates had been spotted holidaying with a showgirl thirty years his junior. Jess was convinced that his loathed long-time rival, fellow TV executive and presenter of *Opportunity Knocks*, Hughie Green, had tipped off the papers. Whether

Hughie Green had exposed Jess to the press or not, the subsequent tabloid furore ruined Jess's television career. He did, however, live happily with his showgirl for nine years, although he never worked again.

While Jess built and lost his career in television, Paula and her mother decamped first to Malta and then Majorca, where, according to Paula's 1995 autobiography, they lived a bohemian life punctuated by Heller's real-life romances and the publication of her bodice-ripping novels. Paula and her father drew further and further apart as her parents' separation lengthened, culminating in the inevitable divorce. In the meantime, at the age of fifteen Paula was sent to Oxford to study for three 'A' levels in a sixth-form college. She passed the exams effortlessly.

Her father still had influence in show business circles and through a contact of his, Paula got a job at Thames Television in London, then moved on to cleaning for wealthy bachelors. By night she would haunt the capital's punk clubs. She first met Bob at a party held for the Boomtown Rats and was instantly smitten. Despite the fact that she was wearing a white wedding dress on that occasion, Bob did not remember her. However, when she turned up at his tour promoter's office to collect some tickets for a Rats' gig, he immediately asked her if she wanted to sit on his knee. She pursued him relentlessly, earning the nickname 'the Limpet' from his fellow band members for her tenacity. Eventually Bob accepted that she was a permanent fixture in his life and they were inseparable for eighteen years.

By the time we had become friends, I would never have guessed that Paula had ever had a difficult relationship with her father. An interesting reversal had occurred in her affections and this, Paula said, had happened when she gave birth to Fifi. All through her childhood years and well into adulthood, she had idolized her film-star mother, yearning for her when she was gone, clinging to her when she returned. When Paula looked at her newborn baby, she simply could not understand how a mother could leave her child behind. Now she blamed her mother for her years of pain.

Her father had come out smelling of roses. His antics with the orange box were forgiven, so too was his obsessive and eccentric behaviour. When Paula now spoke of her father, it was always with incredible pride. She told me that her last visit home had all but completely healed any remaining wounds and she was delighted that he had made the house where she had grown up a shrine to her and her children. All around the walls and on every surface there were pictures of her, Bob and the girls, their wedding day when Jess played the organ, and all her magazine covers. 'He was proud of me in the end, I at least know that,' she smiled. 'The more my father and I got to know one another again, the more we both realized how much we were alike, with the same sense of humour; we were so in tune that we were able to finish off each other's sentences.'

For the past two years their relationship had blossomed and Paula described it as a close friendship in which there were no secrets. In the weeks that followed his death, she talked often of her dad and how fond she was of him, how funny he was, how much he swore. It was obvious that Bob was affected by Jess's passing and Paula told me that he was being a tower of strength. 'My dad loved Bob,' she said, explaining that they had a very similar sense of humour and a mutual delight in the liberal use of profanity. They also shared a deep love for Paula and supported one another's roles in her life. Bob in turn had always liked her father and became very fond of the old man over the years. Jess was wonderfully eccentric, but clever, articulate and amusing, and these were all qualities that inspired Bob. But Bob and Jess shared more characteristics than colourful language and a sense of humour; both were strong, domineering men, with a need to control.

Bob's mother had died when he was seven and his father was often away, so he was brought up by his two sisters. Paula always felt that she and Bob were drawn together through their strange childhood experiences – she wanted a 'perfect family and he wanted a real home'.

Both Bob and wonder-nanny Anita had worked hard over the years to heal the rift between Paula and her parents, maintaining and encouraging her contact with them. Paula always credited Bob for her reunion with her father and Anita was diligent in sending letters and photos, and encouraging the girls to write to their grandparents. Anita was a keen amateur photographer and most of the photos that Jess had on display were her work. Jess, too, had actively sought to rekindle a connection with his daughter and he adored the girls.

The flamboyance and eccentricity of Paula's childhood could have contributed to her own eclectic tastes in fashion, and the austerity of her childhood home, as she described it, was in sharp contrast to the opulence and comfort of the family home she had created. Paula's devotion to and constancy with her girls was also very different from the model of motherhood that she had experienced in childhood, and yet she shared so much in terms of her own talents and ambition with her glamorous parents. She was reaching a crucial stage in her life – little wonder that she had become confused and depressed.

Paula was now convinced that the recurring box dreams had been some kind of a premonition of Jess's death. These dreams had driven her to look for answers in therapy, and ultimately the therapy had contributed to mending ancient rifts with her father, just in time to say goodbye.

———— ◆ ————

Jess Yates's funeral was a quiet family affair. Only two mourners seemed out of place there – a twenty-two–year-old girl standing with an older, unknown gentleman. Periodically Bob stretched an arm round the young girl as she wept. This was Serena Daroubakhsh, Jess's girlfriend of four years.

She and Jess had met when she was eleven and Jess was dating her mother. Serena claimed that by the time she was twelve she would slip into bed with Jess for a platonic cuddle, as he was a naturally tactile man. She claimed that they had shared a bed since she was fifteen, though they did not consummate their relationship until a year later, when she had conveniently reached the age of consent. But the way Serena tells it, this was not a relationship predicated on the physical union – it was a tender and romantic companionship.

Jess and Serena went to visit the Geldofs in London, four years before he died. Unsurprisingly, Serena had been apprehensive about meeting Jess's daughter but, to her relief, the visit could not have gone better. Serena said of Paula, 'I felt like a member of the family. Paula has a great deal of charm and the ability to make you feel you are the most interesting person she has ever met – I'm sure she gets that from her father.' Paula put them up in Fifi's room, together in a double bed, and Serena felt entirely accepted as Jess's partner. Bob, too, went out of his way to make Serena feel comfortable and she adored him. When Serena left with Jess, Paula gave her a 'fond' kiss.

In Paula's autobiography Serena becomes a 'strange nineteen-year-old girl, who just arrived in the pouring rain' who blackmails Jess to let her stay. Serena then takes over his life, tidying the house and generally inveigling her way into his affections. In Paula's version, Jess 'who was very honest with [Paula] about his sex life…' swore that there was no relationship, physical or otherwise.

After Jess died, Serena claimed that she spoke with Paula every day, sometimes twice a day. Though there was little consolation they could offer one another, their contact seemed appropriate to the real grief they both felt. They would talk about family things, reminiscing. I don't remember Paula mentioning this; I only remember the aftermath of the funeral.

But as the funeral approached, the tide turned for Serena. Paula told me that the family wanted to hide Serena away, scared that the press would pick up on the story and carry on where they had left off from the Jess Yates 'showgirl' scandal. Serena received a visit from Jess's brother Edward. In her own words she described how 'He said that they wanted a family funeral which didn't include me. They didn't want me there because I would stick out. It would be embarrassing for me, there as the "grieving widow." She wanted to go however and was chaperoned by her father so that she did not stand out so obviously.

The next morning the tide had gone out completely. Paula had never considered the possibility that Serena might feel she had any right to remain in a house that had been her happy home for over a quarter of her young life. Considering Paula's public condemnation of her childhood and her parents, Serena never guessed that Paula might place any sentimental value on the estate. But she didn't reckon on Paula's head for business. To be fair, it was a stance that she had perhaps been forced to adopt for the maintenance of her family. And Paula did now place emotional value on the house in which she had grown up, the home that now symbolized her revised childhood with a father she had elevated to the pedestal left vacant by her mother.

Serena received a letter from Paula's solicitors in which was stated: 'It is not accepted that you have any claim on the estate or any interest or right to occupy the property. At no time has our client or her uncle considered that you would be a benefactor of the estate or entitled to any inheritance... Nor is it accepted that you were supported by the deceased.' Serena, whose father was a 'wealthy landowner', consulted a solicitor and challenged Paula to a fight for her father's house and possessions. On top of all this, Serena sold her story to the newspapers for a tidy sum and allowed the Welsh manor to deteriorate. I know Paula was furious about Serena's challenge for the house, intensified ten-fold by Serena's eligibility for legal aid. Paula could not get her hands on any of the contents of the house, as Jess had not made a will. She was incensed that she had to pay thousands of pounds to pursue a stake in the estate. Paula's steeliness came as quite a shock at the time. She seemed to be so serene that nothing could perturb her peace of mind. It was almost as if she was above losing her cool. But in her efforts to stake her claim on her father's estate, she demonstrated an ability to turn stone-cold and cast any who opposed her wishes as the enemy.

Her hackles were raised still further by Bob's attitude. It was Bob who had put his foot down and insisted that Serena be allowed to attend the funeral. He impressed me with his emotional support for Serena in the face of his wife's indignation. For one reason or another, Serena received the attentions of a compassionate Bob; Paula said he had bought into her false timidity. Whether he saw her as a cause or recognized her vulnerability, it's impossible to say, but here it seemed that their roles had reversed for a moment, Paula becoming controlling and uncompromising, while Bob supplied the care and understanding. Paula said it was another example of Bob's lack of concern for her sensitivities, concentrating as usual on everyone else's needs.

Paula's therapy got her through the dark period following her father's death, but it had released more than she had bargained for. She sacked two therapists in a row because they cut too close to the bone. She did not like the talk of co-dependence at all, with all its rules and judgements; after all, she had only started therapy to help her unravel a dream. In the end she settled for the gentler approach of a woman in Harley Street, and together they were working through the memories of her childhood, her parents and all the confused emotions that these issues evoked. By turns she found the process fascinating and frightening. It answered some of her questions and raised others. But she was clearly inspired, and optimistic that the big emotional dips of the past year were being smoothed out.

'I have to chant this funny sentence first thing in the morning when I wake up,' Paula told me. '"I am not a bad person, I am not a bad person." The other morning Bob, half asleep, repeated, "I am not a bad person", to which I said, "No, you bloody idiot, it's me that's in therapy, remember, there's nothing wrong with you – God's perfect."'

Through the summer Paula and I saw very little of one another. She had been abroad on holiday and at her home in Kent. She had started a biography of Jess six months before he died. The research had awakened renewed pride in him but, even several months later, she was finding it difficult to continue – she told me she kept seeing her father in the street. She mentioned that Lew Grade (Head of ATV) wanted to do a documentary on Jess's life just before he died and she was considering producing the project herself. But she had other book projects on the go, her therapy had kept her optimistic, so she was surprisingly buoyant.

The contact we did have was mainly by telephone. My own life had been difficult around that time. Paula's calls were characteristically humorous, but I remember apologizing for my own lack of spunk and she chastised me for not telling her sooner about what I was going through. I thanked her for the occasional bouquet of flowers that appeared at the door.

——— ◆ ———

One Sunday evening that autumn, I received a call from my naughty and complicated friend. There was nothing quite like an upbeat Paula on the end of my telephone to ease the 'Ouch' in my life. 'The "Owie" has been well and truly stroked to sleep today,' Paula announced triumphantly.

We had nicknamed our stretches of melancholy: Paula's was the 'Owie', mine was the 'Ouch'. 'I've just spent a thoroughly thrilling afternoon with Rupert Everett on my bed,' Paula chuckled. 'Perhaps you could loan him to me,' I groaned. 'Our legs entwined like Virginia creeper stalks as we fed each another Fifi's gooey fudge cake, finished off with Rupert quoting Byron,' she teased.

Bob had disappeared again, Paula said, on a mission to try to revive his flagging music career. 'Bob utterly loathes Rupert, since he suspects I had an affair with him,' said Paula. Paula had told me about Rupert's first appearance in her life in the early 1980s. It could not have been more perfectly timed. Bob was away a lot then too, on tour mainly, and he was not very telephone-friendly to his then girlfriend. Meanwhile Rupert was genteel, warm, sensitive and very romantic. He made Paula feel special, interesting, and wanted again.

Rupert had apparently announced that Paula was the only woman he had ever fallen in love with. 'I cherished him,' said Paula. 'Enough to think very seriously about leaving Bob. Going out with a rock star was a bit like living with a long-distance lorry driver,' she said. 'Did Rupert really ask you to marry him?' I asked. Paula laughingly replied, 'I was pretty sure it was a proposal at the time, though he was treading the boards, so it was difficult to gauge whether he was in character or in Rupert. I can remember through the fog of the drama, a lot of getting down on one knee to re-enact Shakespeare's premier love scenes.'

Paula and I giggled together at the thought of poor Rupert's rehearsal for his next play being misconstrued.

———— ◆ ————

In late October 1993 Paula and I were sitting in Quaglinos, Terence Conran's cavernous restaurant in the West End of London. Paula was taking me out for a treat, as she called it, and a treat it was, as neither of us was a regular reveller: Paula was always concerned that a late night would interfere with her four o'clock rising. That evening she ordered three green leaves and a couple of tomatoes, topped off with a sprig of garnish that justified the exclusive price. Her diet of salad and mineral water was clearly how she maintained her perfect figure.

'Forcing me to drink an entire bottle of champagne myself is unthinkably selfish of you,' I joked, feeling like a hardened alcoholic compared with her total abstinence. I was always incredibly impressed by Paula's discipline around alcohol and drugs. Her iron resolve to touch no stimulants was noteworthy, particularly as she had spent much of her youth around people on one drug or another. The alcohol had not yet taken affect, so I felt rather sheepish when I confessed to enjoying an occasional joint.

Paula laughed when I admitted to naughty indulgences. She liked that in people, it made them much more interesting, she said, and she never criticized even the most bizarre behaviour of the music crowd. It was like theatre to her and she liked to watch but not take part. However, she had seen at first hand the tragedy drugs had caused for some of her friends and their families, and there were signs that the glamour of showbiz excess was losing its appeal. Bob was unequivocal in his condemnation of drug-takers: 'They're wankers... you try it, you move on,' he would say whenever the subject arose.

Paula's own explanation for her self-restraint was: 'I don't really like feeling out of control or even abnormal, and anyway, I'm petrified I'll get to like it too much. I have that kind of personality that pursues everything to extremes and for me it's safer to stay extremely clean.' That night we decided on 'perfectly imperfect', as the title for a pilot for a self-help programme we had discussed doing together. Paula insisted that this would be the first of many ideas she would produce under the banner of her own production company.

Paula was in incredibly good spirits. She was still grieving the loss of her father but it was of the positive influences of his unique style that she talked now and even mentioned that she had enjoyed reminiscing with her mother. She laughed fondly at the thought of Jess playing his golden Wurlitzer in heaven with all his old friends.

On more than one occasion Paula told me that she had lived with the constant fear that she might have inherited her father's depressive illness. She was subject to bouts of frenetic creative energy followed by serious downs. She recognized these as patterns she had seen in her father's behaviour. She believed that she had to fight tooth and nail to avoid a life of manic depression and constant medication. But his passing seemed to have liberated her from her childhood oppressions and this new-found power came with a profound sense of relief that she had survived his death without any sign of mental illness.

Perhaps Jess's death was actually a blessing for her marriage too. Ever since, Bob had been visibly gentler and more attentive, though it was not necessarily getting through to Paula. She was now chanting 'Bob is wrong' in the mornings, presumably under her breath. In therapy she had moved on from the exploration of her upbringing and was addressing more current issues. Her therapist asked her why she took on so much responsibility and why she had lost her voice, not in a literal sense but particularly with Bob – she would not speak out or challenge him. That evening, she explained how she had come to realize that she was once a little girl who attracted domineering people, the most extreme example of which was the man she married. 'He's the most controlling person I know,' Paula said. 'I liked it when I was in my twenties. I thought it meant that I was being taken care of; I liked the stability it brought me. Bob made me feel safe; he always knew the answer for everything. His word was the word of God and I believed him, but if I didn't I wouldn't have been able to argue. You can't argue with Bob.' Paula followed through with: 'I don't give a fuck about all that anymore. I want to be myself and not constantly trying to please everyone else.'

Paula was changing. She was feeling the power of unlimited possibilities. She remained light-hearted but there was a new resolve and assertiveness about her. I wondered if Bob might try to hold on to the old

Paula with whom he had been comfortable for years. I hinted again that she should encourage him to join her in therapy, as too often a couple would split if one found new strength to challenge the status quo. Anita might also find an empowered Paula difficult to accept without a fight. She ran the house and, to a degree, she ran Paula too. Paula had been quite happy to allow Anita to dictate the children's diet and agenda, and Anita thrived on the responsibility.

Later in the conversation I heard less resolve but a chillingly cold assessment of her role in the family, a role of which, it was clear, she was tiring. She summarized it as follows: Bob had always been adamant that she paid her way, but in fact she played husband, wife and mother. Paula would rise at 4am, sometimes earlier, to pursue her writing and complete her commissions. Her earnings from these projects and *The Big Breakfast* paid the mortgage and the house bills (which were all in her name). She had even invested in Planet 24 before *The Big Breakfast* contract was signed.

The role Paula played behind the scenes of Bob's chequered professional career was impressive enough, but she had played it without ever expecting or accepting credit. It was what she did for her family. Far from seeking the limelight, she actively discouraged publicity, unless there was a fee. She seemed content to have always played this role, leaving the path clear for Bob to shine so brightly. In their house there was a photo of Bob with Mother Teresa, but few realize just how fundamental Paula's role was in the success of Live Aid. While Bob did not take a single penny from Live Aid, she supported him and the family, financially and emotionally, for the whole two-year period and refused to give an interview after the event.

For all Paula's new-found strength, there was an incongruity between what she thought and said and how she behaved. She continued to act as the person Bob wanted her to be. There would be no quick fix, but perhaps with a good shrink, a willing heart and plenty of patience Paula could get to the real root of her discomfort. Failing that, she could carry on slipping on to the bed for the occasional platonic petting with Rupert Everett.

3 the discovery zone

'THE DISCOVERY ZONE' IN CLAPHAM was a children's activity centre; an indoor adventure playground of padded scaffolding, tubular slides and troughs of multi-coloured plastic balls. It was a sanity-saver for me – my children loved it, the entrance fee was less than £3 and it was a short drive from my home. Late in the autumn of 1993, I was queuing for a ticket when I spotted Bob slouching past me with a plastic cup of 'house instant' in one hand and a cell phone shouldered to his ear.

I caught up with him encamped on a bench seat, hunched over his bean juice, like a tramp in a laundromat. 'You look like you're enjoying yourself!' I teased. 'Yeah, right,' he replied flatly. The upward glance of acknowledgement was so swift I wondered if he had seen me at all. He continued staring at the floor through his drink. My better judgement suggested I leave him to his self-indulgence, but I tried again. 'Not your scene, I take it,' I prompted. He shrugged and shot the room a sideways glance, rolling his eyes, in that universal expression of boredom. I felt crushed. I forced a last show of courtesy and bid him farewell. Bob regarded me straight. His eyes were cold and his jaw-line protruded with stubborn indifference that did nothing to relieve my wounded pride. 'Bye, then,' he whispered under his breath as I walked away.

'Hi, gorgeous,' cooed a familiar voice from amongst the tables and chairs. The sight of Bob's decidedly better half immediately lifted my spirits. Paula had a handful of chips in her mouth. At the time it didn't register as odd that some of the time she would starve herself and at others she would binge. We moved to a free section of wall in the corner of the room, well out of earshot of passers-by. She hiked her flimsy white cotton dress up over her knees as she slid cross-legged to the floor.

Paula said that Bob's bad mood was down to his disappointment at his thwarted attempts to break back into the music business, but I didn't buy it. After some encouragement she added that Princess Diana's brother, Charles Spencer, had come round to their house with roses. As Paula would have it, she had made him laugh a couple of times at a charity dinner. But Paula wasn't flattered. She knew that Charlie wanted entertainment. She sighed exhaustedly: 'I'm not a performing dog. Done that. I can't sing for my supper any more. It's time someone entertained me for a change, or better matched my thirst for fun.'

I gave her a hug. Of course they had not been rowing, because Bob did not permit rows, but whatever the encounter had been he'd definitely come off worse. Paula looked defiant, her eyes clear and mischievous and there seemed an added sparkle I hadn't seen in her for a while. Biting her bottom lip nervously and arching a determined eyebrow she said, 'I've actually had enough, Gerry.' And I just knew she really meant it this time. She wasn't looking for a reaction. Paula brought her head closer to mine and whispered: 'I'm not the seventeen-year-old Paula he once knew anymore, I don't need to have someone tell me when I can use the telephone or ask permission to speak ...I'm leaving him.' 'What...when?' I mouthed, deeply shocked, even though she had hinted at this so often. She shook her head in resignation. 'That one, I haven't quite worked out yet, but you know on my fridge...?' Paula ventured, eyebrows straining upwards, pregnant with meaning. Why had the conversation turned so suddenly to her white goods? 'Don't answer!' Paula warned, chewing on the inside of her cheek with nervous concentration. 'What's the only thing on my fridge that exudes, oozes, trickles sex on legs?' she urged with drawn-out melodrama, meeting my dull incomprehension. I pictured a rather short and sticky male model squatting atop her kitchen appliance. 'M...H,' she breathed.

I got it, though what of it? A magazine clipping, stuck to the door? I looked at her expectantly and her cheeks flushed. 'Can't talk now, he's coming over,' Paula motioned with her eyes. She maintained a self-conscious composure, bracing herself against the approaching form of her husband. His whole demeanour looked thunderous and I guessed that our whispered conspiracy had provoked him further.

M.H.... the picture on the fridge. The image hung frozen in the space between us, so vivid I feared that Bob might catch sight of it. The sticky male model on the fridge was Michael Hutchence. Looking decidedly guarded, Paula flicked nervously at the pop magazine resting in her lap (under which hid *The Spectator*): 'He's here in London.' 'Have you seen him?' I enquired urgently, without moving my lips. 'That's what I wanted to talk to you about,' she replied, glancing nervously towards Bob, who was now only a few paces away and staring directly at us. Paula nudged me in the side and said under her breath, 'You're seeing me tonight, right?' 'What?' But that word did not escape my lips, I just thought it very loudly. Not because I hadn't heard her but because, for a second, I wondered when we had made this arrangement. Then the way she was staring at me, her panicking eyes, her imploring expression, signalled that I wasn't the one she was seeing that night. Though it was undeniably intriguing, I was far from comfortable with the role that had just been thrust upon me. I was now the official alibi for Paula's subterfuge.

Bob stared blackly down at us. I felt as if guilt was oozing from every pore in my face. I could feel that Paula was maintaining an icy composure, as if someone had left a fridge door open on my right. 'What are you two old wives nattering about?' he asked, an attempt at humour that utterly failed to mask his contempt. The tension was broken by the sudden appearance of their daughters, who rushed at Paula with excited glee. She struggled to her feet, dragging the girls with her and flung her arms around Bob in a show of affection as genuine as ever. Looking at me, she smiled a joyless smile, palpably relieved at the interruption.

Paula never made it a secret when she was going through a periodic crush on a man, usually very young and always very 'beautiful'. It seemed strange to think that, from the age of seventeen, Paula had stuck like glue to Bob, this highly intelligent but nevertheless Neanderthal-looking man, who stood up for the neediest human beings. Yet she hankered after the opposite in slick and immature boy-band pin-ups. However, the photo of Michael stuck to the fridge door since their fated *Tube* interview was a shrine to Paula's most persistent crush. One day, after years of indulging her imaginary suitors and never protesting at Michael's half-naked body thrusting a languid pose over his electric guitar every time he went to the fridge, Bob defaced the 'Love God', writing 'twat' across his forehead in red felt-tip. Paula replaced it with another equally provocative likeness, and this picture remained unmolested, clearly guarded by the twinkling fairy lights around it.

Paula arrived at my house a few evenings later in a flurry of conspiratorial gestures. It must be said that Paula could be surprisingly prudish about seemingly common-or-garden taboos, such as swearing and discussing sex. We were not the kind of girlfriends who regaled each other with blow-by-blow accounts of our private lives… but suffice it to say that, in the state she was in, Paula was in the mood to share some details about her and Michael's intimacy. According to her, everything was mystical and beautiful about their union. They made love in hotel rooms, making frequent calls to room service for supplies that weren't always used as food; Paula had also flown to Paris for a night of lust. But she went to great pains to emphasize that it wasn't all about sex, although there was plenty of it, and he was huge, she giggled, putting the cushion in front of her face to hide her embarrassment, as she blushed easily. They would talk for hours and she laughed about the fact that she had made him sit through the whole of *Gone With the Wind*. She said Michael was more than willing to watch it with her and she thought this little pleasure was wonderful, made all the more significant because she would usually have to settle for what Bob wanted to do.

I listened with a mixture of embarrassment and envy, gripped and begging for more, as Paula described how much Michael made her feel cherished and feminine. On one occasion, foreplay went on for three hours, and on another he massaged her buttocks until she reached a climax that they were both convinced could be heard in adjacent rooms. It was a sure way of losing your inhibitions, she enthused. Glowing with pride, she described the size of his penis and how he could keep going all night long. I had to agree that ten orgasms was extraordinary. From the picture she painted, he was an artist of 'lurve', who made her feel that every time was the first. It's rare, she told me, to find a man selfless enough to do all this for you and then caress your body until you fall asleep.

I winced a little when she told me about a recent visit to the doctor, suspecting she had caught some venereal disease. The doctor diagnosed a form of thrush caused by too much penetration. Next time they were together she told Michael that he couldn't go there and why. As an absolute example of Michael's total understanding of the female genitalia, she told me that he was unperturbed, giving extra time and attention when he went down on her. And periods didn't stop him either; they turned him on even more, though he wished he could take the pain away for her. This cemented it for Paula – Michael made her feel understood and valued, and that he was committed to her. Besides, she had just spent almost two weeks with him and he was phoning her every day. This was a far cry from the years of his blowing in and out of town, when Paula would only know that he was in London when Bob came home with INXS tickets.

Michael fulfilled all her fantasies and gave her more. She had been sexually awakened, loved, showered in flowers, talked to, listened to, stroked and petted. She was concerned she might be pregnant and I was worried she was about to feel more pain than that. Of course I revelled in her happiness, and egged her on for every detail, but Michael was, after all, a renowned playboy. He never stayed anywhere for any length of time and he had a girl in every port. Paula knew this better than anyone, but would not acknowledge it, because she had pixie dust in her eyes.

◆

By Christmas 1993 I was a regular at the Geldofs' Chelsea house. Invariably Anita would be there, the talented and complex über-nanny, and we became firm friends. She was very bright, warm, funny and acutely wise. The other mothers at school responded to her easy charm and realized that Paula, although devoted to her children, did not run their daily diaries.

Anita was in her mid-twenties with perfect skin and a full head of bouncy black curls that she sometimes wrapped up in a large coloured handkerchief, which made her look rather funky. The studied air of authority let you know loud and clear exactly who ran this ship. The children called Anita 'Ninoor', and the adults called her 'Mary Poppins' for her uncanny all-round talent. She could turn a yard of material into a stunning outfit, create hand-crafted invitation cards for the children's parties and cook sumptuous, nutritious meals for the whole family. Perhaps her greatest accomplishment, not forgetting the obvious love she had for them all which was reciprocated in abundance, was, through painstaking gentle encouragement, to coax the two younger children to utter their first word by the time they were eight months old.

But Anita drew the line firmly at cleaning. Paula wanted the house to be spotless at all times, so a cleaner was engaged to work all day, every day. In fact, it was possible Paula bordered on having a cleaning obsession. So if the marriage was not as perfect as she would have the world believe, the house certainly was, with its sumptuous velvet curtains and gilt-mirrored opulence, rows of books on shelves that lined every available wall space not hung with magnificent oils, watercolours and etchings. A log fire burned continually through the winter and the scent of vanilla wafted from the oil lamps placed discreetly about the place.

The three Geldof girls would spend most of their time in the basement kitchen: painting, making cakes, doing their homework and generally pining for Saturday to arrive, when they were allowed their pocket money and weekly sweet treat. My two loved going to the Geldofs'. It was indeed a fantasy setting; my daughter Sophie loved Peaches's mini-canopied bed adorned in a traditional rose-print fabric with tiny fairy lights surrounding the frame. Television was mainly banned and reading encouraged; Tom was most impressed that Peaches had the entire collection of the *Goosebumps* books. There were the normal sibling squabbles, but as a family they were remarkably harmonious. Fifi, the eldest, had the patience of a saint. She was a most agreeable ten-year-old, a 'Head Girl' in the making, her teachers decided; she was always helpful, polite to the point of humbleness, and apparently unaware that she was the daughter of famous parents.

Though nearly every other word Bob uttered was a swearword the children never copied him. Instead they'd chastise him and, when they realized they could make money, fined him for his bad language, becoming particularly vigilant in their policing. He would just laugh and tell them to draw up an IOU. They would plan holidays in the Caribbean and armies of Barbie dolls on the promise of proceeds that never materialized, though they were convinced that one day they would be millionaires!

All my worries about my children spending Christmas with their father and the lack of funds I had for presents were banished by the wafts of cinnamon and nutmeg trailing up from a pan of mulled wine on the oven plate. I might have thought Paula had employed a professional set designer to make the house resemble a Christmas extravaganza, had I not known that this was one of her favourite times of the year. She had talked about little else for the past month. Her plan, she had told me, was the same every year: 'If the children think last year was fab, wait till they see what I do this year.' Her excitement carried her off, almost daily, to the shops to buy yet more presents and glitter, traces of which could be seen twinkling on pine cones, cinnamon sticks and Flossy, the overweight golden retriever. Oodles of mince pies, huge bowls of pomegranates and tangerines covered nearly every surface, and the aroma of spices, burning in rings atop low-lit lamps, wafted throughout, carried on the strains of Nat King Cole.

Paula returned from Christmas shopping and we retired to her drawing room for a chat. She didn't use this room very much and my normal visits were either spent in the kitchen or up in her bedroom, which was equally stunning. The vast Christmas tree was almost invisible beneath a thick layer of lavish decorations; it was a tower of tinsel, glass baubles and tiny wrapped giftlets balanced on an unruly mound of presents. Fairy lights seemed to cascade from the tree across the walls, and the red velvet curtains, that fell the full height of the room to an artistic crumple on the floor, formed the perfect backdrop to this glittering sculpture. It was a real spectacle and, as I sank into an armchair by the fire, I could just make out what seemed to be a watercolour of the Queen Mother with her two little princesses sitting either side of her. Paula told me it was an original and a present from Bob. She was a great supporter of the Royals. On the dresser there was a photo of Paula's mother. It looked as if it had been taken by Cecil Beaton and showed a glamorously beautiful young woman.

Paula's blonde shock of hair hung damp in a tousled mess, and smudges of black mascara could be seen underneath her eyes. The chipped nail varnish and traces of pink lipstick applied a good few hours ago suggested she wasn't bothering very much about her appearance. I was concerned about her. Paula said she was fine but I knew this was about Michael and I pushed her on it. It was obvious she was more affected by the affair than she was letting on, perhaps even to herself. She said that she was trying to play the perfect mistress, making no waves or demands, but she was confused. She didn't know where she stood.

At the beginning of their affair she might only hear from Michael occasionally, then something changed. He stayed in London for a week or two at a time, spending more time with her than anybody else. When he left, he called her three or four times a day, but now she hadn't heard from him at all for quite a while. Paula tried unsuccessfully to convince me that she was objective about it. It was just a fling for him and she had to live with that gracefully. She said she accepted that Helena Christensen, his supermodel girlfriend, was still very much in the picture, but in the same breath she was adamant that Michael and Helena were not getting on, and that Michael was increasingly unhappy with her. If on the other hand the newspapers were right, Michael and Helena were one step away from walking down the aisle at that time. The deepest cut for Paula was that he would be with Helena for Christmas, doing all those wonderful things he did, but with her.

According to Paula, Michael's career was flagging, INXS were not in the ascendant and he was fed up with being on the arm of a supermodel, rather than the other way round. He had given Paula the impression that he felt that Helena treated him as a fashion accessory, expecting him to be there at the catwalk, supporting her meteoric career. He wasn't used to playing bass guitar to anyone else's lead. Here was Paula with this boundless positive energy, praising him, looking up to him, hanging on his every word. It was a shot in the arm and each time he returned to Helena he was more and more aware of the contrasts between the two women. Though Paula's relationship with Michael undoubtedly increased her dissatisfaction with her marriage, it was not the reason for it. Even now, when she felt very negative about Michael's level of commitment, she asked: 'So, Gerry, come on give me some tips, how do you cope out there on your own? How do you honestly get through it?' I could tell by her tone that this was neither idle curiosity nor real interest in my life, but more about how *she* might succeed on *her* own. I told her that I believed and tried to accept that everything happened for a very good reason, and trusted that better things were round the corner. I hoped I was through the hardest bit.

'Divorce?' Paula enquired. Divorce, I reminded her again, wasn't necessarily the answer and implored her to try again to persuade Bob to re-think his attitude towards getting them both help. 'He doesn't think we have any problems,' Paula replied. So I changed the subject: 'The house looks great, you're very clever.' 'I'm going to Faversham tomorrow to get the house ready there…. I completely, absolutely and utterly love this interval of family union. One exquisite, festive, fantasy month,' she sighed, her eyes still fixed on the glow of the real log fire, on to which she had tossed some pine cones and cinnamon sticks, 'a time of unbounded frolic in the pleasure ground of childhood's most innocent and delicious pleasures.' She smiled bashfully as if she thought she was talking too much.

Bob and Paula had an old rectory in Faversham, Kent, called Davington Priory. Paula told me that Bob had paid for it with the proceeds of his autobiography, *Is That It?* Paula spent most of her weekends and holidays there with the girls. It was a place that guaranteed her tranquillity. It was also the inspiration behind her book *Village People,* a parody of country life featuring a mother and her three daughters. Her love of the country was a further example that Paula was not the party girl that everyone assumed. She frequently complained about having to attend some star-studded function when she would have preferred to stay at home with her girls, reading *The Chronicles of Narnia*.

Although she talked of looking forward to Christmas, evidently all was not well. I was a little curious at the extent of her clearly forced determination to play 'happy families', varnishing over the cracks with this 'Partridge family' act that she had kept up for so long.

She was facing a dilemma. She'd gone through the tunnel of her father's death and come out the other side. *She* was different, but her *situation* hadn't changed. But the alternative carried high risks and no guarantees. Leave or stay? She wanted to leave but she worried about what it would do to the girls. She wasn't sure that they felt very close to Bob, with his frequent absences, but without doubt they loved him as their father. Staying meant living a lie. Each option seemed booby-trapped with inevitable misery or disaster. Paula's feeling of imprisonment was heightened by the pleasure of her affair with Michael, but as he seemed suddenly unavailable as a viable escape route, the only possibility appeared to be for her to sit tight and make the most of it.

She was simply trying to convince herself that it would work out with Bob if she just put a little more effort into the role she had played for as long as they had been together.

4 love me or leave me

FOR THE FIRST FEW MONTHS OF 1994 the distraction of Paula's colourful life moved to the backburner as I had some freelance PR work to keep me busy. The odd chat on the phone and exchanges at school were kept brief, promising one another that we would find time to 'catch up'. There were times when I felt concern for Paula's situation, but my fears were always allayed, as she seemed exuberantly happy. On one occasion I even had a warmer response from Bob. I bumped into him in Sloane Square. He was carrying neat little bags from the 'Knickerbox' underwear shop. He beamed a grin that could have warmed the hearts of most girls at twenty paces, a far cry from my experience at 'The Discovery Zone'.

Bob looked as if he had shaved twice this morning with one of those hi-tech four-bladed razors built from aircraft parts. In the process he had left long thin sideburns, trimmed to impossible spikes, pointing straight down to his trademark jutting jaw-line. Today the uncharacteristically clean, bouncy hair fell in a mingling of soft wavy curls. Mischievous glints of copper in his irises caught in the Easter sunshine and softened the harsh contours of his face. He is hardly classically good-looking and not someone to polish his appearance for the benefit of anyone but himself. However, he has a powerful and compelling presence and on that particular day I got the full Bob Geldof charm-offensive. The bags, he explained were full of surprise gifts for Paula, and we laughed as he acted out the shop assistant's attempt to hide her reaction to his choice of bra and knickers in black lace, pink silk and mock arctic rabbit fur.

We walked up the King's Road to where my car was parked and said goodbye with a warm embrace. 'Lurve the skirt,' Bob called after me. I smiled back. 'Thanks,' I replied. I found myself two roads away from the Geldofs' house and decided to pop in. Within seconds of ringing the doorbell, Paula stood before me in her uniform of the moment: gold-rimmed pebble glasses, her hair scraped back from her face with a pink gingham Alice band, more 'flustered librarian' than '*Tatler* front cover'. She could have been Fifi's older sister rather than a mother of three, standing there in her bare feet and child's T-shirt, stretched and skimpy, brandishing 'Take That' across the front and back.

'You look great... like Doris Day at a teeny bop concert,' I chuckled, taking a gentle pot shot at her 'Take That' T-shirt. She attempted to pull the cloth out into a tent, looking down as if realizing for the first time what it was she had thrown on that morning. 'Oh, yes....' she giggled, 'Robbie gave me this last week for one of the children. Peaches yelled "HRT" at me and then gave me one of her indignant looks that says, "I think that's too young for you, mummy."' Paula shot me a knowing smirk, widening to a full smile, which she covered with a dainty hand; a habit, she had told me, that developed as she became conscious of her slightly crooked teeth. She had never had them fixed, but then a large part of Paula's fascinating allure was her child-like freedom, unfettered by convention or self-consciousness.

Paula was obviously working on a writing commission as her typewriter was out on the dining room table. It was a black and gold 1940s Corona typewriter, with its round keys and confusion of rods and levers like the collision between a cash register and a saxophone. She wrote all her books and articles on it, quite a feat in this age of word processors with their infinite editing facilities and all those wonderful tools for writers. It had been a present from her father when she was six, after he found three manuscripts under her bed, '...probably about running away from home on my imaginary pony, named Bolt,' she explained. 'Anyway, Dad must have thought they had potential and gave me this for my next birthday. I love the romantic weight and clunk of it.' Her voice was tender as she recalled her late father, and her anecdote changed from a joke to a source of sadness in two sentences: 'Miss the old thing terribly.'

Paula always credited Bob with kick-starting her writing career. Once he had the bit between his teeth he introduced her to a few editors and, in her words, 'sang my praises, then threatened them to hire me.' He told them that if she wrote the way she spoke, her column would be the best thing in print. Bob was right – her pieces were always irrepressibly humorous, quirky and intelligent. After that, she said, it was easier than she expected, but then she always made everything that she did look easy. She wrote mostly about her friends and their antics, which was then, as now, a highly saleable commodity. It was impressive how she managed to do this and maintain her friendships. But she was no showbiz editor, scrounging for juicy tit-bits to expose; she was part of the scene, not looking in from the outside. The clever bit was that she was kind. She always flattered her subjects and she had a reputation for her ability to write anyone up into a sex symbol. As a result, people rang her endlessly to pass on the latest gossip.

My mind wandered back to Bob, out shopping for knick-knacks. I wondered if he was guessing at Paula's restlessness or appeasing some recent row. Going on her previous attitude, it would take more than a bag of knickers to rekindle her belief in the relationship. I mentioned that I had bumped into Bob earlier and how buoyant he had looked. 'He can have his good days like anyone. Deep down he's the kindest person I know. But... there's a lot more going on, the deeper down you dig,' Paula replied. 'His manner prevents people from finding or wanting to know what's really eating away at him... well, he puts people off and me... I've just had enough of wading through the shit to reach the sunshine.'

I remember all this as it will be forever linked in my mind with what happened next. The doorbell rang.

Paula looked towards the window that looked on to the street, and went to receive her unannounced visitor, Michael Hutchence. Her whole body language was alive with excited energy as she introduced us to one another. 'Hi, Gerry,' Michael strode over with easy confidence. He was thinner than I expected, but then all rock stars are virtually anorexic, I mused to myself, as I awkwardly received a warm embrace usually reserved for greeting long-lost friends. Paula slithered sexily into his chest and ran her hand down the front of his black Armani-sleek silk shirt. Michael was lost in Paula's eyes and caressing her face as if they were newly weds.

Feeling like a spare wheel on a bobsleigh, I suddenly remembered Bob. I wished I had been more specific when I had mentioned meeting him. I had a sense of dread and a feeling of collusion, and that I was in a position to avert disaster if only I could say or do something. Involuntarily I glanced towards the door, convinced we would hear a key in the lock, imagining the terrible silence of Bob's imminent arrival. Would his Irish temper overcome him? Perhaps Michael was here to tell Bob that Paula was leaving him and the children, right there and then. Michael didn't look like he was bracing himself to break up a family judging by the relaxed cooing noises he and Paula were making as they continued to revel in one another. Michael pulled away for a moment as he tilted his head to light a non-filter-tipped cigarette. 'Aaah! That's good. I hate smoking outside,' he hummed through a wide smile as he pulled on the cigarette. The perfect white teeth disappeared behind a thick curl of blue smoke and I was tempted to march over and frantically wave it away, to eliminate any evidence of his presence.

'I'd better be going,' I muttered. 'Don't leave on my account,' Michael protested. 'I have to. Sorry, kids to collect, and that sort of thing,' I replied, masking my emotions with a false smile. 'What time are yours back?' I fixed Paula a look, imploring her to snap out of her happy haze. 'Bob's taking them to circus club,' Paula replied, missing my telepathic message. 'Oh, shit! I completely forgot, mine will kill me if I don't take them. Tom's nearly mastered walking on a ball,' I said, remembering at the same time that it was Bob who had taught him. 'I'm really glad to have met you, Gerry,' Michael said, giving me a penetrating stare. 'Yes... it's good that

I've met you, too.' I was unable to reciprocate with the same relaxed generosity. Michael went to pick up one of my carrier bags. 'Let me help you out with these,' he mumbled over his cigarette. He picked up my bags and vaulted lithely over the coffee table in the direction of the door, leaving a trail of ash. I hastened after Michael to the door, praying that Paula would have her can of polish out to remove any trace of ash on the floor. 'I'll call you when you get back,' Paula smiled dreamily.

'Great boots.' Michael's voice cruised along the syllables like a well-fed lazy water snake taking an afternoon swim. I looked down at my battered pink cowboy boots, pleased in my fluster that he had noticed. 'First time these old things have had a compliment in ages. I bought them years ago, haven't seen a pair like them since,' I replied. The compliment momentarily distracted me. I replied because he seemed so genuinely interested and because he was making such a monumental effort to be nice to me even when I was acting so jittery. 'I always get two pairs, just in case,' he said, sticking out one foot to show a pair of black open-toed sandals. For a second I stopped, transfixed. His big toenail was painted a deep maroon. 'These are one of those just in case,' he chuckled. His accent seemed more influenced by time spent in America than Australia and I was struck by the soft mellow tones. I had imagined his voice to be louder and rougher, from the strength of his singing. He clearly liked to look after himself: with his perfectly toned body, year-round tan and hair that resembled a late 60s hairdressing advert, he looked more like a member of the elite Hollywood Brat Pack than a Rock God. I retrieved my bags. 'See you, then,' I shouted as I let myself out of the front door. In an hour's time I'd be sipping tea with Bob, talking about the weather in a strained attempt to forget what I knew, while we watched our children master this week's lesson of juggling balls or learning to be a clown.

Meeting Michael that day stirred up for me so many varied and complicated emotions that I decided I should create some distance in my relationship with Paula. I started a letter to myself to explore exactly what all this meant to me and it turned into a letter to Paula, explaining my disappearance. I told her that I needed time out for myself, that this had nothing to do with her and everything to do with a whole string of personal situations stretching into my past. I wrote that I felt angry at Michael for marching into their family home as if it were his own and at their irresponsibility, that their behaviour could affect the lives of so many people. What if Bob had returned, or the children? What kind of memory would that leave for the girls?

My instinct was to condemn her actions but, for a while, a nagging doubt persisted. Paula appeared so at ease with Michael's sudden appearance that I wondered if he was an accepted and frequent visitor to the house. In any event, Bob had taken the girls to circus club and Paula was secure in the knowledge that his return was not imminent. The apparently casual visit was of course carefully timed. I mailed the letter to Paula but it had already served its purpose for me. It was a brain dump and it had cleared my head. I did hold fast to my decision not to see her, but inside I wavered – I keenly felt the absence of her company.

I could see that there was a powerful attraction between Paula and Michael, but I could also see that, though Bob was controlling, moody and arrogant, he did have many positive qualities as well. If not, why would Paula have stayed with him all that time? After a few weeks a note came from Paula saying she understood and that she hoped we would be in contact when she came back from a short spell away. Several weeks passed, then I received a phone call. Paula had returned from her trip in a miserable state. She had broken up with Michael and all but taken herself to bed, leaving the children in Anita's care. Working entirely on instinct, I responded to the call and went to visit Paula.

Like a punk Miss Havisham, her tormented presence haunted the house, defying Anita's efforts to breathe life back in with a daily order from the flower shop on the King's Road. Anita looked very worried and complained of Paula's increasing insistence on feeding herself only on organic ice cream. Paula's feminine pink boudoir smelt stale, permeated by the scent of her latest perfume. I stalked into the gloom, between discarded clothes and a plate of uneaten dinner, to find my friend in a foetal position on top of the duvet. Even Bob was concerned, occasionally popping his head round the door to ask if he could get us anything, but then he disappeared into the night, assured that his help was not required. Paula complained unconvincingly that everyone was fussing too much, as if she was suffering from a particularly virulent cold and had taken herself to bed for a couple of days. With nothing to go on, I said very little at all.

'All I need is time to readjust, muster the strength to get Bob and me back on track. It was good once, it can be again,' Paula said, trying more to convince herself than me.

There was something so vulnerable about her, but I knew there was nothing I could really do to help her. Had I contributed to Paula's decision to finish with Michael? Had I been responsible in the preceding months for influencing her to question her marriage because I had been so blithely open about my own failure? I had relished hours of gossip with her, encouraging, laughing, and begging for more. I felt I had never seriously suggested she should make a go of her marriage. I could not help feeling like an accomplice. One thing was certain – I was here with

Paula as her friend, not to wave a magic wand over the misery she was feeling. I clung on to the hope that both Paula and Bob would face their problems together. After all, Paula was back here, maybe not in the greatest state, but nevertheless ready to make the effort to take the first step, to try to regain the happiness they once had.

Where was Michael? I could not say, and Paula could not bear to have his name uttered. 'I have to get over him, Gerry' is all she could say. 'My heart's sore, not broken,' but this only served to heighten my concern and I lay down on the bed next to her in an awkward act of sympathy. The lunchtime sun shot through the bedroom and Paula covered her eyes with her hand, revealing pale blue nails, chipped and tortured-looking. Paula's voice was a crushed whisper: 'It's a bit too bright.' And I drew the curtains a little further into the middle again. She rearranged her delicately printed dress and looked up with beseeching eyes. I spotted fresh tears sliding down her pale face. I took her into my arms and held her while she sobbed uncontrollably for what seemed an eternity.

———— ◆ ————

The on/off pattern of Paula and Michael's affair went on for months. They would be intensely involved for a time, then would decide that it couldn't work, and that they would stay with their respective partners. But Michael couldn't stay away and in no time he was back on the phone telling Paula to be patient, to wait for the tour to end, that he needed time to let Helena down gently.

When I had first met him at Paula's, Michael had been staying in London for a couple of weeks, overseeing work on his house in Smith Terrace, Chelsea, which was undergoing extensive refurbishment by a top Sydney architect. He was dropping round quite regularly to the Geldofs' house which was just a few streets away. Bob thought nothing of it – he and Michael went way back, and there was mutual respect. Bob loved to go to INXS gigs when they were in London, and Paula told me he would comment on how talented Michael was, even though she thought that he was mildly jealous.

Michael had always breezed casually in and out of Paula's life, careful not to give any quarter to her to demand more. But by May something had changed, the stars were in alignment and the high-octane fuelling of the liaison had increased. When I got to know him, Michael told me that Paula enthralled him. He had had his fill of the superficiality and skin-deep perfection of the fashion world, the petulance and egocentricity of it all. By contrast Paula had depth and breadth, culture and education, wit and style, and above all he loved her *brio*.

Although Paula had actively pursued Michael, on at least one occasion turning up unexpectedly at his hotel and persuading him to get rid of the girl with him, it was not just Paula making all the running. I knew only too well that Michael was calling her mobile several times a day, because it often happened when I was with her, and I would be left waiting, sometimes for up to thirty minutes, or have to endure her gurgling down the phone to him. I was allowed to listen to some of the more innocent messages; she delighted in letting me hear how gorgeous he sounded and giggled with acute embarrassment when I accidentally heard one that was clearly for her ears only, like: 'I'm going to lick you out till you scream, go crazy, die!' 'I'm going to tie you up and torture you with pleasure' – that sort of thing. Arm-loads of beautiful flowers would arrive at the house. Luckily, as Paula and Anita were regulars at the flower shops on the King's Road, the extra foliage would not have been remarkable to Bob's eyes.

When Michael was around and in contact hourly, Paula was ecstatic, but the moment there was a lull, she sank into gloom. Michael was still with Helena, and though Paula was convinced that their relationship was not going well, he would not comfort her with a date for Helena's departure; quite the contrary, he was concerned that if he left too abruptly, Helena would fall apart. So he vacillated between his unconditional and devoted mistress and his 'Danish Super-Frau', as Paula called her.

Whenever Michael went back to Helena, to hold it all together, Paula became confused. He was giving out wildly mixed messages and her only defence was to play at letting him go. The act was unconvincing. She was in love, but under no real illusion that her relationship with Michael was going anywhere. Also, she was still in the midst of an increasing dilemma at home; determined that things should change, but having difficulty with the idea of leaving. Her real concern here was the children's welfare. Once again, it seemed that she was resigned to making the best of her current situation.

I wondered if Paula had discussed her dilemma with any of her other friends. I knew for instance that Jo Fairley and Paula had been the closest of friends for many years. They met when Jo was editor of *Honey* magazine and requested an interview. The chemistry between the two of them was instant and the friendship forged on that day continued to be one of the most important in Paula's life. Jo adored her; the camaraderie between them was infectious. Jo wrote books and magazine articles like Paula and she was a respected newspaper journalist. Jo matched Paula's intellect and though, for me, she did not quite have Paula's wit, neither was she dull.

To the outside observer the two women appeared to live on different planets. Paula's non-conformity and eccentric dress sense was bizarrely contrasted by Jo's conservatism and cut-glass English accent. Nevertheless, it was clear to everyone who came in contact with them that this was a friendship that was going to last – and it did. It was Jo who organized the flowers for the Geldofs' 'rock'n'roll' wedding and who was maid of honour.

One of the first things that struck me about Jo was her unusual complexion. Paula called it 'perfectly peach-like'. Paula would often announce proudly of her best friend, 'Jo never eats or does anything remotely unhealthy, preferring the get-yourself-to-bed-before-ten-o'clock-and-drink-plenty-of-water lifestyle.' This probably accounted for her silken skin, glossy blonde hair, clear baby-blue eyes, and for her looking a good ten years younger than she really was. (Jo is now best-known for her books and magazine columns on beauty.) 'What does Jo think?' I asked her one day. 'The same as you...that I should stay with Bob,' she replied, shrugging her shoulders and rolling her eyes with a deep sigh. 'Made my bed, I suppose,' Paula sighed. 'Jo, with all her journalistic experience, knows better than anyone what the press will do to me.'

Jo was strongly advocating that Paula stick it out with Bob and suggested marriage guidance. As a journalist of some renown she spoke for the press in general when she outlined how they would spin it if the Geldofs officially split. The gist of her argument was that the press must always take sides and in doing so must tip the balance of opinion as far in the direction of their champion as possible. Bob was a 'Saint' and a 'Sir' for his great achievements, so they must cast Paula as the sinner, the ingrate, the insane and adulterous Jezebel. It had happened to Diana, Princess of Wales, and to Sarah Ferguson, the Duchess of York, Jo reminded her. Even though women have had the vote for years and the campaign for equality has raged even longer, Jo argued, in this country there is still a gaping chasm between the treatment of the sexes; and a woman walking out on her husband, regardless of how she might have suffered, is still viewed by many with contempt. There would be no reasoned argument for the possibility of an equal complaint on her part.

Apart from the press response, Jo feared that as hard as it was at home, Paula would find it immeasurably tougher out there on her own. What man would be interested in her with three kids in tow, anyway, and what would it do to the children, to be separated from their father? Jo was also emphatic that Paula's career would suffer severely, detached from Bob and at a time when she would be dependent on work to support herself.

Obviously Paula had not told Jo about Michael. It would seem that Paula had fallen out with Jo some years before, in similar circumstances. She had been contemplating leaving Bob (around 1987) and discussed it with Jo. Jo had been discouraging in her rejection of the suggestion, and scathing about Paula's rumoured affair. In retaliation at disloyal criticism, Paula froze Jo out for a number of years and their friendship had only just been re-established. Neither of them would want to go there again.

'Anyway, what's the point… there is no Michael,' she said irritably. 'It's not about Michael, it's not like I was happy with Bob and then the Love God from Down Under comes along and turned my head.'

She did think it ironic, however, that this particular friend was trying harder than anyone to keep their family together. Apparently Jo was not Bob's greatest fan. Naturally she respected the heroic work he did in Africa, but he behaved towards her as he did to many others. He could, so Paula told me, be rude, arrogant, oafish, inconsiderate and domineering, and in his behaviour towards Jo, these traits became more obvious. The feeling seemed to be mutual, as Paula told it. 'Jo doesn't suck up to Bob,' she said, going on to complain, 'But then he doesn't like any of my friends.' Although Jo obviously had Paula's best interests at heart, these reasons to stay with Bob seemed to fall squarely under the category of living your life by what others think. It was not striking out and being yourself, which Paula's every fibre was compelling her to do even without the added spur of Michael's attractions. Her heart was already halfway down the road, but her head was still in the kitchen, and her body didn't know which to follow.

If I tried to suggest that she could weather the split and all the ensuing unpleasantness, that perhaps it might not be as bad as she expected and it was bound to blow over once there was nothing more to say, Paula would vehemently remind me of what happened to her father. Paula seemed terrified of a press free-for-all. This was prophetic as it transpired, but she could never have guessed at the intensity of the scandal to come. At the time her fear was fuelled by the memory of her father's ruin. She had witnessed the devastating effect the adverse press attention had on his state of mind.

Quite incidentally, it was about this time that Paula told me she had received a peculiar call from a journalist, who told her that Hughie Green, her father's arch-rival, was going to shed light on the showgirl scandal. The journalist didn't elaborate; he was interested in Hughie, asking over and over if Paula knew him and what kind of relationship she had with him. Little did she suspect the awesome significance of this random enquiry.

I encouraged Paula to challenge her fear of her father's experience at the hands of the press. I argued that people are not so easily taken in these days, that we know there are always two sides. 'Nope…I've made my decision and I'm shit at confrontations,' she laughed. 'I don't know how long it's going to take to get over darling Michael, but I've got some great mates, my children of course and… I've decided to join you at one of your meetings. I'm seeing my therapist; you'll see, I'm going to make it.' But, of course, it wasn't all over with Michael. When he could snatch time in London between tour dates, he spent some of the time staying with a friend, who worked for Bob as the producer of *The Big Breakfast*. Paula had told me about her in not particularly glowing terms. I seem to remember a power struggle between the two of them as, strictly speaking, she was Paula's boss, but Paula had friends in higher places... Suddenly the producer was Paula's best friend. They were hanging out, going shopping.

It must have been around June 1994 when Paula suggested we go to LA together, because Michael was playing there and he had a few days off. From my perspective this was a lunatic suggestion and it showed me just how little Paula, together with many other of my friends, was able to understand the parameters of my life. I couldn't possibly afford a weekend in LA – we'd have been eating freezer ice for months afterwards. Paula went with the producer instead and they both had their belly buttons pierced. Body-piercing was such a novel practice in England that the event was picked up by almost every paper. Few were complimentary, but it demonstrated once again Paula's ability to act as a conduit between the mass media and alternative culture. Before the story hit the papers she wore a full length T-shirt, even in bed, terrified of Bob's reaction. When she finally worked up the courage to show him, he was thunderous and said, 'Don't you ever show me that again!'

Michael finished the Dirty Honeymoon tour in late July 1994. He had been on the road for a solid year with no more than a few weeks off at a time. He was on stage most nights, travelling to the next gig by day and performing to crowds of up to 100,000. He had toured the States, Australia, the Far East, South America and Europe. Now he was exhausted, Paula told me, and going to Paris for a rest and a supermodel. Michael told Paula that Helena was hearing wedding bells and he could not burst her bubble so suddenly, so he was avoiding the subject all together. Paula went to Kent with the girls for most of the summer. Despite this break from one another, at the beginning of September Paula told me she was again actively 'courting Michael' and it was weighing heavily on her wallet. She was sending him hampers (and he was saying he wanted to spread the food all over her). The rollercoaster ride was on again.

On the morning of 31 October I flicked on the TV for my customary background viewing of *The Big Breakfast*, while I got the children ready for school. But I had to stop everything when Paula's interview slot came up – she was on the bed with Michael. I hooted with amazement at her shameless audacity: not content to conduct her affair in the safety of hotel rooms, she was flaunting it to the nation as they ate their cornflakes. And while everyone choked on their toast at the sexual chemistry that oozed from their screens, as if the two of them had just stumbled upon a soulmate for the first time, I was in fits, because Paula had told me the day before that she was staying with Michael that night. This was no arbitrary guest with whom she discovered she had a remarkable rapport, this was the continuation of their night together. Popular myth has it that this was the beginning of their affair. Channel 4 received hundreds of complaints that day and the papers were outraged, but Paula had fallen deeply in love with Michael and I think it was reciprocated as sincerely as his temperament allowed. For so long, the relationship was ultimately insecure for her – he had been so unavailable, on tour and with Helena – and a less passionate person might have taken two steps back, let go or waited. She was waiting for Michael to give her a sign, for Michael to see her soul and choose to stay.

———— ◆ ————

The season of goodwill was upon us again, so too was the annual rumour that Michael and Helena were planning to wed. But this year the stories did not have the bite for Paula that they had had twelve months ago; it was her opinion that Helena, aware that she was losing her grip on Michael, had engineered the rumours. Paula was in regular phone contact with Michael, as he enjoyed a family Christmas in LA and she was convinced, when we spoke, that Helena's marching orders were in the post. Michael remained concerned for the supermodel's feelings and would make no fast moves, but Paula kept me up to date with their long-distance yearning, cooing and phone sex.

In between snatched phone calls with Michael and updates to me, Paula maintained the pretence of happy families for Christmas. She had itchy feet but she was no stranger to acting and for a few more weeks… for the sake of the girls. Into January, she was emphatic that she was packing her bags and leaving Bob. I should have known that the one time you don't believe it is the one time the wolf is really coming… but I didn't. Even when both she and Anita separately told me they were looking for a flat to rent, it still seemed remote. Anita had been supportive to Paula for a while in her move to leave Bob, but she didn't give the affair with Michael more than a few months, Paula told me. In the long term, she thought, his rock'n'roll lifestyle would never mesh with Paula's love of homely isolation, but she had warmed to him after initial suspicions that he was just another unscrupulous good-time boy. Along with everyone else who met him, Anita could not deny Michael's unusual charisma.

She became excited whenever they talked of their liberation, she and Paula out on their own together. Maybe, Bob didn't then live up to her high expectations for parenting. By her standards, he didn't read bedtime stories enough, he didn't take the girls to the park, he didn't share the parenting very much at all and he made Paula miserable. How difficult was the decision to make? But I only started to give credence to these plans when, one day in Paula's kitchen, some time in mid-January, she put her arm around Anita and said, 'It's just you and me now. We'll get through this. We've brought the girls up OK so far.' I knew that Anita would ensure the disruption to the girls' lives would be minimized, and that they would see Bob all the time. Paula was of the same mind, and beyond this she insisted that the divorce would be amicable, she was after nothing – no money, not even the house.

On 22 January, Michael's birthday, he flew from LA to his villa in Nice. Paula's spirits took a nose-dive as the spectre of the other woman reared her beautiful head again. But it need not have, because in no time Paula was on the phone to me, jumping up and down – Michael was on his way to town.

When Michael arrived in London in early February, Paula went quiet for a while. Later, she told me they were snatching as many moments together as they could, mostly at night in his room at the Halkin Hotel in Belgravia – they could not be seen out together. But this wasn't enough for them and they wanted to venture into the daylight. Paula was viewing a property in Chelsea Harbour and she wanted Michael to experience some of the perks attached to the deal, enticing him to stay. So she asked me to arrange 'day passes' for us all at the Chelsea Harbour Club, an exclusive health spa and hot rendezvous of the time. This was a bold move, not least because the Chelsea Harbour Club was swarming with well-known faces; Princess Diana went there every day, and so photographers camped in the pot plants. Paula could not just arrive with Michael or meet him there on her own; they needed a cover, and guess who the stooge was to be?

It was carefully planned. I was to meet Michael at the Club and Paula would join us a little later, turning up as if by chance. No journalist could snap a bunch of friends having lunch and expect a pat on the back from his editor. The plan was simple but effective…except I was thirty minutes late. I took an urgent call from Paula on the mobile: 'Where the hell are you?'

When I entered the Club, Paula was sitting in the reception, apparently absorbed in reading promotional bumf. After a convincing act of girly surprise at bumping into one another, I sat down with her, squirming my apologies; she cut me short: 'Will you shut up and go and see him!'

Michael was reclining in his chair, perfectly relaxed. There was no hint of the urgency Paula was transmitting, just a serene amusement, as if he were quite happy to hold this moment of titillation for the rest of the afternoon. I was making my way towards a man I'd met only once before, whom I now had to pretend I'd known for at least ten years. I asked him very loudly (for the benefit of the pot plants) if he would mind if Paula joined us.

The idea that anyone watching would fail to suspect that this was a set-up was ludicrous. Their embrace lasted far longer than my nerves could stand and a sexual static crackled between them. Michael was fascinating and I was beginning to appreciate Paula's driven desire for him. I had been worried that I would feel like a superfluous accessory to their secret rendezvous, which I'm sure Michael realized, as at no point did I feel excluded from his delicate attention. He greeted me with perfect gentlemanly politeness, which never faded with each new meeting, and his focus on me when I spoke seemed sincere. I watched his many-layered interaction with Paula: his hand traced lightly down her back that somehow gave *me* goose-bumps; his enchanted smile and knowing eyes when he looked at her and listened to her. This behaviour continued through the lunch, but he remained attentive to our conversation, which after a while agitated Paula and, picking up on this, he increased the level of attention to her instantly. I began to feel that I was surplus to requirements after all, for though the three of us continued to converse, there was a carnal communication between the two of them that made me wonder why they had not just met in a hotel room in the first place. This was fore-fore play, a ritualistic dance in the danger of the daylight, with someone there to watch.

The Chelsea Harbour Club became the venue for a series of such arrangements. There was a strange inverted logic to meeting there, as if its very vulnerability to press intrusion provided cover for the most scandal-worthy assignations. And so the carousel went round and round. Michael and Paula continued their super-clandestine affair, employing every tactic possible to ensure absolute secrecy, and they used me as their cover.

Whenever I spoke to Paula she was dancing on air, but rather exhausted, as her usual sleep pattern had disintegrated into snatching catnaps wherever she could. The effects of her relationship with Michael were beginning to leak out into the public domain. Paula's bosses at Planet 24 noticed her characteristic professional punctuality was sliding, she was ill-prepared for her guests on the bed and she was not giving her usual perky performance. Even the guests were noticing: the comedian Lenny Henry ventured that Paula was looking a bit beat, and she replied with a naughty smirk, live on camera, 'I had a hard night.'

Paula told me she had been cutting it a little fine in the mornings, leaving Michael's hotel in a taxi as late as she could, to catch up on sleep. Bob challenged her about the late nights and she said he was being rather bolshie about it. He was beginning to be suspicious after the much publicized interview on the bed and asked her if she was seeing Michael, but she managed to convince him that she was out partying with Take That.

Bob went away for the weekend, during which he phoned home to speak to his wife, and Peaches (aged eight) answered. She told him Mummy was upstairs in bed with Michael. When Paula came to the phone she managed to convince Bob that they were merely having tea together and their daughter was confusing the sofa with a bed. But the seed of doubt was well and truly sown. When Bob returned, he happened to bump into Michael at a friend's party and accosted him aggressively: 'You leave my wife alone!' Michael was shaken and Paula furious. She berated Bob, insisting that he was paranoid and that he must apologize to Michael, who was bewildered and a little hurt. Her smoke screen must have been convincing to pull that off, and Bob did phone Michael to say sorry.

Bob, as I know from later conversations I had with him, was very confused at this time. Relations with his wife seemed fractious, disintegrating, but between bouts of mistrust and acrimonious discussion, in which Paula was demonstrating an increasing willingness to show her teeth, she was also being incredibly loving and attentive. So it came as quite a shock when she told him she was leaving. He challenged her once again about Michael and she vehemently denied that he was the reason for her departure and she told me that Bob believed her. Increasingly desperate, he said: 'You can't leave me, you've taken vows before the eyes of God.' Paula replied, 'I never knew you were so religious.' This was indeed surprising, coming from such a self-confessed anti-establishment figure; surprising, too, as he wouldn't marry her for ten years, though she had hoped he would from the moment they met; surprising because they had taken their vows in a $50 Marry-Mart in Las Vegas, and Bob had forbidden her to tell the press. Paula was incensed by this hypocrisy, but in the end Bob begged her to reconsider and, in a moment of sympathy for him, she said she needed space to think it over.

Bob went off to Ireland to give her time to reflect, and Paula breathed a temporary sigh of relief, but she told me her decision was made. While Bob was away, she called to give me her new address and phone number at a penthouse in Bayswater overlooking Hyde Park. I couldn't believe it – after months of talking, she and Anita had finally done it, moved out of the house with the girls and their belongings.

This was a big bold move for Paula – the first time out in the world on her own since she was seventeen. Sure, she was making £5,000 a month for her slot on *The Big Breakfast* and her writing would supplement her income. Sure, she had run the house with little input from Bob, but emotionally and spiritually she had leaned on him for eighteen years. Was she really ready to stand on her own two feet? Despite our conversations, I didn't think that she would have been ready to make the move without a new element in the dynamic of her relationship with Michael. Michael had told her to wait for the tour to end, Michael had told her to wait for him to end his relationship with Helena gently and although Michael was here with Paula now, I guessed she could feel his feet getting their first itches and she wanted to be able to go public with their affair, so that it would be harder for him to leave her.

As they left the house in Chelsea, suitcases in hand, Anita asked if she would miss her home. After all, it was Paula's house: she'd chosen it, bought it, paid the mortgage and put her heart into every lick of paint and yard of carpet. But Paula said no. 'This is nothing to where we're going. We're travelling first class from now on. Michael could buy a hundred of these...'

5 little miss trouble

IT WAS A SUNDAY MORNING. Paula phoned me in unfeigned hysterics – she could barely speak. Something awful had happened; she repeated over and over, 'What am I going to do?' It was 11 February 1995. The night before, her PR had called Paula and Bob for an emergency meeting at their house (the £20,000-a-year retainer Paula paid clearly made him available after office hours). He sat them down for some bad news: Paula's affair with Michael was to hit the headlines in the morning. During the week, Bob and Paula had already briefed him in a joint statement that they were going to separate for a while, to get some space. It was to be released to the press on the Monday.

Their PR man was grave; that statement would not be enough now. It had passed its sell-by date while it was still on the shelf. He informed them that a tabloid was running pictures, captured during the week, of Michael and Paula leaving the Halkin Hotel in Knightsbridge together.

Paula was distraught. This was not the way she had planned it. Michael was playing his own game of letting Helena down softly, and she had denied the affair for so long, what would Bob do to her? She was terrified of his reaction, but above all loomed the spectre of her father's destruction under similar circumstances. It was all her worst nightmares coming together on a single night. She was calling from her new flat in Bayswater; Anita was with the girls. Her hysteria rose anew as she relived the night before and though the words came out in a steady, logical flow, I could hear that she was hyperventilating.

Bob had exploded at the news, his anger was in direct relation to his hurt, but it was directed squarely at her. Paula told me she had run sobbing hysterically from the room and locked herself in the bathroom. She recognized that this was the response of a teenager and had no difficulty making the connection with the pain her father went through, which she had witnessed at an early age. She was terrorized by her phantasmagorical imaginings of the impending consequences, intensified in no small degree by guilt. Shaking uncontrollably, she fell to the floor, paralyzed by the fear of what might be waiting for her on the other side of the door.

Bob plumbed the depths of his boundless compassion in a way that perhaps only Bob Geldof can. Her reaction had totally hijacked his own – he amazed Paula with his heroic kindness, putting on hold his undeniable distress to look after her. Paula told me he kept vigil by the door for over an hour and eventually coaxed her out. She could tell he was in deep pain and bewilderment, but by some superhuman force of will, his first concern was for her. This display of nobility entirely relieved her anxiety that he was about to slit her throat (or his own, for that matter) with a kitchen knife.

They sat and talked in their house, numb with shock. He cried and begged and professed that he was still madly in love with her. She told me this was unbearably painful for her to watch – the warrior disarmed, with all his armour removed, pale and vulnerable. Her pain at the end of their marriage had been and gone months, maybe years ago; this was *his* pain and it was awful. For herself she knew there was no going back. Bob tried to persuade her that affairs can be forgiven, that he could change, that they could seek counselling together. She cried with him, as she knew it was all just way too late. Bob was also alarmed at the media frenzy that was about to erupt and begged her to save the girls from that. In the face of his desperation, she could not maintain her resolution indefinitely and conceded to his plea that they go away together as a family and try to work it out.

So there she was on the other end of the telephone, bracing herself for the morning papers, the waiting cameras and a family holiday that she was dreading. I could feel her fear and confusion in waves that reached me all the way across the River Thames. I suppose I might have guessed that, sooner or later, it had to come to this. But always there was the illusion that it was all under control, that somehow there would be a perfect, painless outcome for all involved.

She and Michael had talked and she told him that Bob was desperate to keep his family together, hoping I think, that Michael would come to her rescue. But he had a frantic Helena on his hands and he was hit by the full horror of the fall-out of their affair. On the spur of the moment they both decided the heat was too much, it wasn't worth the pain. Michael would try to put Helena back together and Paula would give it one last shot with Bob. Sobbing, Paula refused to believe that it was over with Michael but had to concede that it was all such a miserable mess, perhaps this was the right thing to do, and she surrendered herself to retreating with Bob. My heart went out to her and I asked if there was anything I could do, but of course, there was no solution to this explosion of grief. In the end Paula did ask me to try to phone Michael in the South of France.

Paula had persuaded Anita to phone Michael with the news on the Sunday morning. Michael was eating breakfast. 'Do you know your relationship with Paula is all over the morning papers?' Anita told him. Michael nearly choked on his croissant. 'Relationship? I'm still in a relationship... Oh, my God. When I spoke to Michael he sounded drained. He asked me to apologize to Anita for him, explaining that it had all been such a shock. He told me that when Helena returned to the villa she had gone ballistic.

'The British press... they're vipers,' Michael spat. 'This is a nightmare; I really can't believe it... I never promised just to dump Helena. I can't. She's destroyed and she doesn't deserve this; we've been together for three years.' He admitted to being confused about his feelings, but his first priority was to Helena and the last thing he wanted was publicly to humiliate her or Bob. 'I'm sorry...' I said to him. I had agreed to call him only for Paula's peace of mind. I was angry at the mixed messages he was giving out to her, but the more we talked, the more I understood his dilemma. 'How is she, Gerry?' His voice was much softer now. What could I say – she wants to die, she can't live without you, um... she's left her husband and taken the children away from their father and the only home they've ever known so that she can be with you? Not wishing to scare him off completely, I replied, 'You know... just as confused as you, I suppose.'

Although Helena was in the pool, he lowered his voice as he told me how deeply he felt for Paula, but he was finding the thought of parting with Helena hard to contemplate. So I accepted that he was desperately torn between the two, wanting to hurt neither, and once again I was struck by what I saw then as Michael's incredible sensitivity. I began to wonder whether his problems with Helena were a figment of Paula's fertile imagination. But then, perhaps, this scenario was not as surreal as it sounds. Michael never lost ties with any of his ex-girlfriends. He was not a typical playboy, moving from one woman to the next without a thought; Michael cared deeply about his girlfriends, and all women, maybe too much.

Paula's affair having been exposed, the *News of the World* wished the Geldofs well 'in their efforts to repair their broken marriage'. With amazing rapidity, the Geldofs obtained a special dispensation from the girls' schools and were off out of the country. Until this moment the children had had an idyllic uncomplicated childhood, but now they were whisked out of school to protect them from the publicity, and thrown on a plane with a visibly distressed father and a mother gone cold. Paula was dreading the whole ordeal. They were flying to Bono's estate in Ireland, fleeing the country as fast as they could; from there they would plan a more suitable escape. Paula was in constant contact with me. She yearned for Michael, the atmosphere was so horrendous and she needed moral support from outside.

Bono and his wife Ali were heroic in the accommodation of their suffering pals. Paula and Bob were billeted in the folly, away from the main house, and she would phone me between bouts of pitiful bargaining. She could only handle the desperation of the situation through the release of irreverent humour. When they arrived in the kitchen, Paula told me Ali was hastily peeling a picture of Michael off the fridge, which did nothing to lift Bob's spirits. To break the tension, Bono said to his wife, 'You're not having an affair with him, too, are you?' Bob added blackly: 'You've probably both had him, knowing you, yer dirty bastard.' It has been said that in their political work together, Bob despairs of the world and Bono wonders at it, arriving at the same place by different routes. While Bob railed against Michael, furious that he had been suckered into apologizing to him, Bono would take no sides. He and Ali were close to Michael too and defended him as a good man at heart. But to Paula's chagrin, he reminded her that Michael was with Helena, urging Paula not to leave what she had, to pursue such an uncertain future. All these words fell on ears deafened by love and longing, for her heart was irretrievably elsewhere.

I watched the press with fascination, as Michael and Helena arrived in London for the Brit Awards. They had obviously got their stories straight because they were convincing as a loving couple again. The papers were buzzing about the event, as Michael was receiving an award presented to him by Patsy Kensit, who, caught up in all the excitement, appeared to have thrust her hand down Michael's trousers. (Later, we found out that the photo had been doctored to give this impression.)

At the opening of a flagship Prada store in the West End, Michael was strenuous in his denial of any connection between himself and the Geldofs' separation. Of the journalists who were reporting the story, he said: 'I cannot believe I have been set up in this way. It's despicable. They surgically removed the truth and added bullshit.' Helena was more off-hand about the allegations, in that unique Scandinavian way: 'Those stories about Michael and Paula are pathetic. I also know Paula, and when I go out for a drink with my old friends in Copenhagen I often sit on someone's lap. That is all it is.' Knowing what I knew, my favourite quote from Helena at the time was: 'There is nothing to forgive him for, it's all lies. Paula is a friend. Michael and I just kissed and hugged and laughed about it…'

Phoning from an airport in the US, Paula was exasperated as her tired family boarded their third flight, but Bob was adamant that they must keep one step ahead of the press, who would spot their destination and have cameras waiting as they touched down. The ploy must have worked as they arrived in Jamaica unmolested. They stayed at founder of Island Records, Chris Blackwell's mother's house and swam in the pool at Ian Fleming's villa, Golden Eye. Paula walked with the children every day on the perfect white sand beneath the coconut trees, but she said that it was an empty paradise without Michael. For Bob it was the killing fields; Paula told me he was having a nervous breakdown. She was exhausted by his swings from grief to fury; it was awful, hopeless, she said, 'Bob has to realize that these things happen and it's over.' He begged on his knees beside her, as she reclined on a sun-lounger. The girls kept asking their father what was wrong, pleading with Anita to stop Daddy crying. My heart went out to the children and I told Paula how lucky they all were to have Anita there, but I suggested that if it got any worse she should send the girls home with their nanny.

Paula told me that one night when Anita could stand it no longer she went to see Bob in his room. He broke down in her arms and sobbed like a baby. She spent the night assuring him that he would never lose the children. Bob's only hope was that Paula might change her mind. I was slightly shocked by Paula's remorselessness; this episode recalled for me Paula's reaction to Serena and the fight for the house in Wales. But Paula explained that the only way she could bear her guilt, and the agony she was causing him, was to shut down every shred of empathy in her being.

On the fifth day of the holiday, Paula phoned me, sobbing. Bob had caught her on the phone to Michael, snatched the mobile away and in a fit of rage, she told me, he had hit her. I was aghast. My sympathies had been stacked narrowly in favour of Paula, but this tipped the balance and reminded me of all the reasons she was leaving him in the first place. If only I had known then that Paula was capable of making up such a terrible lie. Later I discovered the truth. 'I didn't know who to turn to, I was so frightened…' she said, 'so I told Michael.'

◆

Paula and Bob had been away for two weeks and they returned to London on separate flights, four hours apart. Paula and the girls returned to Bayswater and Bob to the house in Chelsea, cold and empty for the first time since they had lived there. True to her word, Anita encouraged almost daily contact between Bob and the girls, and he was a regular visitor to the flat. But these were brief recesses from his misery, home alone, calculating the pros and cons of remaining on the earth. Soon after, his closest friend Howard, an antiques dealer, moved in with him and kept a constant vigil against any unfortunate accidents.

Contrary to public appearances, as Michael told me later, he was enduring endless punishment from Helena. She had accepted that Paula was just a passing fling, like so many others of which she must have been aware. But he had been a bad boy and was now on a leash, attending all her fashion functions with her, as she metaphorically walked up and down on him in her stilettos. But when he and Paula talked, the sun came out, she made him laugh. Paula told me she was taking no chances. Having agreed to go back to their respective partners, she was following the letter of the plan but perhaps not the spirit. She complained to Michael of Bob's belligerence, while turning on her dazzling charm. It didn't take Michael long to answer the call, faced once again by the contrast between Paula and Helena. Paula was overjoyed to be back in his arms when they met for the first time since the tabloid revelations, now that the coast was a little clearer for them to meet. The whole Halkin debacle, the ensuing emotional wreckage and the collar and leash around his neck had brought Michael to the important realization that he was in love with Paula... and he told her so.

Meanwhile she and I met in the many gaps between Michael's availability. I trailed Paula round West End department stores, watching her strategically reinforce her wardrobe with slinky outfits, silk camisoles trimmed with fur, three-inch, high-heeled slippers and strappy stilettos. She was luxuriating in a retail frenzy of truly magnificent proportions.

But Michael had still not fully resolved things with Helena. She was constantly calling his mobile. Michael and Paula were more paranoid than ever at the pervasive presence of the press and had to concoct ever more elaborate plans to avoid a repeat exposure. They could not camp at Paula's flat because there were newshounds across the street, twenty-four hours a day. The epic reconstruction of Michael's house continued and he was staying with friends. So they met at the homes of mutual friends and had sex in spare bedrooms. Michael was looking for a flat to rent in Belgravia, searching for that perfect, safe, secluded apartment, three floors up with deaf, dumb and blind neighbours. This would take a while, but Paula took it as a pretty strong sign of an evolving commitment.

It must have been all the creeping around in the capital that prompted Paula to suggest a few days in the country, in the most romantic suite, in a most idyllic hotel, not ten minutes from the Geldofs' Davington Priory. When she wrote for the *Sunday Mirror* in 1994 on Britain's sexiest hotel rooms, Paula actually recommended the Chilston Park Hotel where, 'for a mere £170 a night, you can languish with your affairee in a king-size four-poster bed surrounded by oil paintings and antique furniture.'

They booked into the Chilston under Michael's full name and retired to the Regency suite. Bob would sometimes take Paula to this suite when she needed cheering up, but she needed no cheering up this time around. Their tryst was about to enter the history books. She was fond of saying that when they first had sex, 'Michael did six things I was firmly convinced were illegal.' She wrote it in her autobiography and she repeated it in interviews. But this was the night she had in mind, the night that inspired Michael's experimental side.

That evening there was a friendly buzz to the restaurant as they took their seats for dinner. They were aware of the usual furtive glances, but otherwise the crowd was civilized. Soon after they had ordered their food, a man approached the table. Paula recognized him as a journalist she liked and respected. He squatted down and said to them quietly: 'Do you realize that every table in this room is occupied by journos?' Paula and Michael quickly returned to their room and had their puddings sent up. 'How the hell do they find us every fucking time?' Michael fumed. But the proximity of the press failed to dampen their ardour. Considering their present company, they decided to cut short their stay and, knowing they would have to run the gauntlet of the photographers in the morning, decided to leave early to avoid the crush. At first light they called down to reception and were informed that there were 'rather a lot of journalists outside on the forecourt'.

Bracing themselves, they left the room and settled the bill in reception. As they stepped outside, they were met by a wall of paparazzi, literally a hundred bodies pressing towards them. It was mayhem; the photographers jostling and shouting like dealers on a trading floor. Their waiting taxi was beyond the pack and, pulling Paula in close, Michael forged forward, shouldering his way through. Then a particularly bellicose photographer blocked his way with an armful of cameras and Michael extended his arm to avoid a head-on collision. Perhaps the block was aggressive, but at the moment of impact a hundred flashbulbs fired. There was a ruck of grabbing and scuffling. Michael managed to throw Paula clear, in the direction of the car, as he went down to the ground. He made it to the door of the cab and Paula dragged him in. And as the car screeched away, Michael thumped both fists against the window and screamed at the pawing press. There on the front page of the tabloids the next morning was 'the boy' throwing a hefty punch at a photographer. The press were spitting, calling him an Aussie thug. I phoned Paula to see how she was. She was barricaded into her apartment against the mob outside on the pavement. Where was Michael? How did she feel? She said she couldn't tell me anything, but that she would come round after her nervous breakdown. That day she eventually ventured out and faced a barrage of questions from the attending pressmen, but she only answered one: was it a temporary split with Bob? 'No,' she said.

Meanwhile, several miles south, Bob was leaving his house to a similar scene. He denied that he harboured any resentment over the affair, 'I guess it's a trial separation,' he said. 'Isn't that what you call it?' As he drove off, he said: 'Life is a very hard thing sometimes. I am a bit sad and disappointed, I suppose. I don't know what I'll do now, I guess I'll just stay in love with her.' One paper quipped: 'Not even Band Aid could patch up the marriage now.'

On the other side of the Channel, Helena received the news from journalists phoning her for a reaction. But before she could reach the masses with any kind of statement, *Hello!* magazine hit the stands after the Chilston story. Continuing a well-established tradition of publishing cosy pictures of couples who are about to break up, they ran a double-page spread showing Michael and Helena entwined in the South of France. She suggested that the stories of his infidelity were part of a plot hatched by the British press. Rumours were rife that Michael and Helena had secretly wed the week before. In trepidation, I was dying to hear the story from the horse's mouth. I had to wait until the crowd outside Paula's apartment building had thinned to a single line. She said she couldn't even talk on the phone, as she suspected it was being tapped.

A couple of days later, Paula came to see me and, over a cup of Earl Grey, she gave me the details in vivid Technicolor. Michael couldn't believe that this had happened, but he was such a hero. They had set him up, she said: one photographer deliberately provoked him, while another was poised to take the shot. They grabbed at her; she showed me the livid bruises on her arm. 'It was very inconsiderate of them,' she said in a soppy voice, 'we'd hardly had any sleep.' Paula was outraged and I have no doubt that the fracas with the press was a dreadful shock. However, I assumed that she was shocked by their discovery at the Chilston and never suspected that Paula had set the whole thing up herself. Her plan was to force Michael to acknowledge their relationship publicly and to engineer a final split with Helena. I would never have believed that she could be so casually cruel to Bob and Helena. When I discovered the truth much later I also found it difficult to square Paula's terror of a press free-for-all with her actions.

For now, Paula told me about the current Michael/Helena situation. There would be no reconciliation this time. Helena was furious at learning from the press about Michael's latest betrayal. They had spoken and he had been dumped; it was over, ended by his girlfriend, which was how it always happened. For Michael the split was no relief – he was going through the mill over Helena.

Slowly the details of their sleepness night unfolded, Paula clearly building to something – and it wasn't the fight on the front steps. She was displaying an embarrassed, almost teenage fascination: 'Michael is a very naughty boy, he's a very, very bad boy.' Settling into her narrative, she described an afternoon of intricate rituals that Michael had performed on her. Practices she had never imagined, let alone experienced. But along with the giggling discomfort, there was a dreamy serenity to her account. Their stay at the Chilston was to be a fantasy break for Paula and, as she dropped her bags in the antique opulence of their suite, it seemed like all the tragedy and heartache that had led them to this perfect moment was

Paula in a typically glamorous pose in August 1983.
She was a devotee of ultra–feminine fifties-style dresses.

TV presenter Hughie Green of *Opportunity Knocks* fame. Paula discovered in 1997 that he was her real father.

Paula's mother, ex Bluebell dancer, actress, writer and artist, Heller Toren (now known as Helene Thornton Bosment), photographed in 1964, when Paula was five.

Jess Yates, presenter of the religious TV programme *Stars on Sunday*, who brought Paula up. She adored him and was devastated when DNA tests proved Hughie Green's paternity.

Paula and Bob in the early days of their eighteen-year relationship. Bob's fellow band members in the Boomtown Rats dubbed her 'the limpet', so closely did she cling to the gangly Irishman.

Paula with Jools Holland, her co-presenter on *The Tube*, which became a cult TV music show in the eighties.

Paula, Bob, Fifi and Peaches at the opening of Disneyland, Paris in April 1992. As usual, Bob strides ahead, with Paula trailing several paces behind.

Paula headlining with sunflower and bee.

Inset: At the 1994 Brit Awards in London, where Paula presented the Best British Group award to the Stereo MCs.

Paula, wearing astro–turf and plastic vegetables, with co-presenter Gaby Roslin at the launch of Channel 4's *The Big Breakfast* in 1992.

Paula and her publishing team at a signing session for her autobiography in 1995.

Paula and Michael with baby Tiger Lily and Peaches at a Versace fashion show in Milan in 1996.

Paula during a visit to Sydney in September 1996.

Michael reads *Che Guevara* while he and Paula try to relax on Magnetic Island, Great Barrier Reef, Australia in January 1997.

Paula, Belinda Brewin and Tiger arriving at the High Court in London in May 1998 for a custody hearing over Paula and Bob's three daughters.

Paula and twenty-six-year-old Kingsley O'Keke, whom she met at Clouds rehab clinic in Wiltshire.

In a bid to relaunch her career, in 1999 Paula hosted a TV special starring Jerry Springer, but the show, recorded before a celebrity audience, disintegrated into a humiliating catastrophe.

Paula and Tiger share a tender moment in April 2000, five months before Paula's death.

Paula's white coffin, covered in deep pink lilies, is carried into St Mary Magdalene's church in Faversham, Kent.

A clearly grieving Bob leaves the funeral of his former wife. He personally arranged every detail of the ceremony.

Paula's friends Catherine Mayer (left), Belinda Brewin (centre) and Jo Fairley-Sams leave Westminster Coroners Court after the inquest into her death.

not in vain. They had escaped, it seemed, they had survived and, what was more important to her than anything in the world, their love had survived. And to her eternal gratitude it was clear that Michael felt exactly the same way. They had champagne and oysters delivered to the room. 'The last time I had oysters I was sick,' Paula laughed. 'It was a platter fit for Neptune himself.' 'Didn't you get embarrassed?' I asked, when she told me about the things he did with the exotic starter. She told me how Michael had managed to lose an oyster in her vagina. I was aghast and Paula had no difficulty feeding my incredulous appetite for more of Michael's novel talent in the bedroom. For her the oyster had been one of the most sensual experiences she had ever known and now she understood why they were regarded as an aphrodisiac. I protested. Shoving shellfish up her fanny didn't sound at all sensual to me. But when she described the whole scene, I had to amend my assumptions.

Michael slid an oyster from its shell and slurped it from between her breasts. Then he chased another down her chest with his mouth, it slipped across her stomach giving her butterflies of pleasure and, negotiating her thighs, he coaxed it into her vagina with his tongue. By now Paula was in fits of giggles on my sofa. This foreplay went on for hours, bringing her close to orgasm but never quite getting her there. She explained that he had the bedside manner of a surgeon, watching her eyes for any sign of fear, balancing her perfectly between resistance and ecstasy. He smoothly moved their play from one experience to another; sometimes it was a straight caress or massage, sometimes it was oral titillation, sometimes it was novel and the anticipation of each new move maintained her rising level of stimulation. With each new revelation Paula no longer squirmed and covered her face with a handy cushion – she was much more open and, I felt, much more alive than I had ever seen her before.

Months later she told me that there were other props involved. He brought her to climax with the stroke of a silk scarf and a feather. And even later still she said that while they made love he gently squeezed her neck until the lack of blood made her temples pump, and the dizziness increased the intensity of her orgasm. Lovemaking with Michael seemed so natural, so magical. Michael had flair, a love of women; he was creative, expressive, with a passion to share the many pleasures he had himself experienced. He celebrated everything about Paula, her body, her mind, the things she said – and his adoration liberated her.

———— ◆ ————

But there was blood in the water. The press were all over Paula and Michael. They couldn't move in public without the sound of running feet, the click of cameras and the clamour of questions. The papers were tearing up their reputations piece by piece. For Michael it was a real fall from grace, he wasn't used to being vilified, quite the opposite: up until then he had enjoyed the generosity of the world's press. In London he could always do what he pleased: he could play the rock star at a club and get all the adulation, if he wished, or he could wear a hat and pass unnoticed down Oxford Street. No more. But however frustrating this was, he was beyond furious about their cruel assassination of Paula. I had seen Paula get uncharitable press before, but I was horrified at the vitriol that was spewing out of the tabloids now. 'The women are the worst, I don't get it. What happened to The Emily Pankhurst brigade?' she complained. My thoughts wandered back to Jo Fairley's prophecy. I suggested: 'They don't know *you*, it's your image that gets up their noses.' It was ignorance that was responsible for the publication of such tripe and I thought that at least someone should pick up on the angle of her uniqueness; there was a strong argument for Paula as a feminist icon. Regardless of her status in the home, her public face was the epitome of girl-power, choosing exactly who she wanted to be: funny, successful and sexy – the original ladette. But she was way ahead of her time in so many ways, I guess it was inevitable: she was being martyred for the cause. Paula would often refer to Lynda Lee-Potter's article – it hurt her terribly:

SPOILT AND SELFISH, PAULA'S A LITTLE MISS HYPOCRITE –
Paula Yates is always playing a role. Perhaps she could now decide to act out the part of devotedly loyal, steadfast wife who abandons her inner yearnings for freedom and stays with her husband and children.

Another female writer said, 'The hypocrisy of the blonde bitch has always set my teeth on edge...'

To his eternal credit Michael braved the jeers to stay and protect Paula. Looking for some respite, he suggested a visit to the Oscar ceremony; *there* was a celebrity hunting ground where their antics would fit right in with those of the locals and receive no attention at all – except the good kind.

Paula must have been in a playful mood, I smiled to myself, as I scanned the newspaper pictures of her negotiating Heathrow airport, flaunting the slogan 'Little Miss Trouble' across her crop-top. Her skirt was equally cropped and her legs looked amazing. She had given birth to three children and her figure looked as if it hadn't changed since she was eighteen. The papers didn't like what she wore, or that she was boarding a flight to LA or that Michael was thought to be following her out there.

'Why do they get their knickers in such a twist?' she asked. But this time she found it quite amusing that they so predictably took the bait. It was a deliberate 'two-fingered salute' to the press, she told me. The girls looked immaculate in their floral-print frilly dresses, white socks and neatly brushed hair, but the tabloids touted the same 'irresponsible mother' line. I suspected that her lightness of heart had a lot to do with the fact that she was about to put 6,000 miles between her and the tabloids.

Her upbeat mood didn't last. The next phone call I received was full of despondency. She had caught sight of an article written by John Junor in the *Mail on Sunday*:

For me, Paula Yates has as much sex appeal as a bag of unwashed potatoes. Her lover, Mr Michael Hutchence, doesn't look as if he changes his underpants too often either. They are both people of absolutely zero consequence. So, should what this squalid couple do with their own squalid lives be of any real interest to anyone – except Miss Yates's three children and her cuckolded husband Mr Bob Geldof, who also always looks as if a good bath would do him no harm?

Paula was exasperated: 'It's so vicious. If we're of such little consequence, why don't they leave us alone?' Before Michael could follow Paula to LA he had to visit a police station and endure the indignity of an arrest in which they read him the charges and required him to appear in court for the assault of a photojournalist at the Chilston. This was a technicality, but the press ran 'Aussie thug arrested for assault,' implying that he had been run in, handcuffed and thrown in the back of a paddy wagon.

Apparently Michael was far more concerned for his parents, than for himself, over his appearance in court; he didn't want to let his mother down, whom he always described as a real lady. Michael often talked of his family; it was obvious that he was incredibly close to them and extremely proud. Paula's last call had worried me but she now allayed my concern by describing her delight with the villa she was renting, at the Sunset Marquis Hotel, with the children and Anita. She was so relieved to be there, California was the antithesis of everything London had come to represent for her – no one knew who she was or what was being obsessed about in that little British bubble on the other side of the pond.

She immediately went about organizing a party for Michael's arrival and, on his behalf, invited all his friends in California. So much had changed over the last year, I could only listen with vague wonder at the life she was leading now. She was paying £700 a night for the villa and God knows how much the party was costing her, with its full complement of serving staff, cooks, bouncers and food fit for the A-list. She begged me to fly over to help organize it, even offering to pay for my flight. But much as I would have loved to escape into her sparkling world, I just couldn't afford to. Paula was making new friends wherever she went: Madonna, John Travolta, Kim Basinger, Alec Baldwin and Brad Pitt, to mention the handful that I remember. I smiled at the stories she told of their reactions to the eccentric English girl in Hollywood. By the sound of it, she could not have been better received. She was glamorous and more than equal to the personalities she was entertaining.

Paula was amazed to hear that Bob had been seen haunting the post-Oscar parties. This was so out of character for him. He had visited Paula and the girls at their villa. He was still hoping for a reconciliation, she said. But the door was not even slightly ajar. He had played with the children and sat with Anita for a whole afternoon repeating the same word over and over: 'Why?' When he returned to London, dejected and alone, all he would say to the eager reporters was: 'She's my best friend.'

Back in town, the media obsession with Paula and Michael showed no signs of abating. Inspired by Michael's taste for chic design, Paula acquired a whole new wardrobe. This, of course, was construed incorrectly as an attempt to compete with Helena. She told me Michael had introduced her to the concept of wearing one ring on each hand rather than each finger. With a new life, a new man, a new flat and a new look, Paula started talking about a new body. She had always dreamed about getting a boob job, but had never dared to while she was with Bob. Now it cropped up in her conversation as an increasing possibility, and Michael encouraged her, but only if it was her heart's desire.

Within a week they dared to be seen going out together. This was their first official date: Janet Jackson's party at Brown's nightspot. Paula told me it was like being an escaped convict. The building was entirely surrounded by reporters. They had to leave by the back alley, but they were still blinded by dozens of flashbulbs firing in their faces, and even with the protection of the female bodyguard Paula had hired, they had to manhandle a photographer who tried to join them in Michael's Jaguar.

Collecting the children from school was an ordeal for all the parents now. The gates were besieged by hopeful photographers for about two weeks and the registrar sent out a circular to us all, saying something like: 'Due to unprecedented media interest in fellow parents, you might be inconvenienced by the press when dropping off or collecting your child. Please try not to clip anyone with your Volvos and please remember to keep the gates closed.' I remember that when Paula and Michael turned up together for the first time, there were no furtive glances, every parent and staff member just stopped still and gawped. Once or twice Bob and Paula turned up together, and I thought it most bizarre that they were hand-in-hand – he looking rather lost. At school sports days they made a convincing show of unity. Like the absence of argument in their marriage, there seemed an absence of malice in their separation. But it was Anita who most regularly did the run and Bob began to make more frequent appearances on his own. Paula was right, he looked like 'an exhausted bloodhound, down on his luck and taken to drink'. His weight loss was shocking.

Sadly the papers had no interest in Bob's part in the breakdown of the marriage, but as frustrated as she was at her own portrayal by the tabloids, Paula was furious about Michael's denigration. 'He's not a beer-swigging Aussie lout, he's an artist,' she insisted in her autobiography. 'He told me he's cried in every major art gallery in the world.' It was impossible to miss the breadth of his interests. Like Paula, he was an avid reader, with several books on the go at a time. They were strewn about the apartment in various states of disrepair and were diverse in their subjects, particularly art, history and politics. I remember him listening to the conversation of someone running down Margaret Thatcher. Michael said that he was not in a position to comment, but immediately rectified his ignorance. The very next day he bought several books on the Iron Lady and consumed them within a week. Thereafter he proclaimed that, though he could not entirely agree with her politically, he perceived a woman who, far from the popular portrayal of a tyrannical autocrat, was deeply sensitive and intelligent.

The three of us had dinner in a restaurant on the Fulham Road. Michael was railing against Bob's unassailable status in celebrity society. He had gone to visit the set of *The Word*, a music show produced by Planet 24, as a guest of Simon Le Bon. But on arrival Michael was rudely ejected by the show's staff, in an act of outraged solidarity for their boss. 'He had a nerve turning up,' they said. 'If Paula shows her face she'll get a similar reception.' There was a time when Michael, the rock legend, would have had the red carpet rolled out for him.

It had been the first time I had seen Paula eat so much. Pasta was her choice that evening. She was eating as if she hadn't seen a square meal in ages. Michael ordered an incredibly expensive wine and talked knowledgeably about the grape to the two of us, who didn't have a clue. I remember noting that his intake of alcohol that night was tame by his usual lavish standards and he gave Paula full credit for encouraging him to slow down; he was only partaking when they went out, he said. Soon after, I met Michael's manager in the UK, who said he was relieved to see him sipping orange juice, and I made sure he realized it was Paula's influence because she would never have taken credit herself.

The conversation about the press that evening wasn't entirely negative; Michael talked about the positive and valid role of reporting news. He commented on the value of aggressive investigation to reveal the ills of the world, and he mentioned Watergate, the end of Apartheid and the Gulf War. When Michael was in London he read the *Guardian*.

After the meal, Paula leaned up against Michael and he stroked her hair and ran his hand over her bare shoulder. In all the time I saw them together I never saw Michael's hands away from her – he was always stroking her, wrapping his arms around her; she never had to make the first move, it was always there for her – affection, adoration on tap. 'It's impossible to feel insecure with Michael,' she would say.

They seemed to have the perfect relationship. Paula had found her soulmate; as well as being madly in love with her, Michael adored her children, whom he was already describing with the pride a father would his own. 'You see, we can't even enjoy a quiet meal with a friend,' Michael complained as we left with a bodyguard in tow. Scuttling photographers were hailing cabs to take them back to their darkrooms and hungry editors.

'It's all centred around Paula's clothes, Paula's hair, Paula's behaviour, Paula's hypocrisy, Paula's children's names, Paula walking out on Saint Bob,' he continued before they dropped me off at my house. None of us, not even Jo Fairley, could have guessed that she would become a national obsession. She was the Princess Diana of popular culture and was receiving the exact same treatment at the hands of the press.

'What is the great thrill about my personal life? Is it just because I deserted my post?' Paula speculated when we all discussed the matter, which we did repeatedly. 'I never promised to be the girl next door.'

———— ◆ ————

The heat on the street was such that we could no longer comfortably meet in public and I saw little of Paula at school. She and Michael mainly went out at night, usually with a bodyguard and always with a chauffeur. I went with them a couple of times but on the whole I tended to spend time with them at their apartments.

The apartment in Bayswater had only ever been a temporary safe house; it was poky and Paula detested it. She desperately needed more space and was looking for a house to buy. In the meantime, she rented an altogether grander residence in Mayfair. It was owned by the Rama Foundation, part of the empire of the born-again Christian multi-millionaire who started the Rock Café chain. Anita had been making concerned noises to her about the finances, too, and Paula's accountant phoned and warned her to rein in the spending or she might go bankrupt.

'You won't believe it,' said Paula in horror, one day, as she greeted me at the door. 'I've been sacked!' Like the Death Star, Planet 24 had struck. After three years as the only good thing on TV in the morning, after she had co-founded the show, promoted it and supported Bob while he launched it, she had been unceremoniously axed with no notice. Paula hadn't been on *The Big Breakfast* bed since the Halkin exposure but she had had every intention of returning. However, there had been an uneasy silence from the production team and she had sensed that she was being frozen out. 'Miss Yates is to take leave of absence from *The Big Breakfast*' the programme's producers announced. It was Bob's partner to whom it finally fell to tell Paula the bad news. He had called her that afternoon and declared that *The Big Breakfast* was a family show and her lifestyle was no longer in keeping with its image. Paula told me that his exact words were, 'You'll never be clean again.'

Michael called it vicious and spiteful. We could have understood them letting her go for unreliability, perhaps, or disruption to programming but this was like an abuse of human rights, to be sacked for leaving your husband and to be labelled a slut into the bargain. 'It's turning into a seventeenth-century witch hunt!' Paula kept repeating. Her anger was clear, but her voice was level. She had used up all her indignation and was in the flat, cold calm of nervous exhaustion. Paula denounced Bob as the architect of her redundancy and, for me, the value of Bob's stock was falling through the floor. Was he deliberately sabotaging her and his children's means of survival? There seemed a touch of lunacy to it – surely Bob knew that if this ever went to court, he would have to find twice as much money out of his own pocket.

They never changed the format of Paula's slot on *The Big Breakfast* bed. We were all flabbergasted when Bob and the management of Planet 24 replaced Paula on the bed with Lily Savage, alter-ego of transvestite Paul O'Grady.

Michael drove himself to distraction over this slap in the face to the woman he loved. He argued that even an ordinary employee would have been given some kind of severance pay, three months at the very least, and that her treatment was especially harsh after all she had done for Bob's career. If I had ever doubted Paula's story regarding the control Bob held over her, I no longer did. Regardless of the anti-Geldof sentiment running rife, I was worrying about Paula's finances, and when Michael left the room I expressed my concern. She was evasive and played it down, fearful perhaps that Michael would return while we were discussing it, but I could see that she was anxious. 'How the hell are you going to afford to buy a house now?' I asked. I knew that she had seen one she wanted, which was owned by a couple she had met at school. They weren't selling immediately, but were planning to do so within a few months and Paula had agreed to pay a deposit to show good faith.

'*Hello!* have been pestering me for an interview and I've told them to get stuffed about twenty times,' Paula replied. She was afraid her words would be twisted. She also told me that her literary agent was trying to persuade her to exploit the new public interest in her life and write an autobiography. 'I suppose I'm going to have to do it now,' she said with hopeless resignation. She then dropped the bombshell that she had given her house to Bob – she'd signed it over two days ago. 'I just felt so sorry for him, Gerry. I told him I wanted a divorce, he was crying and telling me that he had lost everything – me, the girls – and he pleaded with me not to take the family home as well.' 'But he has a sodding great big pile in the country. How many does he need?' I replied, feeling anger surge up in me. I remember her looking up at me with an embarrassed, helpless expression, and then the full import hit me like the hook that follows a boxer's jab. 'But he's just had you sacked!' and Paula nodded dumbly. I could hardly speak through my rage. Paula obviously needed to get her hands on some money immediately and now the *Hello!* piece looked like manna from heaven. I pointed out that *Hello!* don't rake the dirt, choosing instead to sugar-coat their articles, and anyway her press could hardly get any worse. But I wasn't sure about the autobiography.

Paula agreed with me, but doing an interview with *Hello!* didn't exactly fit with her 'Little Miss Trouble' approach to the press. But they were offering £25,000 – did she have a choice?

Hello! gave her eight pages on which to 'set the record straight'. The interview was gentle, the pictures sumptuous, but what impressed me most was the dignified restraint with which Paula conducted herself. There was not a hint of malice or blame in the piece. She said, 'I so wanted my marriage to work. It did, after all, last for eighteen years, which in our business is extremely rare and certainly means you've tried as hard as you can to keep it happy for as long as possible. But then there just came a point when I knew in my heart that it was over. Every woman who has had to end a marriage knows that it takes a huge amount of courage to do anything about it.' Paula claimed she was unable to say what exactly had caused the break-up: 'All I know is that during the past two years I was beginning to feel more and more unhappy.'

The tabloids responded predictably. How dare she speak out, she was manipulating people's sympathy, and so on. Regardless of what the media threw at her and Michael, Paula didn't regret leaving Bob for a second, she told me. She had never been happier, and no matter how hard it might get, she swore she would not break. 'How could I when I have Michael's arms around me to protect and love me?' It was true; as bad as it was, she was more content than I had seen her since we had reconnected in 1992.

'If only people could see, perhaps they'd understand. This is the purest thing I have ever experienced. Why do they make it sound so dirty?' Paula cried. 'Michael's given me my life back.' He was helping her understand how vital it was to express how she felt. She could challenge him, disagree, argue with him, without fear, because Michael rejoiced in all her emotions. She felt that he was educating her to rejoice in her womanhood. He loved going shopping, according to Paula, never complained and took a keen interest while she tried on endless frocks. If she had a doctor's appointment, he offered to go with her, and when she had her first appointment with the plastic surgeon he wanted to hold her hand, but Paula thought that his presence at the operating table might rather spoil the impact of showing off her augmented breasts. She had been for various pre-op consultations, chosen the shape and groped the implants. As I remember, she chose the saline-filled, which the consultant said were less robust than the silicones, but she chose them for their natural softness.

When she came out of the clinic she was like an excited schoolgirl. 'Don't they hurt?' I asked her. 'Don't you have to wear bandages and all that stuff?' not quite believing that she'd really had them done. I was amazed that she was back to business as usual, as she put it, so quickly. The doctor had given her an exhaustive list of after-care instructions: keep them strapped up in the bandages for at least a week, do not touch, the swelling was natural and would abate after a few days, and so on. Paula didn't follow any of them. She had the bandages off as soon as she got home and Michael had enjoyed them right away. Then she had squeezed them into her new low-cut black Prada dress and they had hit the town together. As usual, she was far enough ahead of the trend to spark debate – the pros and cons of plastic surgery, and the cons of Paula Yates. 'Here we go again,' Michael complained, 'why can't she have them done without a load of bile? Anyone else and it would get ignored.'

While Paula revelled in her new cleavage, the press were not as amused: *She's always had an over-inflated ego, but now she wants boobs to match. But do they make them barrage balloon size? And will she be supplying her own hot air? God knows there's been enough of it over the years.*

The only cosmetic surgery I really consider worthwhile would be an operation to reduce the size of Paula's mouth. Oh, and perhaps the introduction of a couple of live brain cells. You never know, they might breed...

The rumour-mongers also touted the notion that her extravagant new assets were for Michael's pleasure and that it was terrible that a woman would undergo such mutilation for a man. This was fundamentally wide of the mark and Michael pointed out how casually the papers trivialized and belittled her. 'It's Paolo that enjoys them; seeing her so happy with them gives me joy. It lit her up, that's a beautiful feeling. Why do they turn it into something ugly?'

Anyway, Michael was not a breast man, he was a self-confessed bottom-man. I saw him on many occasions smoothing his hand over Paula's pert butt. He described it as the best ass he had ever seen. 'I want to paint it,' he said. Michael had no part in encouraging Paula to go under the knife; he merely encouraged her to follow her heart. She did it for herself and her obvious pleasure in them was plain to see. After the op, Michael's only mention was to coo to her: 'You love your new breasts, don't you, honey?'

It was a couple of days later that I plucked up the courage to ask her if I could see them. I was asking her if she needed to wear a bra, if they felt heavy and if she was still stimulated when Michael touched them. We were sitting on the sofa with a cup of tea; she was in a pink camisole even though it was the middle of the day, and I was dressed sensibly for the cold weather outside. Without hesitation or embarrassment she lifted her breasts out of her skimpy satin front, holding them with her hands as if offering them to me. They were astounding, not a hint of artificiality. They had an authentic softness which I had not anticipated and they looked and felt entirely natural, unlike others I'd seen with the shape and consistency of marshmallow teacakes. 'It's amazing what you can put on American Express!' Paula said, as they went back into her nightwear. She said they were the best things she had spent her money on and I could see her point, even though I was thinking about her bank account again.

It was clear from Paula's expression that she was trying to hide her anxiety. The only work she had done for weeks was hosting Mr Gay UK at Manchester's Hacienda club, for £5,000. That paid for the boobs and the two ribs she had had removed to slim her already wasp-like waist. But it didn't cover the £20,000 for the caps on her teeth, so that, she joked, she could 'wear white without looking like Dracula's mother'. And it didn't cover just about everything else I could see around me.

I knew we weren't getting the complete picture of her financial crisis and I guessed she was keeping Michael in the dark too. I assumed that along with the press harassment, she would not add to his burden with her petty cash receipts. 'Even the journalism has dried up,' Paula said. She told me that she had no choice but to decline the offers of magazine work. The editors expected her to use her columns to dish the dirt on her own affair and were no longer interested in her views on the world. A couple of programme ideas had gone by the wayside and her planned appearance as a 'manager' on *Fantasy Football League*, a show hosted by Frank Skinner and David Baddiel, had also been dropped. 'I'm sure Bob was behind that, he knows the producer,' she said. I considered for a second that perhaps Paula's whirlwind romance had interfered with ideas and deadlines, but that was irrelevant now. She was in a mess and she needed my support.

At home I went through the people I knew who might be able to help. I guessed Paula's best chance for good cash would be TV work, at which I thought she excelled. I made one phone call. I came off the phone buzzing and optimistic for Paula's prospects, where before there had been none. I had been talking to my good friend Sophie with whom I had worked at Henson Enterprises and who had been responsible for selling their programmes worldwide. Sophie was now the general director of programming for FlexTech Plc, the company that owned the British cable channels: Bravo, UK Gold, TTC, Living UK, etc. Together we had evolved a strategy for improving the public's perception of Paula, a prerequisite, in Sophie's view, for relaunching her television career, and I went straight round to see her with the good news.

'Not all the doors are closed,' I enthused. FlexTech did not have the audiences of the terrestrial channels, but they did have a solid reputation and large budgets to spend on advertising and would pitch programmes to Channel 4. Hence, if Paula were to do some presenting, it might first appear that she was taking a step backwards, but in time her face would be on billboards and, with better press, she could make it back to prime-time presenting. Paula told me that Bob had been trying to get a foot in the door at FlexTech with some of his own ideas and it amused her no end that we were already in the boardroom.

She was excited, although she didn't really want to work in television any more; she still wanted to do what she loved best – to write. But she told me that although there were other books her agent was trying to push, the publishers were fixated on her autobiography. 'In the end, it doesn't matter what I do – I just have to work.' I told Paula that it *did* matter what she did. I thought the autobiography would be a publicity disaster for her. Sure, it would earn a fast buck but the fall-out would be horrendous. I explained that the TV work was a long-term, slow-burn solution. It would not yield immediate results but gradually she would get less hassle from the press and slowly get her career back. This time it would be on her terms, on her merits, and out of Bob's control. The response to the *Hello!* piece had been bad enough – if she went ahead with the autobiography, the same thing would happen again only it would be ten times worse. And I could just see how it would be marketed…

Rather defensively, I asked Paula what her own PR person was proposing, but he hadn't been in touch – 'conflict of interest,' she said. He would be engaged with Bob and Planet 24 exclusively. 'There's no one else out there – will you help me make this work?' she asked.

For a moment, I thought about the part of the conversation I had had with Sophie that I had not shared with Paula. Although she had no doubt that I could turn Paula's press around, she was adamant that it should be on a professional basis. 'If you do this, Gerry, make sure you draw up a contract with Paula. I can help you with that. I know these people, they'll suck you dry for nothing in return. Don't do anything without a contract.' I valued Sophie's advice very highly, she was a businesswoman and a professional. But the few phone calls I had in mind to help Paula were not about business, they were about friendship.

'What about Jo Fairley?' I suggested to Paula. 'She must have loads of contacts in the press.' 'This is going to take a little more than a few words in mates' ears over lunch,' she replied. 'And right now, not even my own mother has a good word for me, she's completely sided with Bob.' Indeed, the tide of opinion for Paula and her lover was at its lowest ebb. 'What about Jools or Annie Lennox? Can't you rally support from a few different quarters?' I hadn't seen any of her old friends visit or heard Paula even mention them for a long while. I assumed that she had been so wrapped up in Michael that she hadn't had the time. 'I still speak to Jools. He'll always be there for me. The others as well, but it's not the same anymore, everyone's so close to Bob, too.' Simon and Yasmin Le Bon were being very supportive, I reminded her, and she agreed that they had been fantastic, especially Yasmin, considering she had been one of Helena's best friends for years.

I felt for Paula, I wanted to help but I could not see how I could possibly do the job myself. I had experience of publicity, but nothing on the scale required here; I had never worked on crisis management and Paula needed Red Adair to put out the fires raging in her public life. But what was nagging at me above all these considerations was her evasion over the autobiography and I could tell that there was something going on.

I told her: 'If you do the book, it will be professional suicide.' But Paula could not see beyond an immediate solution to her pressing problem – finding the deposit for her house. I condemned her approach in no uncertain terms. She didn't need me to help her screw this up, she could do that all by herself. If she thought it would work out, I told her to go ahead, she was more than capable of doing her own PR. 'I don't have the luxury of time,' she said. She meant that she didn't have time to do it right, but what was more important than getting her career back on track?

Michael was. He consumed her on every level and I started to wonder what else she didn't have time for. I asked if the children were getting the attention they needed. I challenged her about the film of white powder I had seen on the coffee table at Michael's flat; I said I didn't care what they did together, it wasn't my business, but it's not good around the girls. I pointed out that she had left one man who'd promised to go into therapy for her and taken up with a serial womanizer who did hard drugs. She became agitated, defensive; she was quietly seething that I had dared challenge her. She insisted that Michael was off hard drugs, that he dabbled only occasionally.

My relationship with Paula cooled for a while after this confrontation. I received a tiny taste of what Jo Fairley must have experienced when she had challenged Paula all those years earlier. We conversed from time to time, but there was a palpable distance in her attitude towards me.

Anita was working full time – days, evenings and weekends – and though she did not directly complain, I detected that she was feeling the strain of her employer's chaotic lifestyle. Bob's best friend was still living with him. The only ray of sunshine in his life was that he was seeing his children regularly and they were all making up for lost time. Bob had never been remotely interested in the celebrity social circuit before, but now he was being partied back to life by his good friends, Jerry Hall and Marie Helvin. They insisted that he must get up and get out, Bob told me later, otherwise he would never have left the house. He was often to be seen on the arms of the vintage supermodels, looking pretty battered but making the effort. 'Jerry was amazing,' Bob told me later. 'She forced me to think about life after Paula.'

On a different circuit altogether, Paula and Michael were often out on the town, and each time the papers found something to talk about: 'Michael Hutchence launched a volley of abuse and pushed the waiting photographers violently. One photographer said: "He totally lost it, he was out of control".'

Michael and Paula spent the summer in the South of France, popping back every so often for various parties, a Rolling Stones concert and Michael being charged with assault at Maidstone police station. They were spotted in St Tropez flaunting their delight in each other; on a rented motor launch with Simon and Yasmin Le Bon – 'clearly very much in love...'

Paula's freeze on me thawed when *GQ* magazine, the glossy lad-culture manifesto, ran a split-panel front cover, featuring on the one side Helena Christensen, all tanned and smooth and semi-naked, and on the other Paula, sans make-up, pre-boob job and looking tired. The caption ran: 'Seriously, would you trade her in for Paula Yates?' Back in London, she called me, crying with rage about the beastly cover jibe, and our disagreement of the month before was totally eclipsed.

Responding to her distress, Michael had just been on the phone, screaming at the editor, defending the honour of both women in a five-minute rant littered with expletives. The unrepentant journalist put the phone down on him. It was interesting that in the reviews of the front cover there was a generous scattering of sympathy for Paula against the blatant sexism of the article; whereas Michael's gallant vigilante action played straight into the hands of his critics, confirming his tabloid reputation as a 'temperamental Aussie yob'. Paula told me that Helena phoned her in an open-handed act of solidarity, but she was suspicious of the call because Helena had been calling Michael frequently on his mobile.

———— ◆ ————

Paula and I put the small blip in our relationship down to pressure and resolved to forgive and forget, so in August, when Paula offered to pay my airfare to Nice, I threw caution to the wind and took off for a weekend, leaving the children with my ex-husband. It proved a pleasant break and it was lovely to be with them both, so relaxed, happy and obviously in love.

The villa was beyond anything I could have imagined. It had none of the garish opulence that one might associate with the rock fraternity; instead there was almost a rural modesty to its rough stucco finish and terracotta pan tiles. It had all the trappings though – a swimming pool, manicured lawns and a stunning veranda shaded by a trellis draped in grapevines. Michael took me on a tour of the grounds and showed me his pet project, an impressive vegetable garden. Inside the house Paula was in the throes of marking her territory, dressing up the sparse Mediterranean interiors with her uniquely theatrical designs. The white stucco walls, that seemed to have seeped in from outside, were splashed with colour tests.

'It's going to be Paoloed,' Michael laughed. Paula took me through all the rooms. Michael, she said, was relishing the alien invasion of Indian fabrics and medieval tapestries. It reminded me how inventive she could be, as I trailed from room to room, each with a different theme emerging, though the work was far from complete. In the kitchen, I was curious to see dozens of pictures of Michael staring straight into the camera, with various expressions, tacked up around the walls and work-surfaces. He caught me peering at them and explained that it was all part of his therapy. It was an exercise in meeting himself, learning to love who he really was. Michael's work towards holistic health went beyond this journey inwards. Paula and I sat out on the veranda in the morning sun, with coffee and croissants, while Michael mixed aerobics, Tai Chi and kick-boxing on the lawn.

During the day, Paula would disappear for stints on her typewriter. She was working on three books simultaneously, she told me: her autobiography, a biography of her father and an airport novel called *Wakey Wakey*, about the antics on a breakfast TV show (the latter two projects were never completed). Propped above her desk was a picture of Clive James, whose wit she admired and used as the inspiration for her own, as she rattled away with never a missed-key nor dab of white-out.

The global rock clan had arrived for their summer stint. Bono's villa was within shouting distance of Michael's walled paradise and he was regularly in and out. Johnny Depp and Kate Moss dropped in for a few days. Meanwhile, Michael tended to Paula's every need, bringing her breakfast in bed, massaging oil into her back and thighs. It was like a honeymoon paradise. This idyllic setting and the absence of external stress to interrupt their pleasure in each other transported the two of them. Michael told me of the latest work he had been doing on his solo album as we sat underneath the vine canopy on the first evening, drinking

Pernod and ice to the sound of the cicadas. Paula's feet were resting in his lap and he stroked them almost continually, even as he rolled a joint with the delicate reverence of an ancient Chinese ritual.

Back in London's sooty version of summer, I winced when I saw the cover of a promotional feature on Paula's autobiography. She had dyed her hair a shocking red and spiked it into two devil horns, and there she was, pictured in the swimming pool, holding an inflatable trident. It was striking, inventive, brilliantly art directed, but tragically missing the opportunity to portray a more palatable image. It was back to 'Little Miss Trouble' but with an emphasis on the bad, whose irony would be lost on the readership.

6 paula: her true story?

PAULA HAD BEEN VERY BUSY. She'd bought a house in Clapham, southwest London, before she went out to the South of France. On returning she had started moving in. When we went shopping for the Indian fabrics together in Southall market, she told me of the horrendous scene a week earlier. She had gone around to her old house, to retrieve her stuff. Bob was taken by surprise but he reluctantly allowed her to scavenge. Paula had a large van waiting; she filled it with everything that she could remotely claim as hers, while Bob kept a careful inventory and returned contentious items back inside. She must have put up a good fight because, by the time she had finished, the house had been stripped. She was most amused that even the picture of Bob with Mother Teresa went in the van. Bob's sister later told me that on one of Paula's return trips, she had pleaded with her not to strip the house completely bare, at least to leave some pictures of the girls, but Paula had told her not to get involved.

It was the day of Pixie's birthday party and Michael greeted me at the door of their new house. He treated me to a huge hug and the proud smile of a father whose child has reached another year. Anita was busy in the kitchen adding the final touches to the pink iced buns and homemade lemonade. The house, as everyone agreed, was looking incredible. 'I did it all in four weeks,' Paula announced proudly. Michael's arm hung lazily around Paula's shoulder; he nodded his agreement with the admiring acknowledgements of her handiwork from the guests. 'She's brilliant at everything,' Michael purred, giving a few lucky mothers a tour of the ground floor, which was perfumed with the scent of the flowers he had had delivered for Pixie that morning.

I think everyone was keen to have a snoop around, not only to see Paula's sumptuous interior designs but also to look for any sign of the fire that had gutted the main room only ten days before. Paula had left a joss stick burning downstairs when she took herself to bed for a daytime nap. Anita said it was lucky she'd taken the girls with her to Sainsbury's because when she returned, the house was surrounded by fire engines, with Paula still bleary-eyed from sleep. I had been round shortly afterwards to see the house for the first time – she had only got the keys a few days before. It was an almighty mess, everything was black and Paula was racing round cleaning up and redecorating. Sometimes her energy made my head spin.

But for a subtle smell of charcoal lingering in the sitting room, there was no sign of the accident now; the house was immaculate. It was clear that Michael adored it and said how much he enjoyed coming back to its Paula-esque quality and loving atmosphere. He was particularly impressed with the hand-made leopard skin carpet running up the stairs, pointing out the detail and quality, relieved that it had survived the blaze after a good shampooing.

Instead of dropping off their children and leaving, as they normally would, all the parents stayed. I watched Michael jump up to greet the next knock on the door and give the same familiar greeting: 'Hi, ooh, don't you look lovely,' bending down to examine another little party frock. 'Pixie, honey, you have another friend,' he said. 'That's Michael all over. Wants everyone to feel at home,' said Paula with pride. This was the first occasion when I had heard Michael talk of Paula and the children as 'his girls', showing off how clever they all were and how Peaches could recite poetry. He said that that he had been looking forward to the party all week and had had to cancel a meeting in LA, and rearrange a studio session for the following week. I was impressed.

The wonderful harmony of the house was abruptly interrupted by a loud knock at the door and the appearance of a dishevelled figure in Paula's hallway. 'Oh, shit. I hope he's not going to stay,' Paula whispered in my ear as she bustled out of the kitchen towards Bob. She greeted him with a polite but not overly welcoming tone in her voice. Bob gave Paula a kind of half-smile, half-grimace, before turning to Pixie, 'What the fuck have they done to yer hair?' he asked gruffly. 'Oh, dad, don't be so old-fashioned,' Pixie giggled. She had found Paula's blood-orange hair dye and dyed her own hair to match Paula's. As Bob made his way into the sitting room, Paula came back to the kitchen muttering, 'This is a disaster. I've got a husband having a Norman Bates moment and my lover is upstairs on the phone to his ex-girlfriend.' Bob sat amongst the mothers like the Angel of Death, refusing to respond to Paula's attempts to make him feel welcome, which she persisted with, despite her silent desire for him to return from whence he came. Anita had begged for him to be allowed to stay, reminding both Paula and Michael that he was still the children's father. Paula had said, 'He can be their father someplace else, instead of ruining my party brooding over the wording of his suicide note.'

'Come on, Paula,' Anita was consoling in her soft voice. 'This must be very difficult for him: the house, the children, Michael. That's all he can focus on.' It was true, but Bob's heavy mood so permeated the room, that no one dared strike up conversation. Michael was now off the phone and muttering obscenities to Anita about Bob's 'self-indulgent' behaviour. He felt very strongly that it was inexcusable not to make a little effort, at the very least, towards the mothers and their children. 'If I stay here any longer,' Michael announced as he left the room, 'I'll do something I might regret.' Later that evening Paula complained about Bob. She had found Michael sitting on her bed, sobbing and asking why Bob had ruined it for Pixie. I thought this was strangely melodramatic, but put his over-sensitivity down to sheer exhaustion with the escalating saga. He had not bargained for this when he embarked on the affair. Paula explained that his deep sensitivity could be his own worst enemy, but it was her best friend. I could see that his was not the usual rock god attitude towards family life – his priority was to protect the children from negative adult behaviour. Months later, when I recalled this event, I wondered whether Michael had been going through some kind of drug comedown. The aftermath of Ecstasy, for example, can make some people very emotional. But if he had been on a drug, there was no other sign of it. He steered clear of booze, and was doing only a little 'puff', which I occasionally shared with him. There was no doubt that Michael's feelings were close to the surface that day, but it may just have been his deepening affection for the girls, combined with the pathos of the moment.

It was certainly obvious that Michael loved being with the girls and they adored him. 'When's Michael coming home?' they would repeatedly ask their mother and Anita. When he arrived, they would mob him, proudly displaying paintings they had done for him. Michael gave them real attention and he did give them lots of time: playing, swinging them around, teaching them new songs and reading to them, which earned him Anita's undying approval.

I asked Paula if she and Michael were officially living together now. Michael obviously adored the house and it was big enough for two families, with its six large bedrooms, three sitting rooms, a kitchen to rival that of a country manor house and its wooden veranda looking over an enormous garden with a tree house into the bargain. Paula replied that he had virtually moved in but she thought his mother was concerned about Michael making this a permanent arrangement, and for that reason they were not broadcasting their cohabitation.

Paula told me that she had liked Michael's mother, Patricia, when she met her, but with a hint of reservation. It had been a daunting experience to meet the woman Michael described with more reverence than anyone else in his life. Perhaps there was a tinge of jealousy, which would not be unnatural. She told me how strong Patricia was, a successful make-up artist in Australia and in America; she had brought up three children on virtually no money and built an impressive business. Michael would tell me later that she looked a good twenty years younger than she was and Paula agreed, adding that she was extremely chic and well-spoken. 'He worships his mother. With Bob, there was no mother to impress, to upset, to get on your nerves,' Paula explained. It mattered to Michael to have his mother's approval, and maybe this niggled Paula a little. In fairness I could understand Patricia's concern for her son – his situation was now a far cry from his bachelor days. He was 'Daddy' to three children, and partner to a woman going through an acrimonious divorce. That would give any mother the jitters.

Paula's financial affairs were a continuing worry. She had borrowed the deposit to buy the house from a friend of Michael's. The advance for her autobiography had been earmarked for the house, but it must have been diverted elsewhere. Why borrow the money from a friend of Michael's? Why hadn't Michael stumped up himself?

Strange dealings and fire notwithstanding, the house was a new start to Paula's life. The vibrant colours with which she had decorated every room expressed the optimism and joy that she was feeling. A vivid purple floated across the walls of the sitting room into a vaporous background, setting off the large oils and watercolours lining its length. Jewelled Indian fabrics fell from the windows, cascading over the vast twin sofas. A coffee table covered in white candles and a large wooden bowl of colourful, gold-tipped Sobranie cigarettes sat next to a Victorian glass urn filled with lollipops. Every corner, every detail, drew the eye, from the gentle lick of the flames in the fireplace, to the dimmed fairy lights drizzled across sequinned tablecloths. Every room was a baroque testament to Paula's flair for juxtaposing kitsch, style and grace. Paula and I made a truce on the wisdom of publishing her autobiography. She was adamant that she had kept well away from anything salacious, that there was nothing in there to worry about, but my attitude remained: 'On your head be it'. She shrugged it off and told me that she had written it in three weeks; Jo had given her a hand with the editing. I knew she was clever, but three weeks? I thought that was really going some. Perhaps it accounted for the cut-and-paste feel to the final product. Reading it did allay some of my fears, however. Could there be a chance for her critics to see some of her worth? The book had a surreal dreamlike quality, always entertaining, and exhibiting a distinctive comic rhythm.

Paula Yates: The Autobiography was written in gaps between the main events of her life and it rarely came up in our conversation, until word of its imminent publication began to leak to the press. It was an eagerly awaited 'kiss and tell', with all sorts of speculation running in the papers. Before Paula was officially promoting it, there were rumours of panic at her publishers, HarperCollins, that she had circumvented anything remotely juicy – anything that readers would expect and relish. 'You don't need to be nasty, just truthful,' they told her. Their fretting bored her, she was not going to give them what they wanted, she would just stall for time and make minor concessions. Her publishers were trying to force her hand, she told me, insisting she include details of her relationships and sex life. Paula showed me a letter in which they listed questions to prompt her memory.

Ironically, in the interviews she gave at the time of the launch, she gave out more that could be viewed as 'juicy' than was contained in the entire volume in its final form. She said Bob was 'incredibly controlling'. He actually admits this rather proudly. He says that, on a day-to-day level, if he is not in complete control of his environment he feels like he is 'going mad.'

Of her father: 'He used to make me kiss him and make me have cuddles even when I didn't want to.' And of Michael: 'He is a really, really good person and then he's the naughtiest, most evil boy I've ever come across, who can't be trusted to walk down the street on his own.'

One interviewer, who had obviously not read the book, asked about its accuracy and she admitted: 'There are millions of things I did not put in. I'm not mad, you know.' But only Paula would have the cheek to admit publicly that it was 'purely a money-making venture'. This was one of those devil-may-care throwaway lines that so riled the nation, perhaps because it too bluntly stripped away the illusion of media integrity. In her handling of all the random and probing questions, Paula showed that the trials of the past months had done nothing to blunt her wit or dull her mind. As an example, at a signing of her book in Harrods, when she was asked what she had that Helena Christensen did not, she answered, 'Michael!'

One reporter asked her if she would go back and change anything? And she said, 'No, I wouldn't, but I'd like to change a lot of things that other people have done.' And to the question: What is your motto in life? Paula said: 'Always hold your stomach in.'

But sadly those are my best memories of the book launch. Paula was head and shoulders above the parapet when a tidal wave of hate broke over her. On the one hand this backlash came as no surprise to me. But I could not but sympathize with what she was going through, knowing how deeply these comments would cut her. The vitriol of some of the reviews made me angry. 'Yeah, I did leave a lot out,' she confessed in another interview. 'I left anything out that would hurt anyone, regardless of whether I thought they'd been hideous. I wouldn't have been able to do it.'

Meanwhile I lamented her lack of direction in handling the exposure – she just focused on the highest bid. The book was serialized in the *Sun*, with pictures of her semi-naked – designed to boost sales, sure to draw scorn. She complained bitterly to Michael, who agreed that they had hacked her book to pieces, but he couldn't see that she had played no small part in this herself. She said that her radical efforts to promote the book had kept the publishers off her back. The readers wanted more than she was prepared to give, so she made up for it by giving them some flesh instead. As usual, they went for the style and missed the content. 'When will someone look beyond the cover of this book?' asked Paula. She was invited on a small tour of TV talk shows. She was excited and hopeful that by getting back on to the box to promote her book, she would receive a much-needed boost to her popularity. It was disastrous. I could hardly watch as the various hosts ripped her to shreds in front of studio audiences and a million viewers at home, cheaply insulting her children's names and generally ridiculing her very existence.

I particularly remember her appearance on the *Clive Anderson Show*. A former barrister, Anderson had won a place on the small screen with his uniquely British brand of acerbic wit. He was one of the most watchable chat-show hosts to appear for a decade, because he had the bedside manner of a hyena on happy pills, and a killer instinct to go with it. But it wasn't so entertaining watching him destroying Paula. That night he took every opportunity to shame her and I watched Paula struggle through, biting her bottom lip to stop the tears.

As if her ego were not receiving enough of a battering from the press, her own mother denounced Paula's account of her upbringing as the fantasies of a spoilt child. This put the last remaining nails in her own coffin, because Paula was already furious with her mother for denouncing her over the split with Bob. Paula was determined that it would be the last time her mother abandoned her.

'I didn't know she was writing a novel – I thought it was an autobiography,' said Paula's mother, now Helene Thornton Bosment. Helene insisted that she and Jess adored Paula, who had a 'very privileged' childhood. Helene suggested that someone take Paula's autobiography to a psychiatrist and see what they make of it.

On 27 October Paula underwent her ultimate humiliation. She was looking forward to appearing on *Have I Got News For You* – the popular satirical current affairs game show on BBC television, then hosted by Angus Deayton – though I was concerned for her after the Anderson mauling. She told me, however, that here was a bunch of people who ignored the sniping of the gutter press and would respect her as a fellow journalist. Sure, she realized there would be some teasing, but this tended to consist of good-natured, ultimately clever digs. And I thought, Paula is more than capable, intellectually, of keeping up with the fast, witty repartee and of defending herself. But from the start, the show did not go her way, and Paula, it seemed, was not armed with her usual arsenal of clever one-line put-downs. Ian Hislop, editor of *Private Eye* magazine, was gunning for Paula in a way that he has only surpassed recently in the award-winning show that followed tabloid revelations of Angus Deayton's infidelity and drug use. Sad to say, Paula could not summon the dignity with which Deayton suffered his humiliation. She tried to hit back, but with no ammunition her retaliation descended to insult.

After a reference to the 'bad-tempered and smelly' artist Vincent Van Gogh, Hislop said: 'I know someone like that' – a veiled reference to Bob, who, Paula had written, went for years without a bath. Hislop then asked Paula point blank if she'd had a boob job. A woman in the audience cried, 'Yes!' and Paula commented that a 'fellow sister shouldn't give the game away,' to which Hislop countered: 'Fellow sister? What about Helena Christensen?' Hislop attacked Paula's autobiography and said: 'It only took six days to write. Did you have writer's block?' by which time Paula was visibly losing her sense of humour. Then she featured in the show's Odd One Out round which showed photos of celebrities with plastic boobs. The camera was cutting to Michael, who was in the audience, watching with increasing discomfort until Paula blew her top and branded Hislop the 'sperm of the devil'. She accused him of 'taking the mickey' and snapped, 'you cheeky little cunt! You're a horrible little man.'

The panellists found this immensely amusing and afterwards Hislop said, 'I was most insulted to be called the sperm of the devil. But I was more annoyed that we lost to Merton and her.' Michael told me later that he found Paula collapsed and sobbing uncontrollably backstage. To his utter outrage, the show's participants had filed past her and not one person had stopped to offer a word of consolation. The audience was divided. 'It was appallingly misogynistic,' said one woman. 'They were three big schoolboys ganging up on the one girl in the playground.' But Paula had made herself an easy target with that cursed autobiography.

A day or so after the show, I saw Paula at school and she looked worse than awful. I went up and gave her a long hug. She clung to me and tried to stifle her tears. 'Have I got a target painted on my forehead? Why is it I get attacked at every turn? Why am I the bad guy? When is someone going to take a crack at Bob, for Christ's sake?' While the children played upstairs at my house, Paula unburdened herself. Far from paying out lavish maintenance cheques, Bob was apparently only giving her £300 a week on which she was expected to keep the girls in the style to which they were accustomed. She had clothes, uniforms and school books to buy, and a mortgage to pay. That was without food, house bills and everyday running expenses. She'd handed over the house *she* had bought with her *Tube* money to Bob. Bob had said that he would continue to pay the school fees. Just running a car to take them in and collect them would eat a large hole in £300 per week. And Bob took the car.

His girls had been brought up as little princesses. They were used to having the clothes to dress up in, ribbons, make-up, paints and trips out. Paula claimed that Bob had said that the kids were spoilt, then he said all a child needs is a T-shirt and jeans, and when Paula told him they were growing out of their shoes and needed new ones, she claimed that Bob said, 'Cut the fronts off the ones they have'. Michael was furious, too; his reaction was to take the girls out immediately to buy them what they needed, and more.

'I supported him all those years and he gives me £300 a week. And he won't even give it to me – he gives it to Anita.' This seemed to be the ultimate abuse that showed Bob's lack of respect for Paula. The full extent of Paula's financial disaster had dawned, compounded, it would seem, in no small way by the extent of Bob's spite. 'Why did you let it get this bad?' I asked her. She said she'd done everything she could to solve the problems herself. She'd done the autobiography, she had two other books in draft…but it wasn't enough and now it was getting on top of her. 'Why didn't you tell me what was going on?' I said, feeling guilty that I had missed the signs, deserted her when she really needed help and taken umbrage when she refused my advice. Paula said she was embarrassed. Now it all made sense. The only blessing I could think of was that she had Michael and he was bound to help. But Paula had not told him, because she had always reassured him that she wasn't after his money, and now she wanted to keep to that promise. She had told him bits and pieces, here and there, and indeed he was taking them out later to buy uniforms for the girls, but on the whole, she said, she brushed off the rumours with plausible excuses.

I was sick with fury. Perhaps it was my empathy for Paula's situation that made me forget her extravagances, the apartments she had rented, the clothes and trips abroad. I had somehow assumed that she was entitled to these, earned them for herself, but that Bob or Michael or both should share the financial responsibility for the home and children. I knew that Paula would prefer to be truly independent, but if Bob's influence was indeed preventing Paula from pursuing her profession, she was trapped in a financial hell.

———— ◆ ————

I got on the phone to my friend in PR with an address book to rival Ivana Trump's. Brimming with ideas as always, he was off and running with the notion of redressing the balance in Bob and Paula's reputations while elevating Paula as a more heavyweight TV presenter. Now he suggested a dinner party where the contacts could focus on the task in hand. Not long after, I was having lunch with David Montgomery, the fabled newspaper executive. As lunch progressed, he enquired about Paula. I knew he wasn't fishing for a news story and as Paula's plight had been playing on my mind, I took the opportunity to recount the awful challenges facing my beleaguered friend. I asked him to have a quiet word with Matthew

Wright, the editor of the *Show Biz* column in the *Mirror*, one of the papers that he controlled, and who, to my mind was relentless in his persecution of Paula. Why, David asked, did Paula do such a daft thing as to write an autobiography at a time like this?

I explained that she needed the money and she'd have got a whole pile more if she'd been prepared to reveal all and dish the dirt on Bob... but she wouldn't. David remained sceptical that Paula could be so desperate for money when she was going out with a millionaire rock star and she must be getting a big fat maintenance cheque from Bob every month. I protested vehemently and explained about the £300 a week maintenance given directly to the children's nanny; how Paula had handed over *her* house to him in return for a quickie divorce; how two days later she had got the sack, and he had reneged on the deal – Paula was now having to sue him for divorce, costing more money and more time.

The press baron was impressed that we really had a story here and suggested Paula do an interview, go for the jugular on Bob. I replied that Paula had been slammed too much already for opening her mouth. So he offered another suggestion: build a relationship with a showbiz column. He told me how it works: take them something they can use, become a reliable source of inside information, then once the relationship develops you're in a position to barter. Get to know the showbiz editor on one tabloid and you end up with a lot of influence, because the broadsheets watch the tabloids for their celebrity leads.

I began to see the possibility of building a bridge between Paula and the newspapers, to give her a voice without it being *her* voice. 'One tabloid's showbiz and feature page is always trying to outdo another and *vice versa* – it's not personal, it's all part of the game,' David explained. 'They try to discredit each other's stories at every opportunity – it's the spirit of competition.' He considered the possibility that if all the papers were agreeing on the Paula Yates saga, then there might be room for an opposite argument. After all, this story was selling a lot of newspapers. He reminded me, however, that he was no longer directly involved in the editorial, he had to avoid the temptation to tamper and the decision to take on the other papers would be down to the showbiz editor and editor-in-chief. It seemed that by default I was now acting as PR consultant for Paula, though I was still insisting that I would just make a few calls. She was excited, thanking me for my efforts, but doubtful that the tide of opinion could ever be changed 'even if I grow wings and a halo'.

Having read the showbiz columns avidly, and listened to Paula and Michael reviling the people who wrote them, I had an image of the editors as a frightening, hard-bitten bunch. So it was with considerable trepidation that I phoned the *Mirror* and asked for the showbiz editor, Matthew Wright. I was pleasantly surprised by his sensitive but direct phone manner. With hindsight I realized that showbiz columnists would have to be approachable to win the trust of a publicity-wary celebrity. I introduced myself as a friend of Paula's and explained that I was confused about the relentless negative press she received. Was it not time for a little journalistic objectivity, to put Paula's side? Matthew listened as I skirted and hinted around Bob's misdeeds, in a bid to swing his opinion. Matthew was charm personified, but I was only too aware that this was the perfect tactic to tease out more than I wanted to give.

'So, who are you to Paula? Are you acting for her?' he asked. I replied, absolutely not, that I was a concerned friend. Then he made the extraordinary suggestion that I might direct my concern into helping Paula get off drugs. That was a punch I had not been prepared for, but reeling a little, I continued my call as if he had just told me Paula had forgotten to bring her laundry in. 'Paula's got kids, she should know better,' he warned. 'I don't know where you get this rubbish from,' I replied, trying to sound relaxed in the face of his accusations. Matthew then proceeded to present his 'evidence' which seemed to centre around Paula and Michael emerging from clubs looking the worse for wear. I thought that was the point of nightclubs, I said, but I didn't often go with them so I couldn't comment. I told him that as far as I knew, Michael's only vice these days was freshly squeezed orange juice, and he laughed, and said that next I'd be telling him that Michael had joined the boy scouts. But he insisted that he 'liked the guy' and thought his music was great, but that he was probably bad news for Paula. The line seemed to have shifted somewhat, away from Paula's total culpability. I felt I was getting somewhere, his interest was piqued and I noted that our phone call was progressing well beyond the polite minimum. Feeling a little safer, I ventured into more details about Paula's side. I told him that she has always been a fantastic mother, my children adored her and that Michael was proving to be a very stabilizing influence on them all.

'If you went to their house, you'd be so surprised,' I coaxed. I reminded him that Paula had stayed with Bob for eighteen years – that was impressive and took hard work. She was a very intelligent woman. It had been the biggest decision of her life to walk out, a decision she would hardly take lightly or whimsically. I pointed out that it was unusual for any family to keep a nanny longer than six months and Anita had been there for over ten years. Paula had given her £4,000 as a down payment on a terraced house near her old home in Yorkshire, because Anita had fallen in love with it. Did this not all add up to a legitimate tale to tell, a right to the benefit of the doubt, innocent until proven guilty?

'She's been a good friend to me, I've been through hell over the last three years,' I added, hoping that Paula was becoming human in his mind, and that would be the first step in altering his attitude to her.

Matthew continued to listen, saying 'Hmm, interesting', 'Hmm, good point.' He agreed that there were always two sides to a story. 'Give me time to think about it,' he concluded. 'If I write any of this stuff in, what do I call you?' he asked. I didn't want my name used and I definitely did not want to be referred to as Paula's PR consultant as, on hearing the term, everyone automatically thinks 'spin'. Matthew suggested he use the words, 'A friend said...'

I watched his column with anticipation. Nothing changed dramatically – there was still the undercurrent of criticism – but I began to notice, over time, that he was bringing into his stories a fairer viewpoint. Paula wasn't impressed, having expected a sudden U-turn. I told her that the angle was gradually changing, and doubts were creeping in about Paula's total guilt and Bob's total innocence.

Matthew's comments on the drug-taking niggled at me. If he were right then I had to pull back – it would be a war no one could win. I had been noticing a change in Paula over the past few months – voice occasionally slurred on the phone, stumbling down the stairs, slightly paranoid and short-tempered, but this could all be put down to stress and late nights. Michael's drug habits were known and almost *de rigueur* in his role as 'rock star', but in him I saw someone looking hard at his past, looking hard at himself, into himself, and I could see he was still off the booze. They didn't have weeping lesions on their forearms, they weren't endangering anybody, they weren't violent or offensive. I knew nothing about Class A drugs, but I had no compunction about lecturing against drug abuse and I didn't have to be in Al-Anon to know it was dangerous.

I tentatively confronted Paula. She admitted that she and Michael were taking Prozac to cope with the stress of the past year, as well as Rohypnol to help them sleep. Paula told me how worried she had become at Michael's stress levels. He was getting seriously depressed and she felt he really needed to see someone, and could I recommend anybody? I was sceptical that the press could be getting him down so badly that he needed anti-depressants. Paula explained that everything in his life was combining to cause him huge stress. It was his career, though, that he most concerned about. He was risking a new direction, away from INXS, and it could be disastrous if it didn't work out. 'He hasn't got a record deal for his solo album yet,' she said. I was confused – he was in the middle of recording and he didn't have a deal? He was under contract with his record company for another INXS album but he was trying to broker a deal for himself as a solo artist. No wonder he was away so much of the time: not only was he a tax exile, but he had two albums to produce and one of them was yet to have any takers.

I could see that Michael would be so exhausted from the recording and wheeler-dealing that he could sleep all day. But Paula wasn't working on an album, so why had her sleeping patterns changed so dramatically? She hardly ever left the house these days, and whenever I popped round she looked as if she was doing a negligée photo shoot, or a session to promote her autobiography in the *Sun*. For school runs she was pulling a coat round her camisole and Michael, whose hair was now growing and getting darker by the week, would accompany her. I had to tell her I was really concerned to hear that she was taking such strong tablets for her anxiety and suggested that she go back to her therapist. Why didn't she take Michael along too? But she didn't want to share her therapist with Michael, she said, she didn't think it would be right. This all seemed fair enough to me; I didn't think anything more about it until later and I promised to contact a friend who knew every therapist between here and Arizona.

My friend did come up with a few suggestions, people he knew who would take a gentle approach and help Michael *through* a difficult patch rather than see Michael *as* a difficult patch.

7 can't buy me love

THE *NEWS OF THE WORLD* CAUGHT BOB in Rome with his new squeeze, thirty-year-old French actress Jeanne Marine. They wrote that the two had met recently. 'It's rubbish that they've just met,' said Paula. 'He met her on the set of *Braveheart* long before we broke up.' Bob had been offered a part in the film, but had had to turn it down because he was touring in Dubai. Paula's mood was as gloomy as the autumn sky. We were sitting in the park with our children, huddled together. Paula was kitted out in more layers than I had seen her wear for a good while, but there was still room for improvement: a warm hat and a pair of boots, for instance, instead of her usual high-heeled shoes, in which, to my amazement, she could still run after the children if she had to.

She told me that a neighbour from the block of flats that overlooked her back garden had told her that the paparazzi were bribing people for access to their bedrooms and living rooms, to get a shot into her house. The photographers had said that if they managed to get a shot of Paula in the bathroom, they would double the money. 'Paula's bum, Paula's tits, Paula's going to go fucking mad if they don't stop,' she said. But this anxiety was eclipsed by her over-riding concern for her relationship, as she was convinced that Michael was hankering to leave her. They had had a big fight the night before. This row wasn't like the ones she had almost come to enjoy, rows that healed her fear of confrontation, of expressing herself. In this row they had fisticuffs. 'I've given up everything for him,' Paula cried. He had told her that he didn't know how much longer he could cope, being with 'the most hated woman in the country'. Then he had left for LA.

Michael had told me recently that he was taking four Prozac tablets a day. He wondered if it was the dosage that was making him feel listless. That certainly sounded excessive to me. I questioned the wisdom of his doctor's prescription. He smiled at me in the way he did sometimes, when he thought I was being naïve. Michael gave me a hug and said, 'You're priceless. So innocent really, aren't you, Gerry-Berry. Paula knows a man who asks no questions, he's well known for his relaxed attitude. She gets her medication in bulk and she's been giving them to me.' Prozac wasn't new to him, he had taken it after his accident in 1992, when he fell off a bicycle and hit his head, fracturing his skull and severing nerves that left him with only 10 per cent of his sense of taste and smell. Friends have said that this was a turning point for Michael's psyche, and led to bouts of depression.

Richard Lowenstein, a noted film producer, who cast Michael as a junkie in his 1986 cult film *Dogs in Space*, about a group of post-punk deadbeats in Melbourne, and also produced the video for the first American INXS hit 'Need You Tonight', became one of Michael's closest friends. In an interview he gave after Michael's death, he said:

Ever since the accident, he was on a decline. I'd never seen any evidence of depression, erratic behaviour or violent temper before it. I saw all these things after it. One night, he broke down and sobbed in my arms, 'I can't even taste my girlfriend any more'. His girlfriend then was Helena. For someone who was such a sensual being, this loss of primary senses affected his notion of place in the world and, I believe, damaged his psyche.

Michael had told me that he resented going back to anti-depressants, having weaned himself off them, once he was on the mend. He said that he had been using kick-boxing and yoga ever since, to combat the gloom, looking for a natural high. But now he felt like he was sliding back, that he remained in a fragile state and the symptoms of the accident were resurfacing. 'Is Michael seeing the doctor my friend recommended?' I asked Paula. She said that he didn't have the time, but that if they got back together she would persuade him to take up the appointment. 'The children heard the row,' Paula told me. 'Pixie keeps asking for Michael.'

I handed her a tissue from my bag to wipe away the tears running down her face. She was begging me to talk to someone in the press, to stop the endless criticism; she was convinced that if the adverse publicity ceased, everything would return to normal. 'They're driving him away. He hates this country now. He hates living here. If he sees another bit of bad press, I think he's going to leave.'

I agreed to phone Matthew Wright again. Paula was desperate, impatient with the slow progress of leaked anecdotal stories and a gradual change in attitude among the press. She wanted rapid results now. I took from her rantings the parts that I thought might be useful and kept the rest between us. 'Tell him that Bob made me ask permission to use the telephone and that if I wanted to decorate any of the rooms I had to ask his permission even when it was my money. Tell him that I supported him financially when his stupid restaurant failed.'

I assured her Michael would be back. He still loved her very much, within days he would be missing her sparkle, and the anecdotes that made him laugh. He would miss her beauty. She cheered up a bit. 'Look at the weight I've put on,' she giggled. 'I'm getting fat.' This was the first time her weight-gain seemed to bother her. She had put on one and a half stone and Michael loved it. He was always running his hands over her voluptuous curves, professing to prefer the 'new Paolo'. 'This is a woman, and this woman is a man's fantasy,' he would say.

I thought she suited the new curves – she had maintained a flat stomach, there were no extra bulges, just wonderful belly-dancer curves that suited her new breasts so much better. 'I want them bigger, as soon as I've got the dosh I'm going to have them done again.' Paula was getting insecure and when she told me that, for months, she had wanted to get pregnant, I had to hide my uneasiness. It was too early to be thinking about babies with Michael. She revealed secret trips to a fertility clinic, as far back as 1994. 'My doctor gave me fertility treatment when I wanted Peaches, he just thought I was wanting another baby with Bob,' she said. Paula had written in her autobiography that she and Michael had shopped for baby clothes together in New York as early as 1988. I thought at the time that it must have been one of her jokes; I certainly couldn't imagine that in the present circumstances having a child was Michael's number one priority. Paula assured me that he had gone with her for the treatment.

I tried to tell myself that this was a sign of his commitment to her but a crying baby, soiled nappies, a large family with money problems, a hiatus in his career, and a press at war with them? A baby had to be the last thing Michael needed. 'Hold off on the baby,' I urged. 'Get yourself and your relationship sorted first.' The advice fell on deaf ears. On 28 November, she presented the British Hairdressing Awards in a dress tight enough to show off her small bulge. The press asked, she denied, and they launched into criticizing her hairdo, which was still orange, and the glasses she wore, dubbing it the 'Chris Evans look'. Despite her denials, I was pretty sure I knew the truth. So, whilst she had fretted away to me about wanting Michael's baby, she had already conceived. No wonder she was obsessing about pregnancy, no wonder she was paranoid about Michael coming back – her emotions would be all over the place for the first three months. There was a rapid change in her attitude when I saw her a few days after the award show, for which she received a fee of £5,000. She was looking exhilarated.

Meanwhile my informal conversations with various newspeople continued. I had been introduced to a couple more contacts in the press. I was feeling more confident about dealing gossip on 'the black market', but I would never allow them to think of me in a professional capacity – my information was always written as 'the opinion of a good friend'. The PR guru, on the other hand, was rather excited on my behalf, and was less discreet than I would have liked about my close relationship with Paula. He soon began introducing me as a professional PR agent representing Paula Yates, and in no time at all a trickle of phone calls became a flood. I did what Paula asked and denied the pregnancy, while she continued to provoke speculation, darting into the nearest Mothercare at the slightest hint of a camera lens.

Bob was going from strength to strength; he still had his doldrum days, but Jeanne had definitely invigorated his life. He never slept with his new girlfriend when the girls were around – Pixie still needed cuddles in the middle of the night and he didn't feel it was appropriate for them to see him in bed with Jeanne. Anita liked Jeanne right from the start. She was careful not to mention her too much to Paula, save the odd comment on how good it was for the girls to see their Daddy happy again and that Jeanne was nice to them.

'Humpf,' Paula would say at the mention of Jeanne Marine, 'he might as well have got himself a poodle. She can't speak a word of English.' Jeanne said almost nothing, the English language was a real struggle for her and Anita said she could say only a few words. '"Biscuit" and "walkies", probably,' Paula said.

I had began to notice a deterioration in Anita's health. 'Ninoor's always been a hypochondriac,' Paula would tell me. It was the first indication that she was becoming irritated by Anita. It didn't help that Bob continued to entrust Anita with the maintenance, on the strict instruction that none was given to Paula, ever. Anita observed the letter of that law, but her personal account was becoming overdrawn, as Paula had been unable to pay her for at least four months. But, regardless, she still soldiered on every day and at weekends, because she really loved the girls and she really loved Paula. Bob apparently didn't pay her at weekends, when she took the children over and stayed to look after them, and in the holidays she spent with him.

'Anita's certainly changed her tune about Bob' – here was the source of Paula's gripe with her loyal nanny. She could feel that Bob was confiding his every woe and hope in Anita, whereas when the couple had broken up, Anita had been unequivocal in her support for Paula. 'She was the one who encouraged me to leave Bob,' Paula told me. This was getting bizarre. The Paula I knew would take great pains to see another's point of view (except where Serena, her father's girlfriend was concerned) and even when Michael criticized someone, she was the first to present a defence. Suspicion abounded. Paula's mistrust was almost palpable. She got very tired when Michael was around and tended to blow things out of proportion. He wanted her to go to clubs all night and then she wasn't there for the children in the morning. When Michael left the house, to record or visit LA, Paula could catch up on her sleep. Now she was pregnant and I was optimistic for the future. Anita loved babies, and even Bob thought it would be good for Paula. 'She's always at her happiest when she's pregnant,' he said.

'The girls want to call her Tiger,' Paula told me when they found out she was having a girl. *Peter Pan* was their favourite movie and they adored

Tiger Lily the little Red Indian squaw. Paula wanted 'Heavenly' and Michael loved the name 'Hiraani'. They all played around with the mix for months, but although Paula's pregnancy seemed the only topic of conversation in the house, it was still a secret to the outside world. Michael and Paula were going to Australia for Christmas and he wanted to tell his parents in person.

'It's only a couple of weeks away, honey,' Michael tried to soothe Paula's natural desire to tell the world. But Paula knew Michael was nervous. They had rowed and he let slip that his mother, his father and the boys in INXS had all warned him on separate occasions not to get too involved with Paula. Making up, he tried to explain that none of these people knew her, they had only his interests at heart, and knowing his history with relationships, they feared for Paula's children. He told her he had told them what he had told everyone: he was fully committed to her and the girls, and his family had all relaxed now, about everything. But the damage was done; Paula was not able to forget. She took it personally and would never quite feel comfortable with his mother, nor any of them again. Michael did wait until they got to Australia before telling his mother, but chose to phone his father with the news before they left England. Kell Hutchence did not whoop for joy, Michael told me.

'My dad thought it was too soon. I told him that we had been waiting ten years for this baby, how could it be too soon?' said Michael, referring to the first time he and Paula had slept together, in New York. He had bought baby clothes for her then, he said, and Paula had kept the dress wrapped in tissue paper all these years, confirming the story Paula had told in her book.

———— ◆ ————

The decorations were up on the first of the month. Christmas 1995 arrived early in Paula's house, because she and Michael were leaving England on 16 December.

We were on the way to her bank to collect £2,000 in cash. 'The house is going to look magical this year,' Paula told me. Michael and Paula called each other twenty times a day. She would fill him in with every little detail, a minute-by-minute brief on every incident that had happened since the last call. Laughter was the sound I heard most often coming down the line. The two of them were joyfully happy, and fears of their parting were banished to the past.

When Paula had called Michael in LA after their big fight, to tell him that she was pregnant, he had been considerably underwhelmed. Paula apparently knew that Michael would find the news difficult, but this didn't faze her, as she was sure he would come round. He did, and within days he was back, armed with presents for her and the girls.

It felt like a lifetime ago since we sat in the coffee shop and Paula first hinted at her unhappiness. And here we were again; only this time with a different story to tell. She was happy, brimming with ideas for decorating the house, and it sounded as if she would need every penny of the money she had just taken out to put her plans into action: a tree in every room, lights to rival the Blackpool illuminations, and a coloured-glass Santa with sleigh and ten reindeer for outside. 'It's going to be fit for the second coming,' Paula laughed.

Paula's problems were behind her now. Everyone had been right – pregnancy suited her, and even Anita was back in favour. 'Anita's baking three tons of mince pies a day, it's no wonder I'm getting fat,' she smiled, tapping her stomach. I knew that meant she was appreciating Anita's efforts to make a brilliant Christmas for her, Michael and the girls. The only thing spoiling the anticipation was Bob's delay in signing the papers for the children to get their visas. Bob was to have the children over Christmas. Paula hated being parted from them, but agreed with him that the girls would probably prefer to spend the festive season at Davington Priory, where they had celebrated it since they were born.

As we drove home, the car full to the brim with the spoils of Paula's shopping spree – ribbons, holly, gold spray paints, cinnamon and nutmeg room sprays and oil burners – she asked me to drive past her old house in Redburn Street. 'I loved that house, it was mine, I can't believe I was so stupid.' Paula loved living just off the King's Road, having its shops just on her doorstep, the park, where she had taken her babies to sleep in their prams while she wrote, the neighbours, whom she had come to know and with some of whom she had worked, the restaurants and coffee bars where she would meet her friends, Peter Jones where she bought the children's uniforms. It was a far cry from where she lived now, surrounded by high-rise apartment blocks and none of the creature comforts she had been used to. It was no wonder she ploughed so much energy into making the interior of her house so sumptuous.

The house looked fabulous when Paula had finished decorating it. Anita had been to Toys 'R' Us and brought back sackloads of presents and we all got busy wrapping them up, to put under the tree. It was in moments like these that the strength and love in Paula's relationship with Anita was most obvious: the time and effort they gave, the laughter and reminiscing they did while wrapping up the presents, recounting old stories about the girls and the glee on their faces when they discussed how happy the girls would be to get this year's presents. Anita constructed the new mini-kitchen in their playroom, because she felt that it was pointless for them to wait until Christmas Day and Paula agreed. Paula never queried anything Anita asked her to pay for, where the girls were concerned. When Anita suggested that a walk-in wardrobe fitted with a carved unit of open shelves for ribbons, hats, scarves, socks, pants, and make-up, could be constructed before Christmas, Paula had it done. When the children complained that their beds were boring compared to hers, she and Anita erected a rose-print canopy, worthy of a *House and Gardens* feature.

Paula was glowing; her hair was back to blonde. Not as peroxide as her trademark colour, but a softer blonde as befitted an exotic expectant mother, and it suited her. She was talking about hair extensions – apparently Naomi Campbell had suggested the idea – but she was going to wait until she came back from Australia. I couldn't imagine Paula with long hair, but she said she wanted it all the way down her back.

Michael was paying Paula special attention the day of their pre-Christmas party. She had been feeling sick and tearful earlier in the morning. I had been concerned that her tears were triggered by our conversation the night before. I was worried by her continuing use of Prozac and Rohypnol while she was pregnant, so when she teetered unsteadily on her feet that day, I questioned her about the drugs and put a case for her to stop. She was very persuasive, however, in her assurance that her staggering was caused by sickness, tiredness and dizziness.

Michael's attentiveness seemed to be doing the trick. He never left Paula's side and his hands never left her body, throughout the entire day. Their kissing and touching became so passionate that at one point their guests, two of whom they hardly knew, looked to me for conversation. Paula was in a panic because Bob was being obstructive about the girls going to Australia. It was 14 December, two days before Paula and Michael's flight and it was looking very much as if the girls might not be able to join them after Christmas as they still did not have their visas.

Michael had rented a house on the beach on the Gold Coast for their stay and he was excited about showing off the girls to his family. But Paula was desperately steadfast: 'I can't go without knowing that the girls are coming. And Michael's going to go ape.' At the eleventh hour, Bob did finally organize the papers. And now there was some complication, which meant that the girls could not fly out until later than originally planned. Despite these and other worries, Paula stage-managed a Christmas party that went with a swing. She had hired an Elvis impersonator, and during the course of the evening she said rather mysteriously that she was waiting for Michael's present to arrive. She revelled in her pregnancy, and the festive gathering, as she snuggled up to Michael and listened to 'Love Me Tender' and 'Are You Lonesome Tonight?'

Paula had received a £1,000 cheque, a gift from a fan who was following the news of her money problems. I feared that it had gone on the party instead. Paula's accountant had been calling, too. His warnings were clear and he urged Paula to tackle her haemorrhaging bank account.

Perhaps Bob had been wise to give Anita the household money.

Paula had invited a good friend of mine to the party, and she and I laughed together at the medley of corny renditions of Elvis songs and retired to the kitchen. Paula didn't seem the least bit bothered when Michael chatted to my friend, who is extremely beautiful, brilliant and talented. Michael weaved his usual magic to put her utterly at her ease, which I gathered from Paula she actively encouraged. It seemed totally genuine and it is uncharitable to imagine an ulterior motive. But Paula had described their occasional three-in-a-bed sessions and I once witnessed them trying to seduce a waitress to come back with them, when we had gone out to dinner. 'Michael loves it,' Paula explained. 'He does what most men would do if they were honest.' Michael's penchant for novelty did not appear to faze Paula. In her opinion every man fantasized about women having sex together, which was obviously part of the attraction of the three-way thing.

'What does he do? And how can you cope seeing him screw another woman in front of you?' I asked, knowing that jealously and insecurity must be factors in this situation. She explained that there was a big difference between sexual jealousy and jealousy of the heart. She said she was sure Michael's heart was with her, even if his dick was with someone else. Maybe drugs *were* playing too central a role in their lives. Paula denied using non-prescription drugs, but what about the stimulants in the mix with the sex? Was their pursuit of thrills fuelled by alcohol or something stronger? Surely she would have to be on something to break down the inhibitions I knew she had… but maybe Paula and Michael had transcended inhibition.

'Michael likes to watch,' she winked, and then she said, 'I've never found women sexually attractive before, but something's been released in me. Now I'm fantasizing about girls too – and these breasts have already given pleasure to the fairer sex.' I asked her if she missed the penetration, and she giggled and told me they used dildos for that. She made it sound natural and normal. As a child, Paula had experienced quite an unusual slant on sex. Her mother was a screen siren who wrote steamy novels, which Paula was allowed to read. Her father, nicknamed 'the Bishop', was nevertheless a serial philanderer, with a penchant for young women.

'It's not grubby, Gerry. Michael loves the female body, it's art to him.' Paula described how he would instruct them on what they were to do with each other and get turned on as they enjoyed his suggestions. Sometimes he masturbates and sometimes he takes photos…and sometimes he falls asleep and lets us get on with it,' Paula said without a hint of embarrassment. She felt that Michael, 'who can be such a girl at times,' loved to experience the feminine within himself, lying between two girls and enjoying soft stroking. She had an impressive understanding of his needs and a total willingness to indulge them. Was this why he always called her his soulmate? I remember him saying: 'I don't know where I begin and where she ends, I know we've been together before, we understand each other more than we could possibly learn in a single lifetime.'

It was about nine o'clock in the evening when Paula led Michael to the front door, threw her arms around his neck and said, 'Happy Christmas, baby'. Outside, we all gathered round, wide-eyed at the brand new shiny red Ducati road bike wrapped in a huge pink ribbon. Michael was so excited that he leapt on it straight away and took off down the road, without a helmet.

Paula said later that it had cost her over £10,000. Maybe the excitement of the day had been a little too much for her? I came out of the bathroom later in the evening to see her grabbing the banisters with two hands as she stumbled down the long staircase. When I asked Michael if she was all right, I felt he looked through me for just a split second before he connected with my question and assured me that she was suffering from an iron deficiency and sickness. 'What about the Rohypnol, is she still on that?' 'Oh, Gerry-Berry, you worry too much, she's really fine,' Michael replied. I was unconcerned that Michael may have been on something harder than champagne, and I was far from sure that he was. If appearances were anything to go by, he never changed, nor betrayed any sign that he was other than happy and straight. But Paula was in no position to be experimenting.

My brief was to deny, deny, deny, if any journalist contacted me about the baby. So it was quite mystifying when the news appeared in the press only hours before they flew out to Australia. I asked Paula if she had any idea who could have leaked it and she gave me a knowing smile. As the plane left the ground, carrying the happy couple off to the other side of the world, the wheels of the press machinery turned old attitudes into new stories:

Cheeky Paula began divorce proceedings last week on the grounds of Bob's adultery. It's an outrageous move considering how Paula has cashed in on her sordid affair with Hutchence and sold interviews about her love life to anyone prepared to pay. Just to prove what a great mother she is, peroxide bimbo Paula Yates abandoned her kids yesterday to enjoy a festive break in Hong Kong with her obnoxious boyfriend Michael Hutchence. Paula, who is always bleating about being a devoted parent, has left Fifi, Peaches and Pixie with poor old Geldof, days after launching a bitter custody battle against him. And perhaps you'll also share my wish that she takes a slow boat home.

I hoped she hadn't read the English papers on the plane – she had promised to steer clear of the tabloids. Her calls to me became less frequent while she was away and I took that as a sign that she was much more settled.

Paula and Michael arrived on the Gold Coast where Michael's mother

Patricia and stepfather Ross had an apartment. Michael employed bodyguards for the journey to the christening of his brother Rhett's newborn daughter on the beach in Byron Bay. Michael drove Paula in his Bentley, which was normally parked in his mother's drive. He was excited; Paula told me he had been looking forward to being with all his family, particularly Rhett.

Paula was getting a little impatient, however, with Michael's insistence that they hold back their own news until after the christening, when the rest of his family would be in Sydney – he didn't want to eclipse his new niece Zoë Angel's special day. He was very surprised to learn that his mother already knew, when he took her aside to tell her. Patricia told him that the news had travelled from England ahead of them.

For the remainder of the holiday, Michael had rented a stunning house on the beach, but they never reached their final destination. Anita had called with distressing news about Pixie – she was running a very high temperature and Bob didn't feel she should travel until she got better. Paula agreed, and without hesitation caught the next flight home, leaving a dejected Michael to watch the sun go down on his own. When a worried Paula walked through the door at home, Pixie came running to greet her saying, 'I feel much better now, mummy.'

That Paula sacrificed two weeks with her cherished man in a beachside paradise for the remote possibility that her child had the flu did not surprise me for a second. That was how she was as a mother. Most mothers would respond in the same way, but more than a few would have waited twenty-four hours on the off-chance of a sudden improvement. Paula hardly mentioned it. There was no complaint, no regret. She was only sad for Michael, who was deeply disappointed to lose her and the girls. Paula was far more displeased by the reaction of Michael's family to their forthcoming baby: 'Let's just say no one rushed to open a bottle of champagne.'

Paula said that she didn't know whom she felt most sorry for, herself or Michael. No one in Michael's family had been openly disapproving – they all sounded far too polite to make it overt – but it was clear enough they would all have preferred him to be involved with a single girl without so much baggage. But it was what they were not saying that bothered Paula the most. Hormones are finely tuned to criticism during pregnancy, I reminded her. I encouraged her to see the situation from their perspective, that their concern for Michael was no slight to her. If they were, as she suspected, trying to split them up by encouraging him to stay in Australia, could she not see that this was their way of looking out for him, and such family support would be in her best interests, in the end, too?

She told me how much she liked Rhett and Mandy and Michael's charming stepfather Ross, and that Kell, Michael's father, was rather tactless in leaving out old framed photos of his eldest son with various ex-girlfriends, including Kylie and Helena, but a little harmless showing off hadn't entirely put her off. It was Michael's mother by whom she felt most threatened. Could she, I asked her, be expecting too much of Patricia, perhaps even be a little jealous of Patricia's motherly relationship with Michael? Did it remind her of what she hadn't had herself? It's a bond, I warned her – it can't be broken. Especially if the man in question was as insecure as Michael.

Meanwhile Michael holidayed with the friends he had known all his life, surrounded by an adoring local press that still called him a rock hero, and feeling the warm sand beneath his feet. It was sad that while Michael was in the bosom of his family, getting all the unconditional love and support he needed to heal the anguish he had been going through over the year, Paula was on the other side of the world, in the dreary London winter days with a daily delivery of hate-mail, alone and with no support at all. Irritated that he could not get through to the house because the phone line was dead (Paula couldn't pay the bill); Michael was beginning to ask questions, and Paula was running out of excuses. Anita had been instructed to ask Michael nonchalantly for a credit card before he went away as Paula had mislaid her own. Paula was too embarrassed to ask Michael herself. Thinking nothing of it, Michael handed over his plastic and it was this card Paula used to pay off the telephone bill so that they could be reconnected. She told Michael that the telephone company had made a mistake and were being obstructive about fixing the problem.

The whole country was against them and now the telephone company. Michael phoned BT and shouted at some employees about their incompetence, which was compounded in his mind by their inability to reconcile what he was saying with what they saw in their records.

I told her that she had to come clean. I was sure Michael was here to stay and reminded her of a conversation I had with him only a few weeks earlier, when he poured his heart out over a kitchen supper at my house. He was still getting negative vibes from some of his band members, friends and family, regarding his involvement with Paula. 'It's not about Paolo it's about me. Look at my track record – three years and then I'm off.' He could see their point, but he wanted to prove them wrong this time. 'We all have our wilderness days,' Michael said, but now he wanted his days on the ranch. 'I love the girls. Having children separates the men from the boys,' he said.

I told him that what he was doing for them all was admirable. How obvious it was that the children loved him, and the rewards would be boundless – which he said he was already seeing. He enjoyed helping Paula with the school run, attending their plays, teaching Fifi to kick box, putting Peaches's hair up in rollers, cuddling them when they cried. He said that he had always known that he loved kids, but never expected to fall so deeply in love with someone else's: 'They're not the problem, they're a privilege to be with.' He thought it a repulsive idea that Paula's children should be described as unwanted baggage. 'They should spend one afternoon with these kids, that's all it would take.'

Michael knew that he had problems sticking in a relationship. It was something he had been examining for at least a year, before he got together with Paula. He wanted to address it. Why did he run from harmonious relationships? What made him happy? He was concerned that he would reach the age of forty, 'a sad fucker, cruising the clubs for the next empty one-night shag.' He had seen a therapist a couple of times. In just two sessions, he started to see that this fear of commitment was tied to his parents' divorce. His younger brother Rhett was the difficult one, who reacted to the tension in the house by rebelling, casting Michael in the role of the good boy. He felt the burden of playing the saint and the responsibility for his mother's pain, which he had soaked up like an emotional sponge.

When Michael's mother decided to leave his father and the family home, she felt she could only handle one boy on her own, and she chose Michael, because Michael behaved and Michael listened and Michael understood. The weight of responsibility for his mother's happiness bore him down, robbing him of the carefree rebel days of teenage in which to grow, and explore himself. So later, with the freedom of manhood, he lived those rebel years to the full.

Patricia and Michael were very alike, except 'she had more balls', he laughed. 'I'm happy she found Ross. My Ma deserves the best.' There was no doubt that he was fiercely protective of her, he criticized the arrangement to leave his brother behind with his father Kell, but he never criticized *her* for the decision. Michael was getting nearer to chasing out his demons and he was determined to do so, realizing that he didn't want to put his own children through the pain that he and his brother had suffered. Up until now he had protected himself from the dilemma by keeping his relationships passionately casual. 'I won't let my kid down, whatever it takes, I won't,' he said, determinedly.

I suggested that he air his feelings to a trusted journalist, citing how helpful it would be to change the public perception of him. But Michael said that he had to project 'rock'n'roll'; his management would have a fit if he suddenly came over all touchy-feely – after all, he had a deal to get for his album. 'I don't have to plead my innocence in Australia; why doesn't this backward country get it?'

In February 1996 Paula had to put the house on the market. The New Year had not brought the changes we had hoped for in the press and in her career. She was more depressed than ever. The taxi firm that took her and the children to and from school cancelled the account; she owed them hundreds of pounds. Then out of the blue, Paula was offered a contract with the *Sun*. It should have been good news, but it conjured up images of the condemning copy that would inevitably ensue. 'You know what will happen…' I pleaded. 'There must be another way of sorting out your problems.' 'I can't turn it down,' Paula replied. She'd been asked to return her chequebook and credit cards. She had a further six months to wait for royalties on her autobiography, and she'd been defaulting on her £1,000-a-week mortgage for a while. 'What do you suggest I do?'

This tense response followed a meeting with her bank manager. He came to the house, as Paula didn't want to provide any more ammunition for press speculation. She received him in the large sitting room, while Anita and I waited for the verdict in the smaller. Paula was just getting over a front-page splash on her new hairstyle – a picture which had been doctored to make her hair extensions look ridiculous. She felt crushed, humiliated, she could do no right; she could not even get her hair done without attracting the worst kind of criticism. And she was furious that it was the hairdressers who had tipped off the press.

Paula, Anita and I sat cross-legged by the fire, staring at the floor, quietly reflecting upon the news the bank manager had delivered.

'Have you got *any* money?' Anita asked, her voice shaky with fear. 'About a fiver,' Paula smiled, attempting a joke. 'Can't you ask someone to help?' I suggested a few people close to her. 'No, too humiliating. You see? I have to take the job.' 'Michael – surely he's going to help?' I continued. Paula shook her head vigorously. 'That's even more humiliating. He's already helped out with the children's uniforms and shoes and he's having to buy a family car.' Bob had kept their six-seater Renault Espace for his trips to the King's Road coffee shops. He had told her: sorry, Planet 24 owns it, which meant that she had no claim. Anita tried to persuade him to contribute to another instead – the taxi fares were crippling them. He suggested that Paula take the Tube. It did occur to me that if Paula could afford the Ducati for Michael she could have a bought a car. Paula looked at Anita and said pointedly, 'All we have is your housekeeping.' 'Sorry, Paula, but I need that and Bob made me promise not to hand it over,' Anita squirmed.

Paula seemed to be giving up. Anita could feel it too. She tried to jolly Paula along with empty platitudes: it'll be all right, we'll find a way, it won't last for ever, Bob's just going to have to give you more. Paula was in a corner, she wouldn't take any more handouts from Michael, her house would be re-possessed if she didn't get the funds in fast, so she had no choice but to agree to take the offer from the *Sun*: a £100,000 contract for a year, to write a weekly column. It was a good deal of money for any journalist, but it was a bargain for them. The *Sun* didn't want Paula's opinions on anything; they wanted a diary of the events in her own life and at the end of her pregnancy they expected the biggie: a picture, an exclusive on Paula and Michael's baby. The only advantage was that there would be one fewer paper openly attacking them. It was with the irony that defined Paula's life that she had been hunted by the press, caught and turned on herself.

Paula was just about to embark on one of the toughest fights she'd ever had – she wanted to get her house back from Bob. It was the only way, or she would end up homeless. She didn't see why Michael had to buy her a house. 'Everyone thinks he's much richer than he is,' Paula told me. 'All his money is tied up.' All of Michael's assets had been put into offshore accounts; investments had been made to ensure the least possible tax deductions and death duties. His business partner had arranged that Michael should have £20,000 spending money a month – a seemingly generous allowance, but for Michael, with his high-flying lifestyle, this represented a tight budget.

8 great expectations

PAULA RANG ME TO CHECK THAT the flowers she had organized for my dinner party had arrived. I had arranged this event to bring together Paula and Michael with my social contacts who also had strong links or influence with the media. These included the high-powered PR person and David Montgomery, chief executive of the *Mirror* group. I hoped that if these people were exposed to the real Michael and Paula as opposed to the tabloid caricature, they might be impressed enough to use their influence to change the press treatment.

Paula arrived without Michael. At the last minute he had been called to an INXS production meeting about the forthcoming album *Elegantly Wasted*. The women privately sighed with disappointment, as a personal appearance by the Rock God of Oz had been a major draw of the evening. Paula was disappointed too, but she was conducting herself with the dignity of a countess and the humility of a match-girl. I placed Paula next to David Montgomery, watching and hoping for them to make a connection. But he did not seem inclined to do anything more than politely acknowledge her existence. The subjects of politics and business were being discussed and I worried that the conversation would get stuck in the outside world and never touch Paula's problems.

Paula had been demure all night, on her best behaviour, fitting in rather than challenging. As the evening wore on, the conversation lightened and we were all having fun. David still hadn't talked to Paula. I did notice, however, that he was assessing her, with the odd sideways glance – scanning, processing, and calculating – while she talked intently to his partner. Eventually, he turned to Paula and said, 'You've been having a hard time of it, haven't you?' 'You could say that,' Paula replied nervously. Paula said very little of what she had been through – just enough to show that there had been damage to her self-worth. They discussed politics, the ongoing peace process in Northern Ireland, the love she had for her children and the blessing of the new baby. I was impressed at her restraint; she hadn't hijacked the party with her woes, neither had she regaled us with her repertoire of side-splitting stories.

The PR man turned to Paula and said that whatever people thought of her, at least she had been honest enough to leave her husband before having a relationship and a new baby. Paula thanked him for his observation. 'We'll chat further about your predicament, Paula, I'll talk to Gerry tomorrow, I might know some people who can help.' He smiled at her affectionately and when she left he gave her a sympathetic hug, to emphasize his intent to help where he could. From a phone call I received the following day, thanking me for the party, I was pleased to hear that David had been very surprised at the difference between the real Paula and the popular picture of her – that was what everyone said, once they met her. Perhaps the evening had gone to plan after all.

However, if I had hopes that my long term PR strategy might start to bear fruit, I was still anxious about Paula and Michael on the home front. Michael was finding the pregnancy difficult. Gone was the initial euphoria he had felt and now he was faced with the reality: an expectant mother with raging hormones, who had taken up the party scene again to please her new boyfriend, but now wanted to spin a cocoon and curl up in it. Michael tried to party on, as if nothing had changed. His gigging and clubbing met with increasing resistance from Paula. One night in February, he dragged her out to a Black Grape gig at the Brixton Academy, and afterwards they joined the revelry backstage. The party was wild but Paula wanted to go home and an argument broke out. She was led out by a bouncer and put in a taxi.

In her paranoia, her desperation to hold on to Michael, Paula had already proved willing to follow him to hell and back. But that night she was feeling sick, and she was getting annoyed and scared that he showed no inclination to cut back on his nocturnal activities. This led to a series of arguments after which they reached a compromise that Michael would go out only once every couple of weeks, and for a while the deal worked. 'He has so much energy, I just can't keep up,' Paula would say. At least everyone could feel a little more relaxed about Paula's money worries, since Michael was now paying most of the household expenses and giving Paula £1,000 a month pocket money (into her bank account, not into the nanny's hand for safe-keeping).

Michael's attitude to his role as father to Paula's girls was becoming more confident. 'Bob only realized he was a dad when I came along,' he said. It sounded arrogant, but in the light of many conversations I had with Michael about the children's needs, he was well-informed and doing the best he could. Only a year ago he had been living a most celebrated carefree existence; perhaps a few nights out with his friends wasn't an unreasonable request. I expected it would all calm down as he came more to enjoy his responsibilities and Paula agreed.

But rock'n'roll continued to take its toll on their relationship. Michael came back from the Brit Awards spitting with fury. This would surely be the one event at which he and Paula could hold their heads high, where all their bad press would be ignored or celebrated. Michael found himself presenting an award to Noel and Liam Gallagher. Oasis had behaved like the new bad boys of rock'n'roll all evening. Now, as he accepted his award from Michael, Noel said, 'Has-beens should not be presenting awards to gonnabes.' It was one thing to have the British press attack you for every step you take, but to be called a 'has-been' in front of the industry and millions of viewers at home was more than Michael could bear. The Oasis debacle wasn't the only disturbing aspect of the Brit Awards. I was staggered to hear from a reliable friend of mine that she was sure she saw Paula snorting coke in the loos, that same night. She had to be mistaken. It was doubly inconceivable as she was famously tee-total and ferociously health-conscious, especially while she was pregnant.

As if she did not have enough to contend with, Paula was still chasing her father's lover, Serena, through the courts. It was not going well, and it was consuming vast sums of money, but as soon as Paula obtained a ruling in her favour, she had all the locks changed on the house. Shortly after, Serena changed the locks again; someone had apparently broken into the house and taken armloads of Jess's memorabilia. 'It stinks, the whole thing stinks,' Paula said, after police questioned her about items that were missing. Paula needed the house more than ever now and she had decided that if she won the case, she would sell up to help clear her debts, but success was not certain as the case was in limbo while the courts reached a final decision. It wasn't just the house she wanted, she still yearned for her father's possessions, she was missing him more now than she had at the time of his death, she told me: 'He'd have loved Michael and given Bob a piece of his mind, if he was still alive.'

Paula's next task was to discuss her financial situation, amicably if possible, with Bob. Through a series of phone calls and meetings, she had tried to get him to address what she defined as his responsibilities, but she met a brick wall every time and it was becoming frustrating for her. Paula had approached him for the house and for more reasonable maintenance, but he was having none of it.

'He's so annoyingly calm and I'm beginning to sound more and more like Minnie Mouse,' she said after one of her telephone calls with Bob. Their relationship was going through a very strange patch. It seemed to me that their roles had completely reversed, and Paula would comment on Bob's softer tone whenever they discussed the children. Anita believed that Bob still loved Paula and would take her back in an instant. Paula was in no mood to hear such sentiments. '"Yeah, I still love her" – bullshit!' she scoffed. 'Why did he call the police on me then? "I just wondered if you could lock me missus up for the night, 'coz I need to show her how much I love her."'

She was referring to an incident at Bob's house when the girls were staying with him. On her way to the Brit Awards, Paula had popped round to her old house to see Pixie who had an ear infection. Once more Paula found herself trying to reason with Bob over the lack of support he was giving her. Bob maintained a calm façade while refusing to budge. Paula said that he was not even prepared to contribute to the cost of Anita, whose services he shared at the weekends, saying: 'Get your boyfriend to pay.' In her frustration Paula lost her cool and unleashed a torrent of abuse at him. Bob slammed the door and in a moment of pent-up fury Paula hurled a stone at the bay window, smashing a pane.

The next morning Bob reported the incident to the police and the stone turned into a brick. Paula giggled when we talked about it later. She described the horror on Bob's face when she finally lost it with him. He could not understand her change of personality, after all those years when she had kept silent through his rants, avoiding him by escaping to her room. Now it took little to provoke her own outbursts directed at him.

One of the blessings of Paula's column in the *Sun* was that she now had a legitimate voice of her own. In it Paula dismissed the event as a minor domestic incident – an argument broke out, a pebble was thrown. But what of the rest of the press? A week after her article in the *Sun*, and two weeks after it happened, the stone-throwing incident hit the *Mirror*. *BOB CALLS COPS OVER PAULA; she hurls rock in bust-up over his lover*, read the headline. Our old friend Matthew Wright had written the piece but it seemed to be taking a decidedly pro-Bob stance.

However, this was followed by another article in the same paper, headed: *I WON'T PAY HER A PENNY*, in which the tone was turning quite definitely anti-Bob. The article outlined Paula's financial difficulties in the wake of the split. Though the writer tried subtly to balance the blame, Bob was coming off decidedly worse. Even his new romance came under attack, in a pleasing parallel, though nowhere near as vicious, with the snipes at Paula and Michael, and Jeanne was cast in the same villainous role that Michael was forced to play. The piece finished with the ambiguous: 'But unlike Bob and Jeanne's romance, Paula and Michael kept their affair strictly under wraps to begin with.' In the context this seemed to indicate that it was more acceptable not to flaunt the new love before the old is entirely over – yet another vote for Paula and Michael.

Paula and I were intrigued. This was the first article in a mainstream paper that seemed to cast doubts upon Bob's behaviour since the affair began. It was quite exciting; though it wasn't entirely flattering to Paula, it really felt like inroads into deconstructing Bob's image of 'saintliness' were being made. The article looked like an open invitation to talk, because Matthew had included so many of the details I had supplied to him, but which he had been holding in reserve. 'Okay, what's the story?' he replied to my insistence that it wasn't a brick, it was a little pebble, and did Bob really need to call the cops over such pettiness? I was surprised by the questions Matthew was asking now, the detail he wanted in order to get a clearer picture of Paula's plight. No more 'she's brought it upon herself', no more 'well, what do you expect from a serial adulterer rock god?' He was talking business, he wanted all the facts and he appeared to want them now. So I gave it to him straight. This was my opportunity to unload everything I had, and I was already feeling more comfortable about the way he was going to use it. He agreed that Paula shouldn't be seen giving an interview directly and that everything I gave him would continue to appear as 'a pal says' or 'friends say' but he said that tomorrow would be another big splash. What was fuelling this sudden change of heart? 'There seems to be a sudden interest in this story around here…between you and me, the editor came up a couple of days ago and wanted the low-down. Then he said, "We're going to make this the biggest celebrity story of the decade…and we're backing Yates."'

That night Paula and I chewed our fingernails together, anxious about the tone that the paper would take in the morning. The next day Paula's money problems were hanging out to dry – the *Mirror* carried its story on page one with a complete outline of Paula's debts: the fourteen High Court writs against her; her £100,000-plus debts including mortgage payments, rent arrears, a credit-card deficit, phone bills and taxi fares; £45,000 for rent and damage from the owners of the Mayfair mansion where Paula had lived after splitting with Bob; £20,000 mortgage arrears on the Clapham house; £1,000 a week to cover the loan; a £23,000 credit card debt to American Express, and finally thousands to a taxi firm which ferried her three daughters to school. The article drew attention to the fact that if this debt were called in, the Geldof girls would face a one-mile walk to school. All of which painted a pretty grim picture, but the blame was put squarely at Bob's door, and his hypocrisy was highlighted: Bob said at the time: 'I really hope she's okay and will help her in any way I can.'

Paula and I were not looking forward to the backlash from the other papers, but now at least we had a conduit to the press, one on which we could rely. We had *carte blanche* to say what we wanted about Bob, knowing that almost anything we said would end up in print. We had afternoons of fun, plotting the next attack, keen to maintain the momentum now we had Bob on the ropes. A couple of days after the *Mirror* piece, we masterminded a lovely set-up.

Matthew phoned, rather pleased with his handiwork. Warming to the task, he was eager for the next story and suggested there was mileage in the possibility that Paula might have to walk the children to school. Ordinarily, Paula would never walk anywhere, especially when four months pregnant, but on 8 March she walked out of the house with the children in their school uniforms and proceeded down the road on foot. Hidden cameras took sneaky pictures and photographers dashed for their picture desks. Round the corner I met Paula and the girls with my car and we dropped them at school. That afternoon at 3.15pm there was a photographer standing on a traffic island in Battersea waiting for a burgundy Renault Espace to turn the corner... which it did, like clockwork, moments later. In the heavy traffic, the photographer had plenty of time to fill a whole canister of film with pictures of Bob in his otherwise empty car. The next day the most delicious article hit the stands:

HOW COULD YOU, BOB?
PREGNANT PAULA IS SICK 10 TIMES ON A MILE-LONG
WALK TO SCHOOL

Though the story was somewhat rigged, there was justice in the message of the piece; after all, Bob had told her to walk to school or take the Tube. It felt for the first time that we were on the campaign trail and we had the chance to win. But there were casualties of this war: Michael could no longer be insulated from the knowledge of Paula's financial hole. She never told me how she broke the news to Michael, or whether he found out with the morning post. His response, she told me, was: 'We will get all this sorted out, Paolo.' He promised he would help her get her house back and talked about clearing her debts.

Paula's accountant was astounded when he received a note from Michael's solicitors informing him that he no longer represented Miss Yates and was to pass over all her books to Michael's accountants. He was a mild-mannered man who adored Paula and had been her accountant for years. They were friends and he had done her many favours, often waiving his fees. He couldn't understand why she hadn't called him herself. He was really upset. He had continued working for Paula for the past months, without pay, trying to rescue her from bankruptcy, and suddenly to receive such an instruction, without even a note of explanation from Paula, was beyond his understanding.

When I broached the matter with Paula, she became annoyed and hinted that there was more to the sacking than she was prepared to divulge. Paula was most definitely never going to call her accountant again. A week later, Paula told me that she and Michael were not at liberty to discuss the matter with anyone, as the situation was with their legal team and they had been advised against disclosure until certain details had been clarified. She was most insistent that I must not probe Michael. It later emerged that Paula and Michael's suspicions were completely without foundation.

Michael told me that the £100,000 from the *Sun*, paid to Paula in monthly instalments, was going straight into paying off the bulk of the debts. He had taken Paula with him to see his accountants, where she spent most of the time in the loo being sick. Even though she was coming up to five months, her sickness showed no signs of abating. Even Paula complained sometimes of how much the pregnancy was taking out of her, but she never once regretted that she was going to have Michael's baby. Though she was grateful that Michael was supporting her now, she felt humiliated by the position in which she found herself. She was painfully conscious that Michael had met her when she was strong, independent, a successful writer and television presenter; now she was sure that he saw her as a failure. Michael might have been doing the honourable thing, but he never looked like someone who found it natural to take command, and did not enjoy it. That had always been Paula's role. She was the strong one, but the days when she trotted through airports wearing 'Little Miss Trouble' T-shirts had given way to the vulnerability of pregnancy. And with this child, her fourth, all she wanted to do was hide away, comfort eat, and steadily gain weight.

———— ◆ ————

It cannot be underestimated just how fortunate we were to have the *Mirror* on our side, in the way that it was. In essence, with the *Sun* on Paula's side too, we had the British press looking critically at Bob's role in the split and it was creating a gradual landslide in Paula's favour. But we had no idea to what extent the *Mirror* was investing in this story until a few days after Paula's walk to school; on 12 March, Edward Pilkington of the *Guardian* wrote an article that tracked the Geldof separation, and the latest developments in the tabloids.

> *In 1985, Geldof raised $100 million for the starving of Ethiopia. Last week his wife, through friends, told the press he was so stingy he gives her just £300 a week for groceries – and demands the change. 'Bob says I will pay for leaving him until the day I die,' she said.*

The journalist viewed the tabloid coverage of the story from above, like the observer of a battlefield. And not for the first time Paula's story was compared to that of the Princess of Wales.

> *Last week Paula set in train her final push for supremacy. Several of her friends are known to have approached tabloid newspapers to tell elements of her financial sob-story. The overall impact has been that of a full-scale media blitz which makes Princess Diana's manipulation of the press look timid.*

> *Hutchence himself went public yesterday when, speaking through 'pals', he said, Paula 'hates the idea of me bailing her out. But if it comes to the point where she and the kids are likely to lose their home then, of course, I'll step in.'*

> *That merely begs a further question. If striving to retain her dignity is Paula's priority, then why is she making such a humiliating public display of her marital problems? As Piers Morgan, editor of the* Daily

Mirror, *puts it: 'She is clearly manoeuvring to gain PR supremacy over her husband.'*

Bob, from his elevated perch, has even further to fall. Once the personification of all that was good, he is now squarely in the tabloids' sights as a legitimate target.

'He's a rich man,' says Piers Morgan. 'However aggrieved he feels, he must realize charity begins a little closer to home than Ethiopia. If he doesn't bail Paula out, and soon, he can kiss that Saint Bob title goodbye.'

Paula was relieved…'Umm, golly, things are really starting to move,' she said. Within days of the *Guardian* piece, came a three-pager in the *Daily Express*; an almost psychological appraisal of the Geldof marriage and separation, full of understanding for Paula and featuring a stunning photograph of her in a black latex cat suit, casually martyred in front of a rough wooden crucifix.

Paula knew the journalist quite well; Susan Hill had commissioned and helped Bob write his autobiography and was therefore a unique authority on the couple. She had not only come to know Bob well, but spent hours in the house in Redburn Street, and surmised for herself the reasons why Paula had left Saint Bob. The piece pointed to the similarities between Bob and Paula's marriage breakdown and that of Charles and Diana, describing them both as 'the disastrous coupling of a controlling, almost fatherlike figure and an emotional blonde full of repressed anger.' It also drew attention to the way in which both women's growing need for love and understanding in the domestic arena was unlikely to be fulfilled by these men of power and influence, describing Bob as seeming 'to have shoulders broad enough for all the world's cares, except perhaps for those of his wife.' Michael and Paula were delighted; the print on Paula had peaked spectacularly with this latest piece. I phoned Matthew to thank him for catalyzing the shift in press emphasis, and Michael sent me a massive bunch of flowers with a note saying: 'Thank you for all that you have done. Love M.'

And for a while Paula and Michael enjoyed the relative tranquillity that the turn-around had brought them. Word spread that I was officially acting for Paula: the *Daily Telegraph* announced my involvement with her on a professional basis in their Peterborough column. From then on, any journalist wanting to check facts, run an interview, write an article, would call me. I was soon collecting an impressive contact list, but as it grew, so too did my work load, as they all had to be kept in the frame. Paula was talking of work again; she still wanted to regain the financial freedom she had enjoyed before. We decided to wait a little, hoping her morning sickness would pass. I took her at her word that she would soon be fighting fit and eager to promote herself. Michael's regular disappearances were still making her edgy, but when he returned they would camp in her bedroom for days at a time. He was pleased with the progress of the new album, giving me the odd rendition when he was in the mood. He wanted to be around more, he would often confide, but his tax exile status forced him to adopt a nomadic work-life, where studios blended into departure lounges in LA, France, Australia and often Dublin – which was a convenient haven from the UK. Unlike Paula's last rock star who had hardly called her while he was away, Michael did, and he sent her flowers every day when they were apart.

When Paula started feeling better, we began to meet to discuss television ideas for her to produce or present, but Michael was never far from the conversation. Her divorce was imminent and she hoped that he would propose. For her birthday he had bought her a ring and a nine-foot wooden fence, which went up round the front of the house to ward off prying cameras. She knew the large diamond and ruby cluster ring was not an engagement ring, but she wore it on the third finger of her left hand anyway. The only items of jewellery she ever wore now were this and the platinum and diamond Tiffany cross he had bought for her last birthday. Why wouldn't he marry her? Paula said that Michael had told her that he still hadn't fully accepted his parents' divorce and he had a fear of marriage as deep as Paula's fear that she might lose him.

Armed with a file full of ideas for Paula to present on television I called my friend at FlexTech. She complimented me on Paula and Michael's rehabilitation in the press and, true to her word, offered to set up a meeting for Paula. She suggested we wait a week so that she could arrange for all the heads of programming to be present. Paula laughed when I told her that we were going to a meeting at the Playboy building, but was very impressed by who had been invited to sit round the table to hear her proposals.

The night before the meeting had been a bad one for Paula, she told me as she got into my car. Michael hadn't called her and she nearly cancelled altogether because she hadn't been able to sleep. Paula was sulky and she kept checking her mobile for a call from Michael. How was she ever going to be able to work with this Absent Boyfriend Obsession Disorder? She repeatedly punched numbers into her phone and slammed it back down on her lap when she couldn't get a reply. The independent girl, who happily maintained a lifestyle full of bizarre contradictions, now had chains round her wrists and was shackled to a phone. The meeting went well, despite my misgivings that persisted all the way up to the door of the conference room. Crossing the threshold, the lifeless waif departed and Paula transformed herself into the Goddess of Television. The Playboy channel offered her a presenting job right there and then, which amused her; she said she would give it some thought. The 'teen' programmer explained that they were having difficulty getting increased ratings; some of their shows had fallen flat within weeks of launch and they expressed interest in producing some of the ideas Paula instantly plucked out of the ether. No one could have guessed at the mental state of their promising star only a few moments before she entered the meeting room. Paula looked stunning in her white Ghost-designed dress, her hair extensions falling in soft blonde waves down her back and a large yellow flower balanced on the top of her ear. Gone were the high heels; instead she had opted for flip-flops with flowers nearly covering her pastel pink pedicure. Everyone at the meeting was dazzled.

Now I was being referred to variously as Paula's PR, publicist and agent, though I could hardly claim to be professional, as I wasn't being paid for the service. There was no money in the kitty anyway, even if I had wanted to invoice her; but that wasn't the reason why I had taken on the job – it would be more accurate to say that the job took me on. Paula did encourage me to keep the fees paid by the newspapers; if I contributed to an article and it went into print, it could be worth £350. However, sometimes I would decline the payment, a strategic move to curry favour with the newspaper concerned, a little entry in my own invisible gossip ledger, a marker to be called in on a rainy day. The periodic cheques that did arrive all helped towards my expenses: the exorbitant telephone bills, the dinner party, lunches with journalists, but there was very little left for my other bills, so I had to do other work to provide the funds to keep me, my children and my new au pair, Marlin, in food and clothes.

I asked Paula to put together her ideas after our meeting at FlexTech. The executives appeared to be interested, but something in writing was needed to present to them, once Paula came back from visiting Michael in Dublin, where he was recording. She called me one morning to pass on a story about Liam Gallagher apparently following Michael around the Dublin pubs, shouting "ere, try to sing this then, if you're so fucking fantastic.' 'He was stalking them,' Paula laughed. Michael was out with Bono that night and their paths crossed with Liam, who shouted abuse at Michael and told Bono he was finished, that Noel was the new star, not old-age pensioners like them. They tried to ignore him and Bono's laughter only aggravated his behaviour. Paula gave me the whole story so that I could call Matthew Wright with it for the next day's edition. Although she was working for the *Sun,* she and I knew the rules – this story would achieve two goals for her: a payback for Oasis and credit-building with the man she recognized as the one person who had stuck his neck out to help her.

Matthew was laughing so much he found it difficult to speak. 'I can't believe he called Bono a "has-been", this is a really good story, tell Paula I appreciate this.' So I fed him with more details of the night. Michael and

Bono had met in 1988 at the MTV awards. Their videos were nominated and it was INXS that took the gong with: 'Need You Tonight/Mediate'. It was also the night that INXS took home seven other awards and Bono shook Michael's hand to show his appreciation of what INXS had achieved. They had been the best of friends ever since.

Paula had spent most of her time on this trip twiddling her thumbs either in their hotel or at Bono's house. She said that Ireland was coming to represent loneliness and misery for her – first that tragic trip with Bob, all the time yearning to be with Michael, and now she *was* with him, she was still yearning to be with him. It was not that they had rowed, but Michael was off doing his thing and Paula had let him go without a fight. I imagined her watching the hotel cable channels, but sometimes when we spoke in the evenings she sounded drunk, which struck me as odd as I had never seen Paula drink.

Paula had still not delivered anything on the television opportunities we had created. The truth was that she was nervous about writing her thoughts down. 'How can I be sure they won't nick my ideas?' she asked. Actually Paula was becoming suspicious in general, which she recognized herself, but in true paranoid fashion convinced herself it was justified for her own protection. Most of the friends she and Bob had shared were now resolutely in his camp. She believed that her PR and former friend had double-crossed her; her mother had publicly disowned her and was spending time with Bob; she couldn't trust Michael to walk down the street on his own, and the papers had been full of hurtful stories for the last year. The list went on. One day I found her obsessively cutting up magazine pictures of Helena Christensen. Paula had just found out about Michael sending Helena a Valentine's card, though Michael insisted it was innocent. He told her Helena was still in a mess after their split and he wanted to give her a boost, to let her to know that she was still a special person, despite the fact he had left her for Paula. The pregnancy was increasing Paula's feelings of vulnerability. Feeling bloated and abandoned, the last thing she needed was competition from one of the most beautiful women in the world, angling to poach her boyfriend back.

My hopes that the baby's birth would stabilize everything were challenged when I saw packets of Prozac and Rohypnol lying on her bedside table. A friend who had been given Prozac to deal with trauma in the past was shocked that Paula had told me she was taking four tablets a day. Paula assured me she was under the care of a top Harley Street doctor, and was attending regular check-ups. Her doctor's advice was that Prozac did not reach the uterus, and that high levels of anxiety would have far more detrimental effects on the baby's development. Even the occasional Rohypnol was permitted, and Paula was insistent that her intake was controlled and necessary.

Paula continued to resist committing her ideas to paper, which frustrated my efforts to advance discussions with *Live! TV* and FlexTech. But meanwhile we discussed setting up a production company to handle her ideas and I was lining up potential investment. I had to deflect my friend at FlexTech with stories of Paula's persistent pregnancy sickness, assuring her that Paula was still very excited and grateful for all her help. Paula had been talking to Jools Holland about a show he wanted to do with her. When I mentioned this to my PR guru, he insisted that I held off any takers until he had the chance to introduce us to his new best friend and protégé, a film and TV producer. On the day of the meeting, Paula dragged herself into the restaurant looking every bit the troubled star, humbled and misunderstood, with her swollen bump only exaggerating her state.

There was also a discussion with Michael playing heavily on her mind. He had been talking of moving his base to Australia. He did not want his child brought up in England nor educated in an English school. His experiences with the press had put him off the country entirely and even though things were now getting better, the scars remained. Paula knew Bob would never allow her to emigrate with the girls and she was certainly not leaving without them. Michael was being a little short-sighted, expecting her to uproot the children and take them away from their father, no matter how poor the relationship between Bob and Paula had become. But he felt he could provide the girls with the fathering they needed and his family would rally round to help. All this aggravated Paula's persistent fear of his departure, and we both prayed that once the baby was born, he would reconsider his plans.

The producer had a wealth of TV experience, friends in common with Paula and a few good tales to tell about Planet 24. He made a very casual sales pitch, he praised Paula's *Tube* days, and slid names effortlessly into the conversation. His performance was a little too rich, but his credentials sounded impressive enough, so his style of delivery did not appear to be doing him any harm. We were joined by Kate Sissons, a society editor and journalist who acknowledged the guest of honour immediately with a sympathetic and self-deprecating quip to Paula about how 'horrid' everyone had been to her. Paula smiled and looked over at me as if to say, 'She's wonderful'. In between her guffaws and stories of outrageous party escapades, Kate announced her serious intent to help Paula as far as she could.

Before long Kate's energy had cheered Paula and they swapped phone numbers, promising to be in touch within the week. Paula was captivated and the producer maintained a remote amusement, somewhat upstaged by the floorshow. During the course of the afternoon two fellow diners came over to Paula to pledge their support. 'Whatever they say, you're a good mum,' one of them told her. Paula said she had received lots of support from people in the street. She said that it had helped to get letters from well-wishing friends and the recent support by certain brave journalists willing to stick their necks out and challenge the halo on top of her husband's greasy head. Kate was so open about herself and her own failings that Paula relaxed and a genuine trust developed between them almost immediately. Paula's instinct was right; Kate never did let us down – whatever we told her 'off the record' never found its way into print. As we stood outside the restaurant to hail a black cab, a van drove by and two men yelled over to us, 'Keep yer chin up, Paula, we love you.'

———— ◆ ————

Within a few days, Paula was calling me about raising some money. She sounded very frightened, her voice was weak and deteriorated into sobs when she said that she couldn't afford to pay her mobile phone bill and Fifi's airfare for a holiday with a friend. 'It's not just the fare; it's the spending money, and some clothes. Bob doesn't seem to realize that kids grow.' I knew that when she flew out to see Michael his management arranged for the tickets, but she could hardly ask them to pay for her children's airfares. She explained that she couldn't ask Michael; he had already paid for tickets to France for Anita and the girls for their trip in a few weeks' time. She had decided to sell her jewellery; most of it had already been sold but it was causing her a lot of pain that the few remaining items worth any money were the three amethyst rings that Bob had given her when each of the children was born. 'Why don't you give this story to Matthew? I'm going to Bond Street this afternoon; when I get there, I'll call you to give you the name of the shop that will give me the highest price,' Paula instructed. 'Perhaps we could split the fee.' 'No, you can have it all,' I replied.

But newspapers didn't usually pay out for at least six weeks, so I agreed to give her the money that I had and to keep the fee for this story when it came in. It was crushing to imagine Paula traipsing up and down Bond Street. Matthew was silent for a while when he heard the story, perhaps realizing the full horror of what had become of Paula Yates, the famous TV presenter who had once appeared to have the whole world at her feet. Matthew called the jewellers to confirm the story. Later he called to inform me of other stories of Paula selling clothes back to the shops she had originally bought them from. 'It's pitiful,' he told me. 'I really do feel so sorry for her, please give her my best.' I said I would, which I did, when I saw her at the school two days later. Paula's smile could not hide the tears welling up in her eyes. She was devastated at having to sell her rings and she retired to her bedroom for two days. The estate agents wanted to drop the price of Paula's house, saying they were finding it difficult to sell. She refused, saying she would only accept the asking price. She suspected they were taking advantage of her public desperation for funds, encouraging buyers to negotiate aggressively, pushing for a fast sale for a fast commission. She might have been right, but Paula was suspicious of everyone.

The producer we had lunched with had given us reason for optimism that he would come back with good news on two of the programme treatments we had pitched him. There was the celebrity travel show that Planet 24 had deemed too expensive, but with Michael calling in some A-list movie star friends to contribute we all thought it could come in on a reasonable budget. But we knew the producer was more excited by the Paula & Jools Café de Paris reunion format, a grown-up and glamorous *Tube*, with the original presenters ten years on. That was much more likely to get commissioned, he told us. He was counting on something coming together with Paula or Michael that might give a boost to his company. He suggested they might go with him to meetings with network commissioning editors, and perhaps Michael would be interested in the Jimi Hendrix documentary he was working on, having acquired the exclusive rights to previously unseen footage.

The hot summer weather had come early in 1996, and by the end of May most Londoners had sunburnt arms and foreheads, but Paula was using a solarium to get her tan. She was virtually housebound when she wasn't travelling to see Michael abroad or visiting me and various other friends (though the visits were becoming rarer as she was tending to complain about most of her old friends). At seven months, her pregnancy was making her uncomfortable. She was bigger than she had been with the other children, but now she wasn't taking any exercise – not even the odd swim. My PR mentor was miffed with Paula and Michael. He said that he felt used; he had believed that the only reason Michael hadn't extended a dinner invitation to thank him for all his efforts was that he and Paula were not going out, but friends of his had seen them in restaurants. He was aggrieved at investing time and money in Paula and Michael's public revival and felt that they should at least call to say thank you.

He had indeed been most generous, paying for the meal when he introduced Paula to his contacts, and hosting a couple of drinks parties where they had met more members of the press (though I had assumed he was having the gatherings anyway). There was also a meeting in his flat, when he first met Michael, and paid for us all to have sushi brought in, with a good few bottles of his most expensive champagne.

His voice was hard: 'And they're nothing but a couple of drug addicts.' He said that people he knew had seen both Paula and Michael snorting cocaine and that he was reconsidering his association with them, to protect his own reputation. This erratic dialogue was worrying; if it didn't end on a good note he might do something detrimental to the cause. I assured him that he was more appreciated than he realized and that I was sure Paula and Michael already had plans to show him the gratitude he deserved. Meanwhile I made a note to talk to them about taking him out to dinner or even inviting him to Michael's villa in the South of France.

Paula had begged me, earlier in the day, to come and help her look over her financial papers, to see if there was anything she had left out. She had spent all week trying to find names of girls Bob might have bedded so that she could dismantle Bob's defence. He was claiming to be the injured party, and that it was entirely Paula's choice to have the affair and walk away from eighteen years of marriage, and that justified his keeping the house in Redburn Street. Paula knew that Bob did not earn a huge salary from Planet 24 – it was still in its development stages and the salary could only just pay the children's school fees and the £300 a week he gave to Anita. The rest of his funds went towards the upkeep of his house in Kent, which was actually held in trust by his father. Further, he wanted Michael to declare his earnings and assets, which Michael was refusing to do and, to avoid being summoned to court, he was spending more time out of the country, which of course did little for Paula's morale. She was now blaming Bob for everything.

For Michael it was the last straw, to be asked to disclose his earnings. Events had reached such a stage that whenever Bob's name was mentioned Michael flew into a rage, and it could sometimes take Paula hours to calm him down. Michael was looking tired, the physical transformation he had undergone from the lithe hipster of a year ago was shocking. His hair was almost jet black, any hint of his natural golden brown locks was barely visible, dark shadows encircled his eyes and he was putting on weight. But Paula hadn't noticed, so focused was she on the resolution of her own anxiety.

She had just finished a call to Michael when I arrived and she was tense, but that was hardly surprising with the court case looming. But she said that her stress had far more to do with Michael's constant Houdini act. Paula was consumed with enraged self-pity. She talked of how everything was going to change when she had their baby and how helpless she felt being pregnant and with someone whose second nature it was to fuck every girl in sight. We'd been down that road before, a couple of months previously. We had arranged to meet a friend for lunch and Paula nearly didn't come because Michael hadn't called. She told me that she knew he was with another woman, and so she was packing all his clothes in black plastic bin liners. Later Anita and I unpacked them for her, once she had cried herself into an exhausted heap. She had adopted a similar tack tonight, but this time she was furious because he had told her that he was very proud of himself for not sleeping with anyone while he was away. 'Proud of himself for not sleeping with anyone? Am I supposed to be grateful for that? Why should it be such a chore not to sleep with anyone when he's got me at home?' That night Paula was uncomfortable, her baby was kicking and she stroked her belly to ease the pain. 'I'm huge, look at me,' she smiled wanly. I reassured her that she looked lovely, sitting amongst the candles and fairy lights that twinkled around her bedroom.

9 my house is your house

PAULA ASKED ME TO TAKE HER for a drive. She needed to get out of the house and clear her head. The weather was amazing, but the London smog was almost unbearable, so we decided to make our getaway to the country. Our destination was a picture-postcard pub on the Surrey/Kent border that she and Michael had visited in their courting days. Paula made a point of leaving her mobile at home – the day was for us. She had been talking for weeks about spending a day like this, but I had doubted that it would ever happen.

She had sold her house at the asking price to a cash buyer with no chain. It was two weeks before the settlement hearing and six weeks before the baby arrived, so she was much less stressed than she had been for months, not least because homeless and heavily pregnant she would have more ammunition in court. Paula was referring to her unborn child as Heavenly now. 'She'll probably want to be called Tina when she's older,' Paula quipped, because Michael was pushing for either his mother or sister's names in the mix with Tiger and Hiraani, especially if the child looked like a Hutchence. We were laughing at the possibility of Heavenly voting for her father's choice, after Peaches and Pixie had recently taken to calling each other Sharon and Tracy in rebellion against their exotic names.

Paula had always been convinced Heavenly would look like Michael; she told me she had seen her in a dream, long before she was pregnant. 'She was so beautiful,' Paula said. 'More an angel than an earth child.' I remember this, because it was one of the first times I heard Paula talk of heaven or God, without a subtle cynicism. To her it was a sign – God had given her a little glimpse, a message that she was to be a very special child. And the vision had looked like Michael, with his hair and his smile. She was so inspired herself that I was sold on the story. She had stopped worrying, too, that Heavenly might have a deformity. It had played on her mind, even though the tests were negative. Why did she fear for her child's health? Anyway, the dream seemed to have eased her anxiety.

It seemed, too, that against the odds my efforts to soothe her obsessing over Michael and his whereabouts were bearing some fruit. I had given her a couple of books on the subject of 'love addiction', far from sure that she would even pick them up, but she told me they had helped in an extraordinary way. 'It really works,' Paula told me. 'I left him alone for a couple of days and he became so affectionate, I got the old Michael back.' She told me that she was trying not to worry constantly about her financial problems. They did appear to be easing – her fees from the *Sun* together with contributions from Michael had all but cleared her old debts, but there were new ones accruing: she would have a significant legal bill by the end of the divorce settlement, to which she was hoping Bob would contribute. We sat outside in the pub garden, in hot June weather, shaded by a couple of apple trees. Most of the locals who had come to enjoy their lunchtime Guinness and a packet of crisps maintained a respectful indifference to their famous visitor, and when one lady came up to ask for an autograph, Paula was amazingly relaxed with her.

There were two subjects that ruffled her calm that day: Anita, and my son Tom going to boarding school in September. Anita was ill, huge clumps of hair had been falling out of her head, leaving defined bald spots, and her doctor had diagnosed alopecia, a stress-related condition. But Paula could summon no sympathy for her. 'She's always around, there's never any privacy, Michael can't stand it,' Paula explained. When she was with Bob, she had been glad of Anita's company; they were close, sharing a common joy in the children. Now Michael was around, she said she wanted Anita to disappear into her room, go out, and generally stop fussing around the two of them. And apparently Michael did not want Anita looking after the baby; he felt that she was too involved with the other three girls, especially Peaches, about whom Michael believed Anita was obsessive. It wasn't until Paula was well into her long list of complaints that the real reason why she and her lover were disgruntled with their long-suffering retainer became clear: Anita had refused to sign any papers regarding Paula's court case against Bob.

Anita's argument was that she had to maintain good relations with Bob because she was the element of continuity for the girls across the divide between their parents. She also explained to both Paula, Michael and later myself that it seemed to her that as a father Bob had changed almost beyond recognition. She was still going to Bob's every weekend when he had the girls, and on a Wednesday night when they all slept over, and Bob took them to school on the Thursday morning. Anita would innocently report back to Paula how much the children enjoyed seeing their father. Anita thought Paula would find the happy relationship between father and children a relief and that their lives would be enriched by it, but instead Paula was angry. Anita tried to explain her position, it wasn't about 'sides' anymore and she wanted to remain neutral. Paula wanted to shoot the messenger.

Paula had been so wrapped up in her own problems that she had neglected to ask me for quite some time what was going on in my life, but today she urged me to give her the update. My ex-husband was insisting that my son Tom, aged seven, should be sent to boarding school – a plan which both depressed Tom and me.

Paula was appalled by this apparently despotic power-mongering. She urged me to stand my ground and insist my son stay at home, suggesting that if my wishes weren't considered, regardless of the fact that they were paying the fees, I should take the matter to court.

She was so much more lucid that day. 'It hasn't been ideal for the girls, it's been a challenging year for us all, but what would have been worst, to stay and show them an outdated blueprint of married life?' Paula asked. She spoke as if she viewed her life as a series of tests, which she was beginning to see as ultimately enriching. She regretted that her marriage had failed, and said that she even sometimes wished she hadn't fallen so deeply in love with Michael, as she recognized he came with a whole set of different problems. 'He's the eternal boy, Peter Pan, and I must be Wendy. But Wendy came back from Never Never Land and I can't seem to escape.' 'And Bob must be Captain Hook,' I laughed – at least, that's who Michael thinks he is, I thought. Paula told me that Bob still wanted her back. 'It's incredible, isn't it? But then I never questioned that he loved me deeply.' I wondered if she ever regretted leaving him. There was a long silence before Paula answered. 'Sometimes I wish that I had never woken up, but once you do it's impossible to go back. He would never have changed enough.' Paula fell asleep on the journey back to London, which was probably just as well as the peace of the drive home was about to be interrupted.

My mobile rang; it was our PR friend. He had promised *OK!* magazine an interview with Paula and he was pushing for her agreement. I had already explained to him that it was not in Paula's best interest to give magazine interviews when she had nothing new to say about herself. In fact, I had issued a press release to that effect. We wanted to wait until she had a television show or a project to talk about, instead of recycling the story of her tangled love life. I had discussed this strategy with him on numerous occasions, but today he had convenient amnesia. He became angry, abusive and bullying but I stood my ground and ended the call without giving in to his threats to damage Paula and Michael's new improved status.

Kate Sissons, the society editor of *OK!* couldn't have been more gracious when I spoke to her later. In a rapid risk management manoeuvre, I explained that Paula wasn't closing the door on an interview with *OK!*, but we had a plan to follow and Paula's commitment to the *Sun* for the exclusive photo on the baby pictures was paramount. Kate explained that if Paula was interested in giving an interview after the birth, it could be arranged in conjunction with the *Sun* and we discussed focusing the piece on her future projects rather than on her relationship with Michael. If truth be told, Paula wasn't giving interviews to anyone. *Hello!* had called, and we had already declined their offer for an interview after the birth. Such offers were coming in thick and fast and the sums being quoted were escalating. Paula was being admirably disciplined in standing by her resolve to wait for the right offer and her decision to remain off the magazine shelves.

The media obsession with Paula and Michael had been reinvigorated by the forthcoming birth. And their net was being cast wider. I was talking to journalists who wanted more than the scraps I was able to throw them about the dynamic duo – they wanted an interview with me, the publicist behind the scenes.

It was never part of the plan that the conjuror reveal his tricks and I viewed the latest development with suspicion. However, I would listen to Paula and Michael spit venom at the treachery of the press, but my own experience had not borne this out. I was having a ball and I now had a long list of contacts, many of whom I knew could be trusted, some of whom I would call my friends even now. But when I brought this up with Paula she said, 'You've never been in the firing line.' I cannot deny feeling a jolt of excitement at the thought of giving a personal interview as a PR professional in my own right, not least for the prospect of wider recognition for the work I had done on Paula's behalf. After all, I hadn't got much else out of it apart from a headache. But I was strictly focused on the impact such a move would have on Paula's image. Paula, Michael and I agreed that if it appeared in a broadsheet, it could work in our favour. So, with trepidation, I agreed to speak to the *Daily Telegraph* where favourable pieces were currently appearing at least once a week on Paula and Michael, and to whom I had spoken on numerous occasions. Though I remained unconvinced that they would find enough to fill a whole piece on me, and suspected that it would turn out to be an opportunity to ply me with drink and get as much out of me as possible about Paula and Michael, I agreed to give an interview, which was now to appear in the Sunday colour supplement as their cover story.

With just two days to go before she was due in court, tensions were running high in Paula's household. She was still intent on discrediting Bob but had failed to find one girl who would admit to sleeping with her ex-husband. 'It would be easier to get someone to admit to shagging the Pope,' Paula announced with frustration.

Anita too was under huge stress from all sides. Paula wanted her in her camp in court but Bob had been incredibly hurt by what he perceived as Anita's betrayal of him and it had taken a long time for her to regain his trust. From Anita's point of view, the balance of parental power had shifted back to Bob. She had become less than enthusiastic about Michael and was referring to him as Paula's 'part-time boyfriend', a nickname, I was to find out later, that Bob had coined for him. We were worried about whether Michael would marry Paula after the baby's birth and confused about his reluctance to buy them a new house, although, I knew that Paula had been asking Michael to draw up a new will to take their child into account.

The press were asking the same questions, clogging my answering machine with every conceivable query about the forthcoming action. We had perhaps overdone the sympathy vote with the sale of the family silver and all the endless references to Paula's penury. It had more than accomplished the aim of turning the spotlight on Bob, but now they were starting to ask about Michael: if life is so dire for Paula, how come he won't step in? We had sold the two of them as the ultimate lovers, soulmates weathering the storm together. Now that Paula was homeless and pregnant – where was Michael? Why wasn't he buying her a house? These questions were deflected for now with the assurance that Paula wanted her own house back and Michael's intervention would jeopardize her case, but the obvious contradictions remained.

I brought the matter up with Michael on numerous occasions – the questions about his house in Smith Terrace and his wealth. This was clearly not a subject he liked to discuss with anyone but his business advisors. His responses were obscured by legalese and talk of business strictures. His money, he said, was tied up in trusts and investments and managed for him by a consultant in Sydney. Of the house in Smith Terrace he would say only that he could not sell it, the escalating bills for refurbishment meant that he would lose money if he sold at that time. Something in me was ignoring the obvious fact that if he really loved her, he couldn't stand back and watch her suffer as she was. Michael didn't understand that the questions from the press needed to be answered on his behalf and he had to give me something concrete or the reporters would be writing the story themselves, to flush out the truth.

Michael said Paula could live anywhere else in the world: the South of France, Australia (knowing she would never leave the children and Bob would never let them go), but he could not be seen to be buying another house in London. Meanwhile Bob went to Paula's lawyers with an offer: £20,000 towards the rent on a home. Paula was furious: 'It's insulting, how dare he?' She gritted her teeth, determined to fight and win.

I helped Paula to prepare her paperwork for the case and we discussed which bits I could extract to leak to the press, to build public sympathy. She jotted down financial arrangements between her and Bob in simple terms: the properties they'd shared and the details of when and how Paula had bought the house in Redburn Street. The high-earning capacity she had built up during the time she had spent with her ex-husband was emphasized. The house had been signed over to Bob when she left and he had taken over the mortgage. She would assert that she had supported him and the household, emotionally and financially, right through the gestation of the Live Aid project. She had always been the main breadwinner and Bob had often referred to her as 'a nice little earner'; he would get up at midday and go to the King's Road to meet friends and drink coffee, as she suppoprted his business plans.

The reasons she would give for leaving sounded like the many conversations we had had in the past year or so, specifically: She was trying to come out from under a marriage in which she had been over-dominated. She had had to ask permission for every move she made, including using the telephone. Bob would be shown as a bully, who would go to any lengths to maintain a rigid regime of control. She would say that Bob had begun a relationship with Jeanne a year before she, Paula, had left the marriage for Michael, so therefore *her* adultery was not to blame for the break-up.

Obviously Bob would deny all these allegations, probably relying heavily on the sympathy vote as the injured party, he would profess his innocence on every single count. He would undoubtedly describe his humanitarian efforts, saving millions of lives in Ethiopia and point out that his capacity to earn had been frustrated as he campaigned to bring the world's attention to the plight of many starving nations.

Unfortunately, I got more than I bargained for as I shuffled through Paula's notes. She had obviously forgotten that Bob had already given her £70,000 towards her mortgage, and a further £20,000 towards the down payment on another house.

I was shocked she had never mentioned this when asserting Bob's parsimony. No wonder he had paid the weekly £300 maintenance directly to Anita, he must have increasingly concerned that Paula was spending to excess and would not want the children's sustenance to be in any way compromised. With a fee from the *Hello!* article, a large advance for her autobiography and the sums Bob had already advanced her, she should have no reason to be in so much debt.

Discreet research on my part revealed that Paula's sacking by Planet 24 may have been because she had been late on many occasions and sometimes entirely absent. Obviously her relationship with Bob would have protected her in the past, but following the split, Bob's partners would have no reason to put up with unprofessional behaviour.

But what of the house? Bob would want to keep the family home, as presumably he could not afford another and needed to live in London to maintain his business interests. I was still worrying about Paula's lack of honesty about her finances and her 'fibs' made me feel very uncomfortable.

After mulling it over, I decided not to confront her with these discrepancies until the case was through, not wanting to add to her burdens, but I was feeling uneasy and the spectre of other possible lies was haunting my memories of the past year.

It was a strictly private hearing that started on 10 June, exactly one month after their fast-track divorce, and it went on for three days. Paula said she was stunned when Bob arrived in an immaculate tweed suit and Church's hand-made shoes. She had not seen this man in a suit since he visited the Palace to receive his knighthood and the only other occasion had probably been at their wedding. There was no mistaking that for Bob this was full battle armour – no other cause he had ever fought was important enough for him to put on a suit. He and his lawyer carried a battering ram, too – reams of allegations, reinforced with crates of evidence including receipts that dated back to the beginning of their romance and love notes that Paula had written to him, plus a video.

Bob was to show footage of Paula's infamous flirtation with Michael on *The Big Breakfast* bed, which had occurred two years before she was claiming that their affair had begun. But Paula got there first with videos of her interviews with Jeremy Beadle and Alan Titchmarsh, showing that she acted just as flirtatiously towards them. She said that if she could flirt with them, it proved she could flirt with anyone.

On the second day of the hearing, Paula was grilled for eight hours on every minute detail of their eighteen years together. 'His lawyers presented a 2,000-page affidavit, that's 557 pages longer than *War and Peace*,' said Paula, exhausted and emotional. Naturally we gave our version of the story to the *Mirror*. It ran a detailed article across pages two and three, covering everything we handed over: '…she told a pal: "It was the worst day of my life." A courtroom source said: "Paula felt she had been torn to pieces in the witness box and Bob didn't want to go through that. He just couldn't face it himself".'

Paula had told me that when she was about to take the stand on the third day, preparing herself for another onslaught, she had said to Bob 'Come on, why don't we talk about this?' They went out into the corridor and came to an agreement in principle, in about three minutes flat. When I spoke to the *Mirror*, I emphasized that Bob had backed down: 'He told her he didn't want to go through the same as she had in the witness box. He completely backed down.'

Weeks later, Bob told me his side. He watched Paula, eight months pregnant, being crushed under the aggressive cross-examination. Some of her stories were beginning to show cracks, she was getting confused, and sobbing. He said he couldn't sit there and watch it for another day and called a halt. Paula was ecstatic; she called me from the court with the news that she had won. Her lawyers informed me that they had all signed confidentiality agreements that precluded any discussion of the case, but it was all good news and Paula could move back into her house almost immediately.

She and Bob had thrashed out an informal settlement that returned the house to her. But Bob had thrown in a final spanner, saying that he was now the one out on the street. During gaps in the proceedings Paula was in moment-by-moment contact with Michael, who was twiddling his thumbs in LA, waiting for the threat to his own finances to pass. In the most bizarre twist to the settlement, Michael offered Bob a six-month stay, rent-free, in his newly refurbished house in Smith Terrace and that sealed the deal – Bob accepted.

So Bob was to move out of the family home, and into a house only 300 yards away, recently fitted out to the exacting standards and eccentric tastes of his ex-wife's lover. The four of them would virtually be neighbours. Friends of Bob's found this amusing and there were comments like 'Bob's always been a tight bastard'. Bob was prepared to take the charity of his rival in love, and move into a space where every surface could not but remind him of the terrible anguish he'd suffered, for the sake of a few months' rent.

Paula and Bob issued a joint statement outside the court; it read:

After three days of complete bloody nightmare in the High Courts of Justice, Bob and Paula have with collective sighs of relief arrived amicably at a half-decent solution to their housing arrangements. Paula and the kids will move into the house in Chelsea. Bob will move into Michael's house down the road. Thank you very much.

PS: Neither of us will talk about this any further, so please don't doorstep us.

That the outcome of the case was a tremendous relief hardly needs stating. After months of gnashing our teeth and tearing out our hair, we had come out the other side – victorious. Paula could now get the children back to a settled and happy family life, while she continued to claw her way out of the disasters of her first experiment in living on her own.

———— ◆ ————

The house in Clapham was being dismantled and Anita's brother Tom Debney and his friends had come to help. Tom was a lovely young man, very close to his sister and fond of Paula. Tom, like all Anita's brothers and sisters, had stayed with Paula and house-sat from time to time – Paula had always been welcoming and over the years had come to think of the Debneys as her second family. Tom was joshing with Paula and giving piggy-back rides to the girls and Anita was laughing, admonishing her brother for encouraging them to say 'bottom' and 'poo'.

Paula was busy. Her energy levels had returned and she was sorting through all her fabrics, contemplating whether she would install them in her Chelsea house. Michael arrived after taking a driving test to obtain his international licence. He was angry with a photo-journalist who had snapped him getting out of the car and he had gone over to lambast him, to ask him to leave them all alone.

'Don't worry,' Paula soothed. 'They just want a picture of the removal van turning up.' She knew that Matthew had arranged to send a photographer for the shot. Michael threw me a perplexed look and asked me why on earth anyone would want a picture of their tea-crates.

Paula knew that I had spoken to the *Mirror* and the *Mail* about the timing of the move. She understood that it was important to keep a flow of communication between ourselves and our new friends in the press – it is in the absence of information that the most mischief is made. But I hadn't told her about a call I had received from the *Express* concerning mysterious packages seen arriving at the house by bike. Packages arrived all the time, I had explained, with demo tapes for Michael and legal papers for Paula. I knew because I had taken them in myself when I was around. So what? I didn't pique their interest by adding that the packages were often addressed to Mr Kipper – anyway, Michael had explained that if they carried his real name, they would never get to him intact, they would be steamed open on the off-chance of a valuable haul. It was put to me that the bikes had been traced to a notorious drug dealer and, without thinking, I declared the notion ridiculous.

Paula was so glad to be leaving that house, with its nine-foot fence and sense of insecurity – they'd had two burglaries in the time that she had lived there. 'The house has been jinxed from the start,' Michael was telling Tom. 'Who'd want to live like this?' pointing toward the wooden fence encircling the house. Michael likened the last year to being under house arrest. This habitat was anathema to him; he was used to five-star hotels and luxury villas in LA, Sydney, the Gold Coast, Paris and the French Riviera.

There had been a time when nothing could perturb Michael's positive outlook, but now his attitude to everything was bleak, even his work on the forthcoming INXS album seemed to hold no excitement for him. He was almost always dressed in black. His gradual transformation into a louche Aussie goth was almost complete – all that was missing was black nail polish. Paula cut off her hair extensions herself and the short layered bob she now wore really suited her. The soft honey blonde complemented her pregnancy and was a definite improvement on the peroxide. But Michael's lank black hair didn't suit him at all – it had aged him at least five years. But his appearance had deteriorated more than could be accounted for by the normal wear and tear of a couple of years. Gone too was that boyish air, the happy-go-lucky guy who lit up a room with his energy and love of life. Now he had mood swings and a new cynicism that was particularly evident when Paula complained about her problems. He was less patient with the girls, too, which Paula tried to mitigate by sending them to the park or other parts of the house with Anita, whose own hair had been buzz-cut to accommodate the small patches that continued to appear.

'It's going to be fantastic when we move back to Chelsea,' Paula smiled. We were sitting in her attic bedroom, waiting for the removal men to come up, while Michael was downstairs talking to his business partner about the house swap. I could tell that his partner was none too happy about Bob moving into Smith Terrace, but I didn't know why. All I heard was Michael saying, 'I had no choice mate, the whole thing was killing her.'

Paula was organizing her stuff to be moved to the truck and pulled out a suitcase from beneath the bed. With a giggle, she casually opened it up and my chin dropped to the floor – it was stacked with sex toys. 'I don't think I'll leave this for the men to carry, the catches are a bit dodgy and I can see the papers in the morning.' Paula was hardly fazed by my stunned silence, relishing as always the impact of her outrages on my convent-educated disposition. She proceeded to rummage through the contents, pulling out various items. 'The girls nearly caught me in this,' she said producing a terrifying black dildo with hyper-real veins, and straps like a bridle hanging from it.

Paula's collection of dildos included a polished chrome truncheon, double-headed missiles and an outsized latex statuette. She held up a black face-mask with a phallus projecting from the mouth, and went pink. So as not to embarrass Paula, I rummaged amongst some of the other items in the case: handcuffs, rope, a riding crop and, incomprehensibly, a vaginal speculum. In a state of shocked amusement, I quipped that I guessed she hadn't been using that stuff for a while and she looked at me as if I'd just landed from Mars. 'We were using it yesterday,' she said.

It was amazing that Paula, eight months pregnant, having survived months of agony and stress, was now happily lugging boxes around for the move, and experimenting with this disturbing array of erotic accessories, without a qualm. Paula said that she had never used sex toys in her life before she met Michael, but explained that the contents of the suitcase were merely the accessories of a complex sexuality and that Michael had extremely outlandish tastes. At first she had been squeamish, but gradually he had introduced her to the dubious eroticism of... I knew not what. 'I always thought this kind of gear was for middle-aged politicians with fond memories of their public-school beatings,' Paula said, but the important thing was that it turned Michael on and she had come to enjoy it, through his excitement.

Then it struck me – the Rohypnol by the bed – something had brought me back to that again and again, and perhaps this was it: Paula had been using Rohypnol to anaesthetize herself, while she performed in Michael's fantasy of erotic violation. I asked her if the Rohypnol had anything to do this. She looked me in the eye, as if the possibility had not occurred to her and said wistfully, 'Perhaps...'

———— ◆ ————

Paula's mood was so elevated when she returned to her own house in Chelsea that I decided to postpone the conversation I wanted to have about the lies she'd been telling. What mattered more than anything was that she could feather her nest, free from anything that could perturb her, in readiness for the arrival of Heavenly. Michael had promised Paula that he would be around more as the birth approached, but he would have to visit the studio in London to catch up with the schedule on his album, neglected by his recent flight from the courts.

We went to a charity party hosted by my PR guru. The press took photos of Paula and Michael and everyone congratulated them on how happy they looked as parents-to-be. I thanked Paula for the effort she was making and hinted at the PR man's complaint of neglect. With an understanding wink, she was quick to suggest that we all get together for dinner.

The *Mirror* and a couple of other newspapers reported Rentokil arriving at the house in Redburn Street. We gave Matthew Wright the story that, on moving back into the house, Paula found Bob had left it in a pitiful mess and infested with fleas. Not strictly true, but it caused Michael's manager in England to have a fit of anxiety about the house in Smith Terrace and he beetled round there for a spot-check. He convinced himself that he could see things jumping out of the cushions, while he kept a safe distance from Bob.

The ownership of Michael's house continued to niggle on the fringes of the press coverage of the bizarre house-swap that had brought the Geldofs' settlement to a temporary end. Michael wanted me to stop the journalists from probing any further into the deeds of Smith Terrace. 'I can't afford to have the journalists prying into my affairs,' he urged.

A couple of journalists had called to say that Michael's manager was most unhelpful, verging on rude, when they asked for comments on the swap. It was an extraordinary situation and they wanted detail: when had Michael bought the house and what was he planning to do with it, now that he was with Paula in Redburn Street? One journalist was particularly intrigued; he had discovered that the house was owned by an offshore company and was simply querying how Michael was able to let Bob live there if he didn't own it. Michael's manager's refusal to comment was drawing attention to the very issue he seemed reluctant to discuss. 'It's nobody's business,' he insisted.

As far as he was concerned Michael's world began and ended with his music. It was his job to protect Michael, his image and his business interests. He went on: 'Michael doesn't own Smith Terrace, it's owned by a committee of investors. He had no right to hand it over to Bob, it wasn't his place to do that, and there are some very angry people as a result.' The plot thickened. It was not difficult to understand that Michael would have his assets wrapped up and protected in commercial companies, but to say that there was a committee on the warpath, as if anyone else's cash had really paid for the house, was hard to swallow. If Michael was merely a favoured lodger at Smith Terrace, why then had Bob been allowed to move in?

He said he couldn't give details but insisted that Bob hadn't moved in, he had been allowed to stay for a short period while he looked for somewhere else. Papers were being drawn up which he had agreed to sign.

With nothing to go on I was unable to help the journalists with the information they were looking for; in fact I learned more about Michael's business from them than I did from either Michael or his manager. Michael appeared to own none of his houses. But the question was: who did and why? Who were these people on their committees? In the end I had to insist that Paula direct all the newspapers to me – I didn't want our relationship with them to spiral out of control and Michael's manager clearly wasn't willing to massage their enquiries with the patience it required.

'This is going to cost Michael £26,000 a year,' he said. It was agreed that Bob's stay was to be rent-free. He explained that as Michael wasn't going to be using Smith Terrace, the real owners had planned to rent it out for £950 a week. 'Smith Terrace isn't a home, it's a commercial concern.'

Whatever the truth of the matter, I had many unpleasant calls with him; I considered that he was often rude and evasive, and though we were supposed to be batting for the same team, I got the distinct impression that he was using me as a punch bag to vent his frustrations at Paula's interference with Michael's career. I remembered Paula telling me that in the early days when Michael was still with Helena and she had wanted to get hold of him, his manager would treat her like a groupie, never giving her the contact numbers and never passing on her messages. Now the boot was on the other foot. Paula would answer the phone to him, when he was looking for Michael, and she would be happy and polite, never revealing that Michael was in the house, and never forwarding the messages.

Within a few days of moving back in to her old home, Paula decided that structural changes were needed downstairs. The dividing wall in the hall was knocked down to open up the sitting room; she had decorators in to repaint her bedroom and moved the family out to a hotel in Chelsea Harbour. 'I hope the work doesn't take too long,' Paula worried, 'this hotel is costing Michael a bomb.'

Paula, Anita and the three children had spent ten days in the hotel, taking three meals a day and constantly ordering room service, but even as she said that it was playing on her mind, I could hear the girls in the background, going though the menu without supervision. They, of course, were loving it.

Michael had mentioned his own money worries to Paula and during the week that she spent in the hotel, Michael hadn't sent her any flowers. He had returned to LA and then Dublin and she was afraid that he might not be back in time for the baby's birth. She had reminded him that in the early days he would send her flowers every day but now, all that had changed. She missed the romance, the constant attention and she let him know that she was finding his lack of interest distressing, especially when she was about to give birth to his baby.

When the builders left, Paula returned to her house to admire a brand new mustard-yellow sitting room, a new row of bookshelves that she had hired a carpenter to install and a beautifully redecorated bedroom. She was sitting on a large packing case when I went round to see her. It was countdown time now, with only a few weeks to go before the baby was due, and she was determined to have the house looking wonderful again. Michael was back for a few days and had made up for his lack of attention by sending round three large bouquets and a box of Fortnum & Mason lavender chocolates packed in a beautiful box of padded lilac silk.

'It's too easy to take us for granted, it's important to point out to them that we are special and deserve to be treated like princesses,' Paula announced as she handed the chocolates over to me.

She told me that the girls were delighted to be back in their home. Michael was out with his mother, who had come to London for a short stop before making her way to Nice for her daughter's wedding, to be held in Michael's villa in France. Michael was planning to be there if the baby hadn't been born, but Paula would not be allowed on a plane in her condition and travelling by train would be too strenuous.

'Spending time with his family will probably be good for him,' I told Paula, thinking that Michael looked as if he was in need of some good old-fashioned home cooking and a rest from his itinerary. Paula did not comment and talked of her own plans to stay in the villa after the baby was born. Michael, as always, was concerned that everything should be perfect for his family.

———— ◆ ————

Before Michael left for the wedding, the PR man and I met him and Paula for the promised dinner in a restaurant in London's Fulham Road. The restaurant was packed and every woman in the room was eyeing up

Michael, which he seemed to be enjoying. We were celebrating the success of the court case and finally thanking my friend for all his help. I had done too good a job of promoting him to Paula and Michael in a bid to encourage them to appreciate his contribution, and now it seemed they saw him as the mastermind behind the help that they had been receiving.

Paula looked beautiful. Michael looked at her with a mixture of pride and deep love, as she described her visit to hairdresser Nicky Clarke that afternoon. She was a little tense to begin with, she made a couple of snipes at Kylie, whom Michael had seen for dinner recently, but Michael took this with his usual magnanimity and put his arms around her. After the meal we sat chatting round the table with our half-filled glasses.

Half an hour later, my friend was looking very comfortable and behaving in an uncharacteristically affectionate way towards me. I wondered if this was a special performance for Michael, whose arms were draped casually around Paula's shoulders, while he criticized Englishmen's inhibitions and their fear of women. Michael talked of his progress with the album and the difficulties of getting a solo deal. He was looking forward to touring, as he was missing the really big gigs and Mr PR was asking lots of questions: how big was his entourage, did he employ a photographer to travel with them, who paid for the travel and promotion expenses and who controlled the PR, looking at me with a subtle smile that suggested I could do it.

Music was Michael's whole world, and that night he was more eloquent than ever on his influences and inspirations. He told us that his music had been such a natural progression from the poems he wrote in his early teens, poems that proved the only reliable outlet for the pain he felt in a family torn apart. He wrote when he was bored and melancholy, missing his younger brother Rhett.

I have since read Michael's biography *Just A Man* by his sister Tina Hutchence and his mother, Patricia Glassop. In it a picture emerges of a sensitive boy growing up in what should have been privileged conditions, but as in so many families the children became the ultimate casualties of the vagaries of marriage. But this is a tale of poignancy beyond the standard fare of marital acrimony, as the two boys were separated when their parents split, victims of a double divorce.

Patricia Kennedy had already one child from a previous marriage, Christina ('Tina') Elaine. Patricia had no money when she left Tina's father but a promising career in front of her. Michael always talked proudly of his mother's modelling days when he discussed her with me. 'Not only was she exquisitely beautiful, my mother is clever, classy and driven,' Michael would boast. By his bedside table in his villa in the South of France he kept a picture of her, looking spectacular when she entered the 'Gown of the Year' awards in 1953.

Michael Kelland John Hutchence was born to parents Patricia and Kell on 22 January 1960. According to his mother and sister Michael was 'adorable' right from the start. In 1962 Patricia gave birth to Rhett Bradley. Rhett was apparently the complete opposite to his angelic older brother – he was cranky and often threw tantrums. As Kell was spending more and more time abroad on business trips, Patricia and Tina were left to care for the two young boys.

In 1965 the family moved to Hong Kong where life was good for all the Hutchences. Michael and Rhett recited their nursery rhymes in Cantonese as well as English, joined the swimming club and the boy scouts, learned kick boxing, judo, archery, chess and studied music. They loved to visit their mother when she was working on film sets. These fond memories of Hong Kong led to Michael's life-long love affair with the place – he always kept an apartment there.

The family returned to Australia in 1972, when Michael was twelve. On his first day at his new school, Michael was bullied by a group of boys because of the 'stuck up' British accent he had acquired in Hong Kong, and another student came to his rescue; this was Andrew Farriss, who would become one of Michael's greatest friends and his fellow band member in INXS.

Patricia and Kell's marriage had been in difficulties for some years, but Patricia had stayed with Kell for the sake of the boys. In 1975, she was offered work in Los Angeles, studying corrective make-up. She knew this was her opportunity to get away and made the agonizing decision to take only Michael with her. She was unable to control Rhett and felt that he would be better off staying with his father, at least until she was settled. Thirteen-year-old Rhett cried and begged to go with his mother, and Patricia says her heart was breaking as they said their goodbyes at the airport. Michael told me that he could still hear his brother crying at the airport and would wake in the night in a cold sweat, having dreamed of that day when he saw Rhett pleading through the glass: 'Michael, don't leave me.'

Kell moved to the Philippines with Rhett, where they were able to employ a cook and staff to clean the house. Patricia was relieved and happy for Rhett, that he was now getting the attention he had always craved from his father. But Patricia wrote: 'Kell's hurt was profound. Kell would not allow Rhett to join us, even for a holiday.' And she did not fight it. It was against the law back then, for a parent to remove a child beyond the reach of their spouse, without consent, and she was scared that Kell might instigate legal proceedings to take Michael back. Michael would say of this period: 'It was when I had to grow up real fast.'

He told me that although he enjoyed the peace away from Rhett's rows with his mother, he was very lonely at times. Poetry, music and marijuana became his companions. At North Hollywood High Michael met an alien culture, and fell in with friends who introduced him to all ranges and styles of music. At school his grades were low, but he was keen on art, music, drama and English.

Richard Lowenstein said, after Michael's death, that his time spent in California was a period Michael regarded as special, steering him inexorably towards the world of entertainment. I always had the impression, when Michael talked of that time with his mother and sister, that he felt guilt that Rhett had drawn the short straw, and struggled under the weight of the responsibility of being the chosen one.

After eighteen months in California, Michael was sent back to Australia on his own after Patricia had a bad fall and ended up in bed for a month. She eventually followed him home six months later. By the time Michael returned to Australia, his best mate Andrew Farriss had already pulled together a band. Michael eagerly joined the group, called Doctor Dolphin, as their lead singer. They practised in garages at the Farrisses' and at Patricia's home. When the Farriss family decided to move to Perth, Michael followed them, and INXS was born.

———— ◆ ————

Michael flirted with dreams of immortality through the ultimate rock god death. He had told me over dinner that evening on the Fulham Road that the only way to become a legend was to die before you get old. He talked of Morrison, Cobain, Hendrix and Lennon. He admitted to fears that his career was sliding, and he longed to play Wembley again, to the adoration of thousands. He was being philosophical, but this was no dream of fame, this was a dream of death. I became animated on the dangers of drugs, and the need to cherish his life: for his friends, his family and his unborn child.

While Paula was in deep conversation with the PR man, Michael listened patiently to my lecture on the megastar myth. I was telling him of my friend James Hunt who had spent years playing fast and loose with his life. Michael said he had been a great fan of James Hunt, loved the reckless determination with which he drove, and his hard-won progress through the ranks of world motor racing. Michael knew, too, of James's drug taking, drinking and womanizing, but then who didn't? What he didn't know was that James was in a similar state to that which Michael was in now but James had been on Prozac and still been depressed. This revelation got Michael's attention.

James wanted to get clean for his girlfriend. His serial womanizing had left him alone and empty, until one day, visiting a hamburger restaurant, he fell in love from a distance with a petite and purposeful blonde waitress. For a whole year, James ate enough hamburgers to put him off meat for life. The girl was working there part-time to help fund her fine arts degree, and when James eventually plucked up the courage to invite her to dinner, she accepted, without a clue as to who he was. She knew only that she was drawn to this mysterious man with his daily newspaper and mischievous twinkle. After a week of seeing one another every night, she moved in with him, and James announced to the world that he had finally fallen in love, which was something he thought would never happen to him.

His new girlfriend deplored his lifestyle, his friends and, even to a degree, his past. She cared nothing for his nostalgic trips to Monte Carlo, for wild parties on yachts with people only interested in the famous. Instead she introduced him to simpler pleasures: long walks together on Wimbledon Common and rides through London by bicycle rather than in his old Mercedes. James built a studio for her in his house in Wimbledon village and she would spend her days painting, while James tended the large garden and his collection of rare budgerigars.

James overcame his need for a different woman every night and let his membership to Tramps nightclub lapse; calls from Nigel Dempster went unreturned, unless he wanted to promote his lover's art shows. But the years of hard living had fed a craving that was now a dependency and she wanted him off everything, including the Prozac. She attended Al-Anon meetings, for the partners of alcoholics and drug users, or anyone with an addictive personality. In time James went to group sessions with us. I introduced him to my therapist and the work began. It was tough for him – coming off the drugs brought a steep decline into deep depression. But with help from his girlfriend, his therapist and a holistic healer, James worked through his problems, reading all the books he could on addictions – narcotic, adrenalin, sex – and on co-dependency, as well as a whole host of other self-help books. It wasn't plain sailing; he would often slip back to his old ways and his girlfriend would find the leftovers of marijuana and pills, but to her credit she would just increase her visits to Al-Anon.

Had my story featured anyone else, a random bod who had chosen life over a history of self-destruction, I don't think Michael would have stayed the distance; but because it was James, a *Boy's Own* god of speed and cool, Michael wanted to hear it. He asked which drugs James had mostly used and which healer he had been seeing. He wanted to know how difficult it was to banish the old friends, who were only around for the good times. 'Enablers,' I said, and Michael asked why I used that particular word. Paula raised her eyebrows at me, in a silent message that said: 'Make the point.' 'Enablers are apparently well-meaning people, who enable you to continue doing things to yourself that aren't good for you.'

Like the wife of an alcoholic, who complains, screams, bribes and begs in an attempt to help her husband give up, but who, when his drinking threatens his ability to do his job, picks up the pieces, protecting him from the consequences. Or the wife who focuses her entire life on her husband, forgetting her own needs and neglecting herself while she enables him to drink, providing all the home comforts and calling his boss to make excuses for his absence. The partner of an addict is normally a caretaker and protects the addict from hitting the crises they need to shock them out of their pattern.

I explained that there were many forms of enabling, but that they always involved maintaining the state of dependence in the addict, by action or inaction. An enabler might be another addict or a kind listener, who enjoys the role of confidant or rescuer. Either way, the enabler has a subconscious interest in the dynamics of the relationship remaining unaltered and is likely to react if it begins to change, particularly if the addict makes any effort to disengage from the addiction or the enabler.

But James got to a point where he could set apart the friends who were good for him from those who reinforced his weaknesses. He valued his new relationship and realized that if he returned to his old ways, she would not stick around, and only the old friends would return. None of the people who supported his recovery, who were working hard on their own issues, would encourage his habit by continuing the friendship while he slipped gradually downhill. And this knowledge kept him going.

The tragedy for James was that it was all too late. Years of abuse of his body and his mind had already set in motion the wheels that would eventually kill him. Although he had been clean for a year, giving up forty cigarettes a day, eating healthily and exercising, he died of a heart attack at the age of forty-five.

'It was the night he asked his girlfriend to marry him, wasn't it?' Paula chipped in. I suspected she was having a subtle dig at Michael.

'He said when he knew he was worthy of her, and was confident that he wouldn't let her down, that he would propose and she had waited five years for that.' His girlfriend was away at the time, her first ever holiday away from James. She had planned it as her last, before they tried for a baby. James called her on the remote Greek island and told her that she was the love of his life and had brought him salvation. She described the conversation as the most intimate moment of their lives together. He talked of booking the church for three weeks hence and friends of his recalled him visiting for a lunch party earlier that day, looking happier than they'd ever seen him before. The depression was gone, he had told them, and he refused the champagne – he would normally drink until it ran out – asking for water instead.

After calling his girlfriend, James played a game of pool with a friend at his house, complained of feeling unwell and went to bed. The next morning his friend found him dead. His lover, meanwhile, had gone alone down to the water's edge, the happiest girl in the world, reflecting on how far they come and all the hard work they had put into their relationship. She was so proud of James for overcoming his demons that she thanked God for the miracle. She told me that when she looked up into the night sky she was sure she saw James, but put it down to the deep connection they had at that moment. She had no idea she would never see him alive again. 'Fuck, man,' said Michael. 'How do you get over that?' 'She hasn't,' I replied. 'When she came home she did go to the church, where James had wanted them to get married, but it was for his funeral instead.'

Call it intuition, but I had felt compelled to tell this story to Michael. I sensed deep down that the dream of oblivion had taken hold of him.

Michael asked me if James had discovered in therapy what had caused his depression and drug-taking: 'Was it his childhood?' 'Partially, perhaps, but whatever it was had fuelled his drive for fame, and he made fame his god, instead of himself,' I replied. 'The message he got from therapy was that the adulation of others was an antidote for the loathing he had for himself – sort yourself out, and you don't need the fame.'

Michael was nodding his head. 'Yeah, man... Yeah, man,' he murmured under his breath.

10 heaven sent

IT WAS MICHAEL WHO ANSWERED the door to me when I arrived armed with flowers and the presents I had bought for Heavenly over the previous months. He took a fat cigar from his mouth and planted an enthusiastic kiss on my cheek. The pre-birth nerves of two nights ago, when he and Paula had come round for dinner in my garden, had totally evaporated. He had been dancing to Frank Sinatra which he put on at full volume in the downstairs room. It hadn't been easy to reach their front door for the hordes of photographers eager to get the first picture, and when Michael phoned to tell me the news he warned me to phone the house as I arrived, so that he would know it was me knocking at the door. I was quick to turn my mobile back off, it was full of messages, and the phone at home had been ringing off the hook for news of the birth. I just wanted to spend time with the new parents and their darling baby, uninterrupted.

'She's beautiful, it was amazing, Paula was incredible,' Michael was dancing. 'She's perfect, Paula thinks she looks like me.' He beamed with pride.

It was a relief that Heavenly had finally arrived without complication, that Paula was fine, and that Michael had been there at the birth. Two nights ago, he had looked like a man who was preparing to bolt. His manner had been strained. Paula didn't appear concerned by his constant disappearance to my loo, and when I asked her if he was alright, she laughed and told me that he was probably adjusting his hair. Now, Paula was sitting up in her bed while she munched on a piece of toast, with Heavenly lying across her stomach.

'Oh my God, you've cloned Michael,' I laughed. Heavenly was the image of her father, right down to her little hands and feet. Even then, just a few hours old, her tiny fingers and toes moved like Michael's. Paula didn't look the least bit tired; she was elated and told me, as I settled down on the bed beside them, how easy it had been and that Michael, with the assistance of two midwives, had helped deliver the baby. 'He was incredible,' she said. 'My waters broke in the middle of the night and a few hours later, Heavenly was born.'

As I cooed over the little beauty, feeling broody and emotional,

Michael constantly floated in and out to give Paula and Heavenly a kiss and tell the mother how clever she was. Her bedroom windows were wide open to let some air into the room, as it was almost unbearably hot, and we could hear the journalists singing outside to Michael's Frank Sinatra songs. 'Matthew Wright will be blowing a gasket,' I told Paula, 'if I don't call to tell him the news.' Of course I knew that Matthew would already know about the baby's arrival, but he would want to hear it with some detail that no one else could get, for tomorrow's edition. And more than anyone, he deserved to have the main scoop, even though I knew that the *Sun* had already been promised 'the picture'. The last thing I wanted to do was work on a day like this. I would have much preferred to settle into the sofa, and drink the champagne Michael had poured, to the sound of him swapping CDs and singing along with every song. But Matthew was top of a long list of those who had helped us get where we were. So I could hardly shut them all out now that the golden child had finally arrived and we no longer needed them.

It was 22 July 1996 and Heavenly Hiraani Tiger Lily Hutchence was the most famous baby to be born since Prince Harry. It was like a royal occasion. Flowers from every newspaper and television company kept arriving at the house and I had to fill the bath tub, where Heavenly had been born, to keep the flowers from wilting in the heat. I looked for a towel in the bathroom cupboard. There, among the bottles of bubble bath and Nina Ricci scent, was a folded slip of paper and a couple of white pills, imprinted with the symbol of a bird in flight. I unfolded the wrap to reveal half a teaspoon of fine white powder. I had a pretty good idea what I was looking at, and I was paralyzed, wondering whether I should put it away somewhere safer, out of reach of the children. Bob had been looking after them down in Faversham for a few days and I knew that Anita was bringing them back at any moment.

I wasn't quite sure if I should do anything at all. What if Michael discovered I had touched it without asking? I couldn't very well go downstairs and ask him what I should do with his stash. I had been discussing the subject with him only the other night, when he had agreed that no one should take drugs around children. I thought of approaching Paula, but decided that it was bad timing and anyway she would probably deny all knowledge of the drugs. And if that were the case, I would only be getting Michael into trouble, causing unrest in this perfect moment. I didn't want to be the bearer of bad news on a day like this, but I also couldn't leave this poison in the bathroom cupboard either; so, realizing that Michael must be on something already and would probably not miss a bit of his stash, I flushed the whole lot down the loo.

In that moment, as I walked out of the bathroom and passed Paula's lawyers on the stairs, I realized that I had become the enabler I had been lecturing Michael about at dinner only a couple of weeks earlier. But I reasoned it away, as enablers do: it was a one-off – after all, I could hardly go and spoil this day for them over a little recreational medication that Michael probably forgot in the excitement of the moment. Could I?

The lawyers had come to deliver some papers for Paula to sign. Then Michael's manager arrived with flowers. He later discussed with them both a convenient time for the photographer to take the exclusive *Sun* photo. Eventually everyone left. Michael couldn't sit down in one place for a second – he was darting about, putting on more music, singing, lighting another cigar and drinking more champagne. 'You must be tired,' I said to him. He had been up all night and Paula had just told me that she had worried that Michael would miss the birth, as he had stayed out all night the evening before. Paula had said earlier, when we were on our own, that she had known Heavenly was coming, from the cramps she had had all that night, and she hadn't been able to get hold of Michael.

He'd been very unsettled since he'd come back from Tina's wedding, she confided. She felt that his family were inconsiderate in their demands on him, expecting him to fly out with just days to go before his child was due to be born, handing over his house and staff for his sister's big day and paying for the champagne and oyster reception. Paula made the event sound like one of biblical proportions. 'Michael even pays for all Kell's holidays,' she said, referring to Kell and his wife Sue's recent round-trip of Europe, which ended with a stay in Michael's villa on the Riviera. This was not really a fair assessment of Michael's support for his family.

Paula's gripe had more to do with Michael's precarious availability for her, his silent threat of spontaneous departure and, in her eyes, his lack of financial support over her housing problems, forcing her to fight so hard to get her own house back with the attendant stress and legal costs.

The people outside were beginning to sound like a football crowd. For a while, Paula hadn't minded that their names were being called out from the street. Inevitably she began to tire of the noise, and she was clearly in need of a good few hours' sleep. I went downstairs to have a chat with Michael about throwing them a morsel to keep the photographers happy. He was on the phone in the hall, saying: 'No, mate. You can't come round now, the place is swarming with press. Yeah, I've got the money, I'll slip round later.'

He swung round to see me standing behind him and gave me an oops-you-caught-me grin, and told me that he had been talking to his mother. He obviously didn't realize how long I had been standing behind him nor that I knew his mother was out of the country. Michael agreed to meet the press without hesitation. All they needed was one photo and a few words from him and they would probably go away content. So he opened the front door in his shirt and shorts, to a round of flashing bulbs, shouts and cheers.

'How does it feel being a father, Michael?' one of them shouted. 'This is the proudest day of my life. I'm on cloud nine. Ask any dad – they'll all tell you the same thing.' 'What are you going to call her?' another shouted. 'Heavenly, because that's exactly what she is, but Paula's already calling her Tiger. Who knows?' It was perfect. This was the first time Michael had faced the tabloid press, the first time that they had got an authorized picture of him, and he was in a good mood, polite, ecstatic. This momentary open-handedness would pay dividends for his profile. They got the full Hutchence charm-offensive and today he was genuinely pleased to see them.

There had been non-stop escalating offers from the newspapers for a photo of Paula and Michael's child. Some were offering up to £100,000 and beyond. One offered me personally £80,000 for a Polaroid of the baby, regardless of quality. *Hello!* and *OK!* entered an impromptu bidding war. The *News of the World* wrote to me, exploring the idea of 'a sympathetic and generously paid super-spread on the Paula and Michael story including the birth'. Everyone wanted *the* picture which was already promised to the *Sun*. But in order to maintain good relations with them all, particularly those who had helped us out, each should have something, and something different from one another.

The most important contact to acknowledge was Matthew Wright. He knew that the deal with the *Sun* was already in place and was conscious of Paula's need for job security, although, through me, he did offer her a similar contract with the *Mirror*. But we realized that if she defected, the guns would be out for her again. So we had to accept that the *Sun* would get the *picture* and the Mirror would get the *story* of the birth.

The *Sun* had Paula on their payroll and her column gave them access to her life, and the *Mirror* had a direct conduit to her, through me. It was a highly delicate balancing act to maintain, particularly as the *Sun* went mad each time they were pipped to a story by the *Mirror*. All along Paula denied any knowledge of the source of these leaked stories that the *Mirror* ran, even saying that she had no idea who Gerry Agar was. She told me that she had suggested to them that she must be under constant surveillance by a stalker.

I was encouraging Paula to rethink her stance on giving an exclusive interview to *OK!* magazine – the highest offer so far. Paula was nervous that she would not be able to meet her legal bills and worried that Michael would again feel pressured to help her out, so she asked me to tell *OK!* that she was seriously considering the offer. The *Sun* were to get their picture, the *Mirror* their story 'through a friend', the *Mail* would be promised something else and I was already trading in futures with other

Michael in a 1990
studio shot.

Michael before his
peak in an early INXS
publicity shot...

...and after global
stardom, at
Wembley Arena
in June 1997,
on the tour he
never finished.

Michael with Australian soap and pop princess, Kylie Minogue, in 1990. She has described him as the love of her life.

With girlfriend Helena Christensen in 1994. Michael left the Danish supermodel for Paula.

In March 1995 the press followed Paula and Michael to the Chilston Park Hotel in Kent. Michael was involved in a brawl with a photographer, for which he was fined. As the car whisked them away, Paula remained composed while Michael continued to rage. Having orchestrated the furore, she demonstrated her steely control in a crisis.

A pregnant Paula walks her daughters Fifi and Peaches to school in March 1996. This photo opportunity was staged to shame Bob.

Paula's house in Clapham, south London. Michael paid for the fence to be erected in a bid to keep out prying camera lenses.

Michael happily greets
the press on the day of
his daughter's birth –
22 July 1996.

The proud parents with
Heavenly Hiraani Tiger Lily
in Sydney in 1996.

Michael cradles Tiger as Paula is
arrested and driven to Chelsea
police station, where she was
questioned about the opium
found at their London home
while they were in Australia.

Paula and Michael leaving their house with eight-month-old Tiger.

Michael's coffin, decorated with hundreds of irises and one tiger lily, is carried out of St Andrew's Cathedral, Sydney by his fellow INXS band members and his brother Rhett, whose striped suit was a gift from Michael.

Michael's mother Patricia is supported by husband Ross (**left**) and Michael's father, ex-husband Kell.

Paula and Tiger with Belinda Brewin at the funeral service.

publications: there would be a Paula interview, perhaps a Michael interview (he had not yet given one to the British press), pictures of the baby at a few weeks old, and one of the strongest stocks on the celebrity gossip market at the time, the promotional interviews Michael would give for the launch of the forthcoming INXS album.

The *Telegraph* had been talking about a feature in which Michael would take a journalist out and dress him, reshape his wardrobe, show him where to eat, where to take his girlfriend – a lifestyle piece. I had been talking to the *Mail* about Paula writing articles for them when she was free from her contract with the *Sun*. They knew it might not be for some time, but they were excited about her potential as one of their columnists, and promised her greater latitude than the *Sun* would allow, however long they had to wait.

'She had everything,' the editors would say. 'Beauty, mother-of-four but still looks fabulous, a rock god for a boyfriend, history, class, humour, *The Tube*, celebrity friends, and she can write.' She was still the Rock Chick Princess and every woman wanted to hear what she had to say.

Paula's press had gone from lynch-mob to fan-club. We had passed through a period of press ambivalence, and now they had become her extended family. When I returned the phone calls that day, I was mindful to explain exactly what I had promised to all the other newspapers, giving my reasons. But it was Matthew who got the bonus prize, when Michael agreed to speak to him directly, on my mobile, so he got the story from the rock god himself, about how he had helped Paula deliver Tiger. Matthew was over the moon. It was late when I'd finally finished ringing round, ensuring the next day's press would be favourable, and I picked up a message from Matthew to call him urgently.

'We've got a problem.' Matthew's voice was glum. He explained that some compromising photos of Michael and a girl had just landed on his desk. I made some comment like, 'Well, we all know Michael's not been a saint.' But Matthew wasn't talking about old photos – apparently these pictures had been taken two nights before the birth, the night Paula had said that Michael had gone missing.

The arrival of Heavenly and the press it generated should have been phenomenal: Michael was the ecstatic dad; the baby's weight; she looks like her father; all the grandparents are thrilled (leaving out, of course, that Paula was still not speaking to her mother and that she had banned her from seeing any of her grandchildren). The questions were inevitable, but we had well-prepared answers, dodging anything tricky, like the marriage, with diversions, and the baby was the perfect smoke-screen for this.

But Michael had been caught coming out of Brown's nightclub with a couple of girls, his arms about their bodies. He had apparently been seen in the nightclub with another girl, and they weren't just talking. Sure, Paula would get the sympathy vote if this story ran. It would be perfect publicity for her, if further vindication were needed, to counter the image of the sluttish deserter. But Paula didn't want the world to see her as a victim and she most certainly didn't want to be seen as a fool. 'Is there any way you can bury this and run the original story?' I pleaded. He explained that if it was up to him he would, but his editor might not be amused to discover that such a scoop had been passed over, just because his showbiz editor felt that it didn't look as nice as 'Michael helps to deliver his child' – especially if the story ran in other papers.

'What if the *Sun* decides that they won't publish, because they'll lose their columnist, never get the baby photo or anything else, including the interview with Michael when his album comes out?' I asked. 'It won't bother the *Sun* very much, they want to get rid of her anyway,' he replied. He had heard from someone at the *Sun* that they were not planning to renew Paula's contract. The reasons, he was told, were that she had been reticent with stories about herself and the copy for her column was always late and increasingly muddled, and she often called in sounding drunk. They were going to wait until they ran the baby photo, before releasing a story on Michael's drug-taking in the studio. He explained that there was only a certain amount that the *Mirror* could do to help, they had already stuck their necks out for Paula and he genuinely felt really sorry for her. 'Look, I'll chance it,' Matthew said at last. 'I don't want Paula hurt, she's just had a baby and this is the last thing she needs.' I collapsed with relief.

Paula had said nothing about the *Sun's* dissatisfaction with her work and nothing about being late with her copy. I had been given to understand quite the opposite: told of their continuing support and gratitude for her work.

I had told Matthew that I was resolved to tackle Michael about the photos, hoping there was some reasonable explanation. I was reluctant to believe that he would be out with other women on the eve of his daughter's birth and Paula had told me that Michael was working hard to curb his promiscuity. Michael had told me himself that he knew he was addicted to sex and found it almost impossible to pass up an opportunity for the thrill of seduction, the release of success, regardless of the consequences. He knew too that he had to address the source, if he was going to tackle the symptoms of this addiction. And in his most lucid moments he was clear that he wanted to remain faithful to Paula and forge a meaningful relationship. But there were two sides of his nature, engaged in a tug of war. It had nothing to do with how he felt about

Paula, he had explained to me, and everything to do with how he felt about himself.

'I'm with you,' Matthew said. 'I want to see Michael as the Renaissance man – he's turned over a new leaf, and he and Paula are made for each other, but these photos are in direct contradiction to all that.'

How was I going to ask Michael if he had been with another woman? Paula had told me that Michael was so pleased with the press I had achieved for them both that he was questioning why he paid over £20,000 to his own PR. He was apparently planning to divert some of that money to me. Not that any figures were discussed, but Paula had agreed to pay me 25 per cent of everything she received, from magazine interviews and television work. So in effect I now found myself with two clients.

So part of my conversation with Michael would be in a professional capacity, challenging the wisdom of his own publicity efforts in frolicking into the small hours, while his partner was at home, feeling contractions. Quite apart from the pain this might cause Paula, it would wreak inevitable havoc with his reputation. When I finally got hold of him he suggested we meet in Hampstead. He was recording at studios on Haverstock Hill and said that it would be nice to continue the discussions we had had in the restaurant. It was too hot to sit outside and Michael wanted to take a stroll over the Heath. When I arrived at the studio he had already arranged for sandwiches and soft drinks to be bought, and in the end we never left the air-conditioned comfort of his car, we just drove to a car park in sight of greenery.

It was impossible to remain angry with Michael for too long. I explained that what I was about to ask him wasn't my business and if we had been just friends, I felt that this conversation probably wouldn't be taking place. He smiled and assured me in his most empathetic way that he understood completely, and that it always touched him, how fiercely protective I was of Paula. But he insisted that those girls that night had been just friends. It was hard to argue with this. He had a mesmerizing energy, and loved the company of women. It seemed that Michael found it impossible to be near anyone without touching them: standing, sitting, male or female, he would be holding their hand, leaning on them, or draping his arms about their shoulders.

He was adamant about his feelings for Paula; he expected that he would always battle with his desire for other women but he loved her so much that he was genuinely trying to change. Then he talked more openly about himself, his ambitions and anxieties and how difficult it was to reconcile his sex, drugs and rock'n'roll lifestyle with his new role in the lives of Paula, Tiger and the Geldof girls.

He mentioned having become fascinated by the story of James Hunt. In fact, he told me, he had thought of little else since the conversation, how awful it must be have been for the girl he left behind and, speaking to some film friends of his, he had pitched the idea of making James's life into a feature. Michael had put a large amount of cash into the Australian film *Crocodile Dundee*, when others had thought it would be a flop. It wasn't, of course, and it subsequently became a box-office hit. He also featured in a film called *Frankenstein Unbound* alongside John Hurt and Bridget Fonda and told me that he had been bitten by the acting bug. He was talking to his American agent about more film work and he was planning to take acting classes. 'I just can't do the rock star kick for everyone else anymore. I'm dancing to too many people's tunes. I want to find out about me,' he told me. We talked of how much had changed since I first met him. The change in his appearance had alarmed me and I urged him to take a long hard look in the mirror and ask himself what he needed. Michael was very receptive. He understood the benefits of therapy from the experiences of friends and family. He realized that his lifestyle was bringing him no lasting happiness, and he was getting a glimpse of how he could save himself. He talked of how amazing it was to be a father and how proud he was of Paula. 'Paula is an incredible woman, I'm never bored and that's always been a real problem for me,' he confided. But in that moment too, he recognized that he had handicaps. The life he had led had insulated him from discomfort – when the going gets tough, just get going: to another country, to a different crowd, a new wardrobe and a new girl. Staying put would be like being caged, with the door always open, and freedom beckoning. 'It's in being in a relationship, sticking with it, through all its mad cycles, that you can really learn about yourself,' Michael said.

'It's having children that really gets you in touch with yourself, in my experience,' I replied. 'It's the best way of understanding your childhood. Every reaction you have to your kids points to something in your past – it's fascinating.' 'Like Paula's need to prove to herself that she wouldn't be like her own mother?' Michael suggested. 'Bob couldn't understand her. I feel completely understood by Paula and I believe that I understand her too. She's unique and very much misunderstood. Our daughter is very lucky to have her as her mother.'

He knew that everyone thought he was going to muck it up, but he was determined to sort himself out. He relished his new family, as he called them; they would be his real source of happiness – shared experiences with his children and his children's children. Michael remembered how it felt to have a father who directed the family from a remote location and a mother whom he felt was never able, for economic reasons as much as anything, to achieve the balance between work and home, becoming tantalizingly unavailable to him. In his unconscious drive to replace what he had lost, he adored and celebrated Paula for her determination to be a mother at home. Then he remembered Bob and his hatred flared; he was still appalled that Bob had never made it easier for Paula to stay at home. 'Now he knows what he had all along, he'll never find anyone like her,' he almost spat. 'If I had to come back to this earth again as a girl, I'd want to come back as Paula.' 'I know,' I replied, 'and she's always said that she'd want to come back as you.'

Michael brought our extraordinary conversation to a close by suggesting that I take him to an Al-Anon meeting so that he could observe the basics of the twelve-step plan. We were both excited by the depth of our conversation and I was amazed and thrilled by his suggestion. Seizing the moment, I said 'Why not right now?' Meetings were never hard to find, anywhere in London there would be three to four sessions a day. Making a silent inventory of his day, he seemed amused by my zeal and entered into the idea, in the spirit of adventure. I took him to a meeting where he would feel most at ease, amongst some well-known faces and in Chelsea near his home, in case he ever felt the need for a quick fix. It was the first time, he said, in the last two years of visiting London, that in a public space no one bothered him and there were no cameras.

'That was so powerful, man,' Michael kept repeating, saying that he recognized so much of himself in other people's stories. A lot of his mates were attending twelve-step programmes and he felt that it had been a useful experience to see how they had managed to keep themselves in check. Michael had been touched, without a doubt. He didn't speak up, but then most people don't on the first visit. Michael told me that it had been humbling and shocking to discover the extent to which drink and drugs had affected people's lives. He seemed to be connecting with his own role in his family, the feelings of responsibility and guilt that he carried around with him. And yet, he still said his use of 'stuff' was to 'just feel good for a while'.

It was plain to see that this brief exposure to a way forward had fired him up, but it required stamina to follow it through. He could find this inspiration again, whenever he wanted to, but these moments were like beacons in the night, and to make it from one to another took a leap of faith and a resolve that was tested in even the most committed and disciplined of people. How difficult would it be for Michael, to whom the world was a playground into which he could escape for any diversion imaginable? And for all his enthusiasm, he had failed to identify the role that drugs were playing in his own life. As we drew up to Redburn Street, Michael expressed a feeling of calm and optimism and he was excited to see Tiger and Paula when he arrived home. I decided against going in with him, and asked him to get Paula to give me a call about her *Sun* contract in the morning.

When Paula called the next day, I put her deflated mood down to a sleepless night with Tiger. In fact, she told me that Tiger had been fantastic and had slept all night. Ordinarily I wouldn't have bothered her, but Matthew's tip-off about the *Sun* had to be dealt with immediately – it was her only source of income, apart from the help she received from Michael. Paula agreed that the coverage of their baby's birth, two days previously in almost all the papers had been fantastic, but she was preoccupied with Michael's continuing refusal to marry her. She had assumed, from the way he was talking about responsibility and settling down when he returned from his afternoon with me, that he was re-thinking his stance on marriage. But he still wasn't ready, he had told her. And his actions said as much to Paula. She complained that he had spent most of the first week of their baby's life in the studio.

Her raging hormones would be playing a large part in her erratic emotional reactions. The first week after the birth can be the worst – everything can seem exaggerated. But I was on a mission to ensure her another year's contract with the *Sun* or she'd have far more to worry about. I needed to know what was happening about the photographic session with the baby and when she was intending to provide the picture. She told me that Michael's UK manager had commissioned the photographer, Alex Keshishian, an ex-boyfriend of Madonna's and a friend of Michael's. Therefore the photo would be going back to him. I brought Paula up to date with the *OK!* negotiations. The editors had no problems with the *Sun* having the first picture, but if she wanted to go ahead with their feature, we would need to act quickly. Obviously, Michael's contribution would make all the difference. Paula was surprisingly hesitant about Michael's involvement but agreed that it would help secure the deal. I put it to her that it would be the ideal way of demonstrating that they were very much together and blissfully happy. Drawing in a deep breath I dialled the number of Michael's UK manager by whom I knew I would be made distinctly unwelcome. However, I was completely unprepared for the shocking news that awaited me.

Michael's manager had sold the picture for a meagre £8,000. My blood turned cold – I knew what that picture was really worth. Paula had just lost £100,000 and jeopardized her contract renewal, though he may not have been aware that the photo was a vital bargaining tool for Paula. But it was done now and I asked him to keep the photo until I got back to him. Thinking out loud I emphasized the importance of Paula and Michael appearing together in the *OK!* magazine feature.

My suggestion had hit a nerve. It was out of the question, not in the interests of Michael, the band or the record label, he insisted. As far as he was concerned Paula could do what she liked, and on her own head be it but, he said, she wouldn't be doing herself any favours because it would only rile Bob if she appeared looking like the cat that got the cream. In these comments from his manager, I could hear Michael's frenzied paranoia about Bob. He was understandably protective of Michael. He wanted his boy back on track with the album and looking like a rock star for the promotion. Paula had been a major complication from the start. To be fair, Michael's manager's job was only to consider Michael in the context of frontman to INXS. He knew that the record label would only sanction Michael to do interviews for the music press; he had lined most of them up for the album launch already and didn't want to dilute the impact. He said he was still struggling to get a deal for the solo album and it seemed my effort to turn Michael into 'Val Doonican' would ruin the mystique of the dark rock'n'roller.

I gained the strong impression that he was playing with a marked deck. Had Michael given him the nod to stand his ground over the *OK!* deal? Perhaps he was beginning to distance himself from his tormented mistress. By my reckoning, with the baby photo, lack of a renewed column contract and the *OK!* interview, £200,000 had been fumbled. This should have provided the financing for Paula's new life. They could have cleared her legal bill and builder's invoices, perhaps releasing her from that burden, to allow her to think more clearly about the future. Now that the photo was sold and the *OK!* interview was undermined, I could only fight the fires that were still ablaze.

The showbiz editor of the *Sun* could only be reached on his mobile. When I caught up with him, he was in LA, hunting down a Madonna story. I told him I was handling the photo and wanted Paula's contract for her column renewed for another year. He agreed to organize an extension for another six months. He arranged for an updated contract to be biked round for Paula to sign and then I would release the photo.

Paula had just finished breast-feeding Tiger – I had still not heard the little girl cry nor had I seen the colour of her eyes – when I told her about the *Sun* picture debacle. She was furious, but effusive in her gratitude for my swift intervention. This was the last thing she needed to hear, but she had to engage and quickly, to avert disaster. Papers from the *Sun* would be arriving shortly and I wanted to get back to *OK!* as quickly as possible. Paula decided to mount one last offensive on Michael's manager, and she promised to call him herself. 'It's not you he has a gripe with,' Paula explained, 'he still thinks of me as a groupie, someone that's ruined Michael's life.'

Paula was looking beautiful that day. Nicky Clarke had been around to dress her hair and she was wearing a flimsy white Victorian cotton nightdress. But her mood was black as she got up off the bed, cradling

Tiger and went downstairs. 'Come on, let's sort this out,' she said. On the phone to Michael, Paula unleashed twelve months of pent-up fury. The poor man could not have got a word in, even if he had tried. She told him about the *Sun* picture: 'He might as well have sold it in a job lot with some old buttons, on the street corner.' Paula, who never normally swore, was at full volume with every expletive she could muster. She brought up his manager's apparent obstruction of the *OK!* piece and said to Michael: 'How am I going to pay my lawyers' bills now?' Then she seemed to calm down – Michael had said he would cover them.

I had never seen Paula lose it before, and wished I hadn't been the messenger. I offered to remove Tiger from the violent outburst, but Paula shot me a warning glare that Tiger was staying in her arms. Paula sank into the sofa. The rage had not subsided but Tiger remained blissfully unaware that her mother had just blasted her father with a tirade that must surely have been heard on the street. 'Oh shit,' Paula said, 'I'd better call him back. This will really upset him and he probably won't come back tonight.'

———— ◆ ————

The atmosphere in Paula's house was strained and the only person in a bouncy mood was my daughter Sophie, who finally had been allowed to see the new baby. Tiger was almost two weeks old and, thinking that now there would be a degree of peace, I gave in to her pleas to see her favourite family. I knew Paula was still seething about having to turn down *OK!*, but she was about to hear that they seemed open to trying again when Tiger was a few months old. The album would be out by then, Michael would have most of his interviews out of the way and his management might be less anxious. But Paula was keen to persuade Michael to think about it sooner and they had discussed a shoot in the South of France, towards the end of the summer.

Tiger was suckling on Paula's breast. Her operation had had no effect on her ability to feed the baby. Paula was wearing a mint green silk nightdress, with cream lace trim around the cleavage. She told me that Michael had bought it for her – he had chosen a maternity style, with delicate pearl buttons down the front. She was keen to lose the three stone she had put on, but it was amazing how fast she was regaining her figure, and I hoped she was eating properly. Her health visitor from the hospital had just left and apparently both mother and daughter were doing very well. She admitted to feeling more emotional with this baby, but that was hardly surprising under the circumstances and, as if to prove the point, she told me she had just received a letter from Bob's solicitors.

She had official papers strewn across the bed; she gathered them up into a pile and flung them into a box file beside her bed. 'I'm fed up with all of this,' she said. The letter was a warning from Bob, insisting that Paula apply for permission before making changes to the house. She had been making some modifications, but she had been awarded the house. She told me he wanted to take the case back to court, to exercise his rights to getting the house back again. 'How could he? I've just had a baby and he wants me out. When is he going to get it – this house is mine?' Paula was exasperated and I was confused. This could have been the perfect opportunity to bring up my discovery about the money Bob had given her in the original deal but I couldn't. I wanted to put her fears and distress before my petty complaints, so I left it and listened instead to the latest of Bob's 'atrocities'. 'He'll never forgive me for leaving him, this will continue till I'm dead,' she said.

Paula was convinced of this. She warned us all that he would hound her until she broke. In her therapy Paula had tried to understand Bob's over-riding anger, particularly when it was aimed at her. Bob had apparently always flatly refused therapy, calling it pointless and unnecessary, but how much had that to do with his fear of the painful memories he might have to relive? Instead he appeared to live his life at a break-neck speed, whether walking or talking or pacing to think, unable to sit for more than a minute, nor listen for a second. A few months after they broke up he had told Paula that she was the best wife and mother anyone could have, and he would never find her equal. In his way, it seemed, he had been as terrified of marriage as Michael. 'He's an angry little boy hitting out at me, when he should be working out who he's really angry with,' Paula said.

When they first got together she knew he was a very mixed-up person, but that was their bond – she could relate to his awkwardness and they thought that they could make a new start together, build a new family that would never fragment, because they were at the helm, no longer passengers on someone else's ship. 'Bob was so scared of falling in love, but Michael embraced the love he felt for me, regardless of the baggage I brought,' Paula continued. 'But Michael is having a problem following through,' I said softly. 'So did Bob, but he did it eventually,' Paula reminded me. 'But by the time he got round to it, the weeds had already taken hold.'

Her bedroom was newly decorated in a light sky-blue, with muslin draping the tall narrow windows, but the rest of the room still looked as if she had just moved in. The four-poster bed had been replaced with a divan, with a narrower one beside hers, for Tiger to sleep in. For a bedside table she relied on a packing case and used shoeboxes to store paper. But it wasn't untidy; she still had her Australian cleaner coming in every day for several hours.

She had a stack of invitations beside her bed. Paula and Michael were being asked to support everything from film premières, to magazine parties, restaurant and shop launches, but they rarely accepted; and yet the press were still calling her an attention seeker, desperate for fame. Bob, on the other hand, was noticeably much more social these days, visible at high-profile parties in almost every society column. His girlfriend Jeanne had just given an interview to *Hello!*, in which she stridently debunked the idea that he never took a bath. While Paula had always worried about Bob's reaction to her giving exclusives on their lives 'at home', Bob did not seem unhappy that his new girlfriend should give a fabulously obvious interview to help redeem his image since the recent press had been challenging his sainthood. Paula had hidden the copy of *Hello!* under her bed and had poured over Jeanne's words many times, when no one else was in the house. 'Did you notice that French poodle had to have an interpreter when she gave that interview? She still can't speak English,' she said. Paula claimed that the few words Jeanne could speak were 'Bob' and 'poor you', delivered with a distinctly Irish lilt.

Paula had a few messages of congratulation – Jools Holland sent a funny note, and a dribble of her celebrity friends sent flowers – but most of the bouquets were from newspapers and work colleagues. Michael was incensed, she told me, about the lack of goodwill from people she once called friends, friends who now opted to side silently with Bob. She told me that she saw more of Michael's mates, but they weren't really her cup of tea – the girlfriends of his few closest friends were dull, she said.

Paula's bedroom seemed a fitting metaphor for where we had arrived – a new lick of paint over the same old problems. The battle for the house was re-emerging. Paula's finances were close to stabilizing, with Michael's offer to clear the lawyers' bills. But she had started spending again and the evidence was here, in the smell of the paint and the new carpets, even though she knew that she had no income.

Michael had taken to ignoring Anita completely and Paula was being more direct about expressing her feelings. There were reports that life at Bob's house in Kent was far more peaceful than *chez* Michael and Paula. The girls chose poems from Bob's library and they would recite and discuss the meaning or the author's intent. Bob was making the time to help them with their homework, while Paula never had the time these days, she was so wrapped up with Michael. Paula and Michael were both highly emotional individuals, aggravated by all the stress, but there was less emotional chaos at Bob's house. Paula and Michael's mood swings were becoming so nerve-wracking that I was convinced they should both be seeing a doctor.

Paula had changed. In the past she had always soldiered on, but now her reactions were increasingly extreme and this worried me. Paula and Michael were like a chemical reaction: when Paula was down, Michael found it difficult to detach and joined in with her complaints, trying to be supportive but driving her deeper. But when they were up, they were really up. On top of which Paula was not getting the sleep that a new mother needed.

———— ◆ ————

It was a column in the *Sun* written by Paula that initiated the long supressed confrontation between Paula and me. Its subject was the iniquity of small children being sent to boarding school. A few days later we had the most almighty row on the telephone. All the tensions that had been building up suddenly overflowed, and the things I wanted to air with her came pouring out. I told her that she could work if she wanted to, but that she hadn't made the effort to do her part, by writing the books for which she had been commissioned, or jotting down the TV ideas she had brought to the meeting with FlexTech. She had so many people bending over backwards to help her sort herself out. She had Anita and Bob sharing the care of the children, Dina doing the cleaning and me making sure no one was saying anything nasty about her, and trying to find her money into the bargain. Once I got started, the words just kept tumbling out. I asked her why her voice was sounding so slurry, had she been taking something? The phone went dead.

Despite this, Paula's profile had to be maintained. It became public knowledge that Bob was taking her back to court over Redburn Street. There had been a couple of enquiries about Paula and Michael's rumoured drug-taking and the marriage question lingered. I didn't expect to be speaking to Paula for a few days and wondered if she would in fact call me to apologize. The sound of her voice haunted my dreams. What disturbed me most was the memory of her lazy intonation – she had sounded drunk. But she didn't drink and never smoked dope – the Prozac would bring clarity not slurring, but maybe Rohypynol in large quantities could have that effect. Now all the fragments seemed to come together: the late nights, the lack of sleep, the days in bed, the mood swings, the paranoia, the brown paper packages delivered under different names, the questions from the press and Matthew's warnings, the rumours of illegible *Sun* submissions – actually, the list was rather scary. The possibility that Paula was submerged in Michael's underground world occurred to me for the first time. If so, I thought, we are all in trouble. Still, I kept up a façade to everyone, telling them how well she was doing and how happy she was with her new baby and her fantastic partner. But I felt none of my original enthusiasm; I had to strain to disguise my real feelings, but with each call the lie cut deeper into my conscience, and became more difficult to carry off.

My friend the PR supremo called in the middle of my soul-searching. This call came with a proposal for us to join forces in some way. He knew that I had been taking on more work and he was very interested. I needed to boost my income. Paula and Michael had said that I would be receiving a retainer from Michael's management, having realized that the work I had done for him should be recognized financially, but Paula still had no money. It was a full-time job for me now; having started as a little helping hand, it had become a full-blown account, with more complications than most. My friend insisted I realize my own value as a consultant, but I had never thought of my work for Paula as a paid job.

'Either stop what you're doing or get paid,' the PR man said. 'You could *easily* find work elsewhere.' I was reminded of the reasons I had gone into therapy: putting other people's problems before my own. This was such a horrendous reality check. He was underlining how Paula and Michael had done nothing but complain about Bob's lack of care for Paula's finances, but never given a second thought to mine.

Paula did call me within a few days. She was warm and positive. I was surprised that she made no mention of our argument, as if she had temporary amnesia. She told me that she and Michael were missing me. 'We've been through so much together, if Michael won't marry me I'll marry you instead,' Paula told me. This was something she would often say to me – it had almost become the motto of our friendship. I knew she was trying to get round me, but her flattery was so endearing, it was hard to resist, like a little girl saying 'You still love me, don't you?' Paula poured affection down the phone, her humour had returned and I was smitten by her charm all over again. She thanked me for the newspaper articles I had sent as inspiration for next week's columns. Paula talked of Tiger and how beautiful she was and we laughed about how much she looked like Michael, how relieved she was that Tiger was so perfect. She was looking forward to going to the South of France, the only downer being that Michael's mother was joining them for the first week. Apparently Patricia had implied her disapproval of Paula's plan for a home birth. But I knew Paula's antipathy to Michael's mother went deeper than minor irritations.

Banished from her daughter's sight, her own mother had been visiting Bob and the girls. Helene had told Anita that she was worried for the children's welfare. Paula scoffed that her mother had cared nothing for *her* welfare when she left *her* behind in that gothic nightmare. In Paula's view, Patricia, like Helene, had put her career before her children. When Paula herself had children, she found she could not countenance how any mother could leave her babies behind. She spoke out about it, and recorded her views in her early baby books. This had caused a storm in the press – working mothers were up in arms against this elitist view, but for her it was a conviction. She said that if Michael had had a stable home life, he would not have half the problems he had now. Michael's aversion to marriage, Paula had decided, had nothing to do with her and everything to do with his mother.

The highlight of her week had been a long chat with Rupert Everett on the phone. She loved to hear all the gossip and she told me that she really appreciated the constancy of his affection where so many others had quietly walked away. He was dying to see her when he came back from LA, but Michael wasn't particularly keen; like Bob, he for some reason felt mildly threatened by their friendship.

Then Paula asked me to be Tiger's godmother. If there was any lingering resentment in me, it was fully dispelled by this sign of friendship. 'But don't say anything yet,' she said. I suppose I might have thought how strange this conversation was, if I had been thinking of Paula as manipulative. In retrospect it is easy to see that she liked to keep her close friends at a distance from one another and the details of each relationship secret. It may have been part of her technique for making every individual feel that he or she was the most special person in her life, or it may have been that she did not want them to compare notes.

I took some flowers and chocolates and a small present for Tiger over to Paula's. Paula had taken the girls out, but would be back later, Anita told me. She must have forgotten I was coming, which I thought was a little strange, as Paula had been very insistent about the time, saying that she was desperate to see me.

Michael was in the kitchen, slumped over the table, cradling his head. When he looked up, it was obvious he'd been crying. 'I can't take much more of this, how much more am I expected to deal with?' Michael cried as I put a comforting arm around his shoulders. He told me that he had asked Bono to be Tiger's godfather, but he had refused. Bono felt that in accepting their offer to be godfather to Paula's love baby, he might jeopardize his lifelong friendship with Bob. 'That man controls everyone, I can't even ask my best mate to be my daughter's godfather,' he said, seemingly desperate. Michael then launched into a tirade, beginning with his feeling that he couldn't take any more court appearances; he had agreed to pay Paula's lawyer's fees, which he said were in the region of astronomical. 'I hate this country. I'm stuck, though, I hate what's happened to me.' He was at his wits' end now, he explained, trapped and with no chance of things improving. He said that he hated Bob and wanted him dead. He knew people, he implied threateningly. If Bob died it would all be over.

'Paula and I could move with the girls, go and live in Australia. I don't want my daughter brought up in England, I want her in Australia with me and my family,' he continued, defiantly. Michael pointed out that Tiger didn't have family in England, that Paula didn't speak to her mother and the only other relations that Tiger had were a two-day flight away: 'We could start a new life. My sister loves kids, my mother would help out with the girls, and Paula wouldn't be attacked there. Paula was fucking breast-feeding when she got Bob's solicitor's letter – it was a real shock to her; he's a fucking evil bastard and no one's got the guts to stop him, not even my best mates.'

If ever Paula wanted proof of Michael's commitment, then she had it now in his willingness to stay with her and Tiger through the horrendous conditions surrounding the relationship. He would have been anywhere but here, had it not been for them. The palpable struggle he was having was moving. The golden eagle had had its wings clipped and was coming to terms with life in captivity. He must love them both very much, I thought.

11 elegantly wasted

MICHAEL'S VILLA HAD BEEN A MOTEL for every friend, well-wisher and distant relative passing through, Paula told me. She wanted the house to herself and she wanted Michael to herself, so they could play happy families together, but there were too many temptations. The rock clan had arrived and everyone wanted to party.

I had been rethinking my visit for a number of reasons. Obviously I didn't want to add to the crowd, I could always go another time and I'd had another run-in with Paula. A couple of nights before she left for France, I had a series of calls from journalists asking me to confirm Paula and Michael's wedding arrangements. The *Sun* was running the news the next day and the other papers told me they were surprised not to have heard about it. These rumours were continual but they rarely made it into print. I felt no compunction in denouncing the story, as I had always done. It was late, but I knew Paula and Michael's day began at midnight. I got Michael first. 'Of course it isn't true; I'm really getting sick of this. Where did they get that from?' Michael replied hotly. I was quite taken aback by the strength of his reaction. He had lived with these constant speculations when he was with Helena; perhaps he was taking a firm stance for Paula's benefit. 'Who is it?' I heard her ask. 'Someone has told the papers that we're getting married. It's in the *Sun* tomorrow.' I had promised to call the *Express*, the *Mail* and of course the *Mirror* back straight away, so I was eager to get off the phone and give them the official denial. 'I'll deal with it directly, Michael,' I replied.

A few minutes later I called him to confirm: 'They've all been told. I can't do anything about the *Sun*, but there will be enough papers with a direct quote from you to the contrary, which should balance it out.' Michael thanked me for my efforts and apologized for his earlier reaction.

I had just fallen asleep when the phone beside my bed started ringing again. I was tempted to leave it, but this caller was relentless and I finally gave in and picked up the receiver. 'What did you go and do that for?' Paula whispered angrily. 'Michael's really cross about all this, you know,' she continued, as if I had leaked the news. 'What are you talking about?' I replied, half-asleep. 'Didn't he tell you? I've sorted it all out.' 'Why did you have to say anything at all?' Paula asked. This was the first time I had heard

Paula talk to me in this tone. 'Michael told me he didn't want it in the papers.' I had previously agreed with Paula that if I received calls in the middle of the night from the press asking to confirm or deny an important event in their lives, that I would check my response with her and Michael first. 'Just keep quiet next time,' she said. I told Paula she was being unfair. 'I've got to go, Michael's coming back,' she hissed. 'Who you talking to, babes?' I heard in the background. 'Jo's just called to see how Tiger is,' I heard Paula tell him just before the phone went dead.

I had worked out what had happened. Paula had leaked the news of their engagement and I'd blown it for her. Instead of feeling angry, I felt sorry for her. It was a desperate ruse, but nothing would propel Michael towards marriage until he was ready. Maybe she really believed she was engaged? She still wore Michael's ring on her third finger and talked freely to the children about their bridesmaids' dresses. She had even asked me to be maid of honour and told me she had started fittings for her wedding dress. When we spoke again the next day, she made light of the event in her usual way, with a series of excuses. A pattern of fantasies was beginning to emerge. She always enjoyed exaggerating a story for effect, which was entertaining at a dinner party but unhelpful in everyday life, and now she was telling bizarre fibs. A pair of shoes that she said were a present from Jools she had actually bought herself. A room she said she had painted would turn out later to have been painted by Anita's brother. Columns I had helped her write after Tiger was born she later claimed she had written in five minutes.

On 11 August the *Sunday Telegraph* magazine ran its interview with me across the centre spread. It was featured on the front cover with a picture of Paula and Michael and the strap line: *The world's worst job: making Britain love Paula and Michael.* It was a wildly fanciful *Ab Fab* portrayal of my professional life, with a photo of me, barefoot, sitting on the floor talking on the phone, surrounded by newspapers. Naturally the article centred on my work for Paula and Michael:

> *This is a job that many people would regard as something of a poisoned chalice. Not Gerry. For her, it is a breath of fresh air: 'I merely have to change the tape in the heads of the British public. They need to stop seeing Paula as the irresponsible mother who ran off with the loony rock star and start understanding her as the intellectual heavyweight that she is. It's very much a drip-feed process, but it's beginning to work,'* I was quoted as saying.

The article meandered through my theatrical behaviour in the restaurant where the interview took place, the break-up of my marriage, my childhood, the décor of my home and back to my work with Paula and Michael. As well as an encapsulation of my strategy for Paula and Michael:

> *She wants to see Paula back on television, preferably doing something a little more serious than lying on a bed. 'She is incredibly well-read,' Gerry*

argues, 'bright to the point of genius and should be interviewing poets, politicians and captains of industry as well as soap stars.' But Gerry knows that the future is not just about Paula. She must also convince the world that Michael Hutchence does more than just sit about strumming chords. He is, she says, a kind man who wants to be a father and he is a clever man who reads Margaret Thatcher's memoirs. In fact, 'Michael is like Oscar Wilde, a total genius – accepted by a small band of gays, artists and aristocrats but misunderstood by the world at large.'

But the interview had been done just before the birth and things had moved on somewhat since then.

Two days after publication Paula called me. She was tense, on the edge of panic. Michael was raging about the article. He could not see all the positive associations that had been artfully woven into the fabric of the piece. The article couldn't have been that bad since, the following day, I had received a call from a production company offering her work, I told her. She was quite excited for a moment, but soon returned to Michael's fury. He was ranting that he would never return to London and that threat had clearly terrified Paula. Why had I done it? she moaned. That horrible front cover. This was becoming absurd, I said, I didn't have any control over the front cover, that was down to the editor. She knew that. And I added that I thought the piece was amazingly positive for them, and in the *Telegraph* too, and that both she and Michael has approved of me doing the interview. I couldn't understand quite what the problem was until she mentioned that Michael's manager had been furious over the allusion to Oscar Wilde, suggesting that it made Michael look gay. I suppose it should have come as little surprise, but I was starting to spin. I said that he was a decade out of date and Michael should stop listening to him – no one's going to think he's gay. It was insane and I thought, 'Wake up, Paula – this *is* the worst job in Britain'. I pointed out that I wasn't getting paid for this. It was no longer about Paula and I working together against the coverage in the British press. With her fanciful wedding announcement it seemed we were locked in a covert PR duel. My throat constricted while I suggested to her that this arrangement was not going to work anymore.

'Oh, he'll get over it,' said Paula, her voice softening. 'We're going places, you and I. We'll be making money before you know it and you'll get paid for all the incredible work that you've done.' She reminded me of our agreement: 25 per cent of everything I handled, and that was a generous percentage. I said I didn't want to join them at the villa if Michael wanted to beat me up. She assured me he would be calm by then, and that she was really looking forward to seeing me. I decided to wait to reach my decision about whether to disengage from them all. Perhaps I just needed a holiday.

Dismayed that the very people my comments were designed to

promote had not appreciated them, I rang round my contacts for some second opinions. The comments I received were overwhelmingly in favour of the Wilde allusion and no one had any difficulty drawing the intended parallels. Other papers had picked up on the article and quoted from it. It was all good PR but Michael's management obviously thought differently.

In fear, Paula had called me the day before I left for Nice and told me that Michael was raging about another article. His manager was telling him that the record company were threatening to drop Michael if his PR did not come back on-message, and she hoped I would be able to smooth things out.

I had explained to Paula that I was just as surprised as they about an article that had appeared recently. It would seem that my PR mentor had made a premature announcement that he and I were handling Paula's and, more to the point, Michael's PR under the auspices of a new joint venture. Now Michael's manager was demanding to know what exactly he and I were intending to do with Michael. Still reeling from the Wilde quote in the *Telegraph* and fearful that *OK!* were about to snap Michael in a golfing jumper, he had roundly expressed his anger to Michael. Paula told me that Michael was ranting all day about how everyone was ruining his life and treating him like a piece of meat. In fact the *Telegraph* piece had been most successful for Paula. Where before we had to knock down doors to get her considered for work (not that she ever followed anything up), within days I was receiving calls from production companies with proposals to put Paula up for television work, and treatments were landing on the doormat several times a week.

———— ◆ ————

The producer with whom Paula and I had been discussing projects met me from the airport and we drove to a beach café in Nice before setting off for the villa. He was fighting to save his company and had been pushing to finalize a deal with Paula. She had suggested he fly out to discuss the next stages. He said he wasn't here to party, he would no longer be mucked around, he was here to close the deal and then he was on the first flight out. I felt sorry for him.

Paula had asked me to sleep on my decision to quit and suggested that we would talk on holiday about how things could be resolved, though I was doubtful about the outcome. Paula couldn't, or wouldn't take her mind off Michael for long enough even to jump-start her own career. Perhaps the producer had suspected this and turned his attention to Michael for ideas that he could get started on.

In the South of France it was open house and Michael laid on everything, playing the perfect host, accommodating the whims of his guests. The villa was a colonial outpost for the rock fraternity. The evening menu, chosen by the host himself, was chalked up outside in the morning – all five courses and Dom Perignon. Every night we dressed for dinner and took our seats on the veranda, an open-air dining room with a ceiling of cascading grape vines. The table was set with slender church candles in silver candelabra and the meals were cooked and served by Michael's staff, who waited at table and filled our glasses. It could have been paradise.

Paula had transformed the house, and every room bore her unmistakable stamp. Only the dining room had been preserved, at Michael's request, recording the original décor of the house, with its white stucco walls, oak beams and *trompe-l'œil* ceiling of trellis and vines. Paula's colours were lavish and rich. She told me Michael's mother was horrified to see that the villa had lost its original charm, but Paula was determined to exorcise the ghost of Helena. It was a sumptuous stage-set of funky Victoriana, like a gypsy caravan, with its red tassels and falling silks flung over lampshades and draped casually across the sofas. The sun played through the layers of tones and textures, and Michael beamed with admiration for her efforts, as he showed new visitors round.

Paula described the original style as John Lewis meets Ikea, themed by Helena as a gallery for studio shots of herself. So a bonfire was lit and Helena's flat-pack furniture was ceremonially incinerated. 'Shame I couldn't do the same with the photos,' she sighed. 'They were everywhere, but Michael took them down without a complaint.' Paula had replaced them with family pictures of herself and Michael with the children.

For all the opulence of the setting, Paula looked like she needed a good square meal. She had lost a shocking amount of weight since I had seen her last, only three weeks earlier. She was wearing a short white dress with a pink flowery print. Her hair was in girlish bunches and she was back in the high-heeled kitten shoes she had worn when she and Michael first began their affair. She greeted me with a warm embrace and whispered that it had all been hellish.

When Michael appeared I braced myself for a showdown, but he too gave me a lingering welcome hug. He looked knackered and puffy and Paula said to me later: 'It's the drink that does that to him.' But I wasn't so sure. His eyes were evasive and his usual grace was marred by wayward coordination. Paula took me to my room, which she told me she had painted herself, a soft lilac washed with a pearl sheen and dotted with *fleurs-de-lys* stamped in silver across the walls. I asked her if she had been eating properly and she explained that she had to put herself on a strict diet to fit into a size-eight dress that Michael had bought her from Chanel. 'Poor baby. I don't think he had any idea that in nine months his pint-size girlfriend could provide enough blubber to end whaling for good.' She assured me that she was not relapsing into the anorexia of her youth, but she was obviously doing something pretty radical to look the way that she did.

We all went to a beach that afternoon. Michael was driving, and he handled the trip well, despite his affable vacancy. We arrived at a roped-off private beach, with its own chic bar and café, and security turning away the public. Bono was there with his wife Ali, and their children would occasionally run up and taunt him, where we sat under a coconut-mat canopy. I hadn't met him before but we fell naturally into conversation; he had a welcoming way about him. The only time I heard Bono refer to his job was when he laughed with Michael about the weight he'd have to lose for his next tour. Other than that, Bono talked families and what we were all going to eat for lunch. Paula sat with us, cradling Tiger in her arms and occasionally feeding her. Then she offered the baby to Michael and he took her down to the sea front while Paula draped her arms around Bono's neck and said: 'Don't forget, you've promised to fuck me first, if you ever get fed up with Ali,' at which Bono laughed, saying it was a deal, then returned to discussing the cost of flying with easyJet.

When we returned to the villa I slipped away to my room and slept. My bedroom was directly over the kitchen and as I lay my head down on the pillow I could hear Michael's voice raised and Paula shouting back at him.

'I just want you to make sure that Tiger is properly looked after,' I heard her say. 'Okay, okay, I'm sorting it out,' Michael replied. After a couple of hours' sleep I went to find Paula. She was lying in bed with Tiger suckling beside her. I knew that Paula believed in feeding on demand, but Tiger seemed to be on the breast even when she hadn't asked to be. 'She's got a good appetite,' I commented. Paula smiled down at her baby daughter with deep affection and giggled: 'She's like her father, doesn't know when to stop a good thing.'

Paula was understandably tired and spent most of the next day in her bedroom. When I did see her I remarked on what a wonderfully peaceful baby Tiger was. She had hardly stirred from the moment I got there, the only sign of life being her incredible appetite.

'It's surprising what four Prozac a day can do,' Paula said. My stunned silence prompted a stream of justifications. She assured me Tiger was quite okay, I just hadn't seen her when she was awake; she was a night owl like her father. Paula said she had made an appointment to see her doctor when she got home, to wean her off the drugs she was taking. Her doctor had told her that if she came straight off them, her depression would return and she was barely coping as it was. Back in London all the stresses awaited her: the lawyers' fees for the case against Serena and ongoing actions with Bob were mounting. Although Michael had promised to pay them in lieu of the *OK!* interview, she told me that he was beginning to worry about money too.

Andy Gill, a top-flight producer who had been developing Michael's solo album with him, was staying for a day or two. By all accounts he hadn't seen Michael for a while and was keen to move the work to its next stage. His girlfriend, Catherine Mayer, a political journalist who was unnervingly bright, talked in great detail about the time they had spent here the previous summer. Andy and Michael looked right together. They could have been best friends for a lifetime, they were so comfortable in each other's company. Of all the acquaintances I was to make on that holiday, it was Andy who appeared to have Michael's best interests at heart. They talked music, they giggled like schoolboys, reminiscing about old times, with many friends in common on the scene, and when Bono came over to the villa it was like the return of the three musketeers.

I spent the next few days reading on my own in unoccupied rooms or out in the garden where I could work on a suntan at the same time. Paula stayed in her room even at mealtimes and I checked to see that someone was taking up food. Michael said she wasn't hungry and that all Paula needed was sleep. Michael danced around his guests, unable to hold the thread of any conversation. His usual geniality had shifted sideways to become a parody of the careless charm that had been his hallmark. Now, when I engaged him, his once penetrating attention seemed to focus some way behind me and he was distracted within a sentence or two as he weaved away to pour some more champagne or roll a spliff. I now knew that he was loaded with illicit substances for most of the day, and on the third day, I was to witness one of his erratic mood dives. I went out into the garden to join Paula and Michael on the lawn, only to catch the tail end of a thunderous outburst. Michael was swearing and Paula ran from the garden, in floods of tears.

Michael had told her of his plans to take everyone to a nightclub the next day and Paula wanted him to stay with her and spend some time with Tiger. He was obviously still as smitten with his daughter, but he had explained to Paula that he wanted to catch up with some friends and celebrate the summer. For the first time I heard him complain about the other children. He was angry that Fifi, Peaches and Pixie had given his housekeeper so much work to do and felt that Anita had been lazy not to help clear up their mess. Paula had suggested that Michael wasn't thinking straight because he'd taken 'too much gear' the night before. She took Tiger out of the sun and moved into the shade by the side of the house where there were some chairs and a small wooden table.

Jo Fairley and her husband arrived and I found her sitting with Paula, still down in the shade where I'd left her a few hours earlier. They barely acknowledged my presence; I sat down with them, open to join in with their conversation. Before long, their exclusive body language made me feel uncomfortable; I couldn't deny that I found it hurtful and confusing. I was bewildered that they would choose to cause such obvious discomfort to a fellow guest. The afternoon progressed with no relief from spiteful undertones.

At supper, Michael was uptight, but eventually bombed himself into relaxation. He supplied the very best champagne, which I quaffed to dull my nerves and I loosened up enough to begin giggling with Andy. When Paula hadn't come down to supper again, Jo decided to take a tray up to her and stayed with her for the rest of the evening.

Michael remained disconnected from the scenes around him. He was not being rude, but seemed unable or unwilling to concentrate his attention in one place for more than a few seconds. His enthusiasm would only surface with the arrival of a new face, or when he was talking about his music. That night the house was full of people. Michael put on the work-in-progress of an Elton John single, produced by his friend, and the general consensus of the guests was that they were impressed. Then Michael put on another track and the room went quiet, until one drunken woman bellowed: 'Turn that crap off and get Elton back on again.' Michael obeyed without protest and the woman swayed and sang to Elton's new tune. Andy whispered to me that it had been a track from Michael's solo album.

The evening ended when a few of Michael's friends from the beach arrived to take him out clubbing. I retired to bed.

———— ◆ ————

Michael was almost coming out in hives at the thought of returning to 'the hell on earth' that was London. He took Paula, myself and the producer out for a spot of sightseeing in Valbonne. It was three days before he and Paula were leaving and his anxiety seemed to bring on a monstrous male PMT – Pre Metropolis Tension. Even though they would only be spending a week in England before going on to Australia, Michael was fixated by the dreaded scramble through Heathrow, and the fight for life beyond. Paula was very quiet that day and said next to nothing on the journeys there and back.

Michael wanted to mark the end of his holiday in a nightclub. I was reluctant, but Andy said it would be a laugh. The holiday had served to awaken my slumbering sensibilities. This rock'n'roll court was no different from any other, with its undisputed king and queen and its courtiers vying for status. Just before we left to enjoy the Cannes nightlife, Paula came into my room and sat on my bed, while I was getting ready. She asked me to make sure Michael wasn't out too late and to keep an eye on him. I had no desire to be out all night anyway, I said, and thought it was unlikely

Michael would risk me seeing anything that compromised his relationship with her.

She asked me if I had enjoyed my stay and I told her it had been wonderful, just what I needed. She looked relieved and apologized for not spending more time with me. I asked her if her relationship with Michael had flourished over the holiday break and if she would consider spending more time in France, as Bob was now doing his share of bringing up the girls. She said she sensed a restlessness in Michael since Tiger had been born and she would have to find a way to tour with him when his album came out. But she hated the idea of being parted from the girls and Michael had told her that he didn't want Tiger on the tour – it was not a good environment for a child. She looked tired and defeated, knowing she had fallen pitifully short of the heady happiness with which she had optimistically split from Bob. And I was sad, too, for all the dreams we had shared for our shiny new beginnings, and for the chasm that was widening between us. We had been moving apart for longer than I was willing to accept, but now I knew we'd chosen diverging paths.

Michael was behaving like he had just been let out of school at the end of term. He chose the black open-top Mercedes jeep to convey his guests – Catherine, Andy, the producer and myself – to the club in Cannes.

Although Paula didn't come with us, she had for the first time joined us for dinner. She looked beautiful – intoxicating, Michael called her. Her figure showed almost no sign of having recently given birth to Tiger and she had it on display in a low-cut and very chic tight black dress. She was in good spirits, making everyone laugh with anecdotes of her television days and of wonderful times spent with Michael. He smiled on, enjoying the response from the audience as if it were him on stage, and anyone could see in this rare glimpse of her former self that this what had turned his head and that he still adored her. He kissed her neck, cradled her in his arms, put on some music that meant something special to them both and sang along to her, looking at her in the most melting way. Buried deep beneath the chaos that passed for their everyday life, they were still passionately in love and he was still captivated. Before we left, he excused himself to go upstairs, to see Paula and 'give her some loving'. He smiled knowingly to us as we all waited in the hallway for him to return. 'What a woman,' he said, as he skipped out to the jeep.

Michael put on Grace Jones's 'Private Life', and sang along at the top of his amazing voice. With its disco funk fusion and Jones's feral vocals, it was the perfect anthem for a dash down the coastal freeway from Nice to Cannes for a spot of clubbing. Michael approached the club at speed and skidded to a halt in front of the entrance. The bouncers rallied as we disembarked and hustled Michael through the crowds lining for admission, leaving us to follow in their wake. Everyone knew him. Michael threw his arms around the manager, who waved us in the direction of the VIP lounge with a deferential look that said 'no charge'.

We crossed the club with the bouncers. Lasers strafed the heaving dance-floor through a haze of dry ice and Gauloises. Snapshots of sweating faces and manic eyes froze in the flicker of a powerful strobe. Like some futuristic war zone, the club spectacle built a visceral excitement. We were escorted up a flight of steps, into a generous mezzanine bar with plush banquette seating and table lights. As we sat, the manager announced in French and waves of his hands that Michael and his guests would drink on the house. With the champagne arrived a straggle of friends and admirers that Michael welcomed into our space. They looked to me like local pimps and gangsters made good, but they were probably young entrepreneurs, or the offspring of international diplomats. After a brief interchange, Michael leaned across and asked who wanted what.

I looked at Andy who had chaperoned me from the start. He shrugged and said Michael was getting some stuff, probably 'Es' because that's what he preferred. Michael was already flying and I thought if he took more, we might be stranded in the club all night. I had a gin and tonic, while glasses of water were handed round. Michael offered me a pill. All I could think of was the story in the news about a young girl who had died after taking just one 'E', and the small white tablet terrified me. He was insistent that I at least try it. The media were stirring up paranoia, he said; it can't kill you, that case was one in a million and, anyway, it wasn't the 'E' that killed her – she drank too much water. Michael nibbled the tablet in half, put it in my hand and I accepted it to get him off my back, but slipped it into my pocket.

Within about forty minutes Michael was jumping up and down on the seats, hanging from the netting on the ceiling and shouting to the music. Michael's friends hovered and people came and went. Someone introduced some young girls, who sat by Michael and giggled at his intimate attentions. The group was in constant motion, shouting in each other's ears, sitting, standing, laughing, dancing. Someone produced a camera and was firing off the flash, while Michael teased the girls for a pose. I sat there imagining the film going to the shop for processing, and all the hands through which the pictures would pass before they ended up in the local paper, or sold to a London tabloid.

'You're off duty,' Andy laughed when I told him how stupid Michael was being – these girls looked sixteen, which meant they were probably younger. Michael leaned over them, all charm and flattery, then he took one off for a dance. I felt as if I was party to a crime; my best friend was at home breast-feeding the baby while her partner played with local girls, only months past having their parents tuck them up in bed. I wished I had never come. 'How long has this been going on?' I asked Andy. 'Michael's always needed women – everyone knows that,' he answered.

Andy's girlfriend Catherine was deep in conversation with Michael's friends or dancing with him on the seats. When I needed the loo, Andy asked her to show me where they were, and we joined the customary long queue for the ladies. We got to talking about the villa and the pool, and that reminded me of the photo taken to promote Paula's autobiography, where she'd spiked her hair into horns and held a plastic trident. Apparently they had been at a club all night and returned to the villa to find a dozen photographers waiting for Paula. They had all found it hilarious and amazing that Paula had been able to carry off the shoot with such panache. I thought that *was* pretty impressive: the Paula I knew would have cancelled and gone to bed for a day. Paula and Michael were famous in the area and I heard someone in the crowded loo say, 'It's amazing what you can do on five 'Es'. Paula's so wild she can outdo Michael's drug-taking any day. He's certainly met his match.' 'There's no one like Paula. She'd play Russian roulette, given half a chance,' Catherine said.

Back in the VIP lounge, Michael called over to me, 'I'm tripping my unbelievable tits off! Are you feeling it?' he asked. 'What?' I shouted back. Andy whispered, 'The 'E'.' 'No,' I replied, but I must have looked extremely glum or maybe Andy had told him I was getting annoyed with his behaviour. He sidled up to me and put an arm around my shoulders.

'Cheer up, Gerry-Berry. What's up?' Michael's words slurred in my ear and his eyes swivelled in their sockets. 'Let's go somewhere quiet we can talk,' Michael offered.

'Come on, what's up?' Michael's lisp was more pronounced and his words slurred around the sympathetic question. I explained that I was worried about Paula and felt guilty that I was supporting what was going on, if only by virtue of not taking a stand. I explained that I couldn't watch him smooching these young girls. Michael laughed and gave me a reassuring hug. 'Oh, Gerry, I love you so much. I love those quaint words you use and I love you for loving Paula so much.' But his words only heightened my discomfort, as I realized his affectionate concern was merely enhanced by the Ecstasy he had taken.

He told me that he would always take care of Paula, that he adored his baby girl and that no one could do for him what Paula had done. 'She understands me, man,' he kept repeating. 'She's being treated like shit,' I said, trying to cut through his narcotic oblivion, 'and you and I know that she doesn't deserve what's happening to her.' Michael wouldn't have it. He was too convinced by his own theories, the self-deceptions of a drug addict. He could accept no part in the downward spiral of their lives; everyone else was to blame – it was all Bob's fault. He spat out the name of his tormentor and his eyes darted furiously from side to side. 'I've got someone on him,' Michael announced. 'Ex-FBI and he knows some scary people.'

He claimed to have employed a private investigator, an ex-government agent, to expose Bob and Paula's accountant. They had stolen millions of Paula's money. There was no truth at all in this allegation but I asked him how he knew all this and he replied that Paula had told him. I had been feeling sad, but now I was seriously alarmed.

The Paula I knew had a beady eye on how much she earned and where it was going. She'd run the finances of the house for all her married life, so how would she let millions of pounds evaporate from her bank account? The fact was that she hadn't earned millions of pounds. Visions of men in black, going through her accountant's filing cabinet with torches in the dead of night should have had me in stitches, but for the fact that Michael was deep in a serious paranoid delusion.

He went on to describe plans to bring Bob to his knees. He would never rest, he said, until Bob was exposed. Michael had the look of maniacal obsession. Anything I could say was in direct contradiction to his beliefs, and to the lies told him by Paula. He told me that his will was going to take months to amend. His business partner was aware of Bob's determination to get his hands on Michael's money and they were hard at work, hiding everything so that it would never be found. 'Paula's right, she's given up everything for me. She's lost her career, she's lost all her money. That bastard has taken it all and no one knows,' he continued bitterly.

These rantings began to make a sort of sense. I realized now what Paula must have told him, to explain her bankruptcy. Now I understood why Michael's accountants had hijacked her books. And why he had ranted continuously against Bob. I didn't need to wonder how far Paula's yarns had gone – the pennies dropped like rain inside my head. It wouldn't just be lies, it would be omissions. Michael would know nothing of the job offers she had failed to take up. Clearly his mind was too addled to divine the truth for himself, and he was awash with the figments of Paula's divisive imagination.

The gossip I had overheard about Paula's drug-taking had awoken me to a reality that, even now, I was reluctant to accept. How much and for how long? Why would she want Michael to see her as this persecuted victim? With a crushing sense of my own naïvety, I knew the answers had always been there. I implored Michael to take us all back home. Michael drove like he was playing a car-chase video game. Grace Jones was back at full volume. I had been deafened by the house music in the club but now I could feel the pulverizing bass through the seat. Andy was still doing his level best to calm my nerves, as I screamed with the others as Michael careered round bends on two wheels and drove full-tilt over roundabouts planted with flowers. But mine were screams of pure terror rather than the hysterical laughter of the other passengers.

We stopped outside a block of flats, in a brutal concrete landscape on the outskirts of Cannes. Michael disappeared inside. We must have been sitting there about ten minutes when two French youths approached the jeep with a package and said it was for Michael. Inside was a brick of hashish. Young boys passing by stopped to admire the Mercedes under the chemical yellow of the street lighting, commenting in French and trying to draw us into conversation. It was 4am, I was tired and on the verge of tears, hoping that Michael would come back soon. Eventually Andy gave in to my fretting and went to fetch him.

Five minutes later, Andy returned with Michael, who remarked, 'Thanks, guys. If you hadn't got me out, I was about to get myself into serious trouble with the missus.' Later I heard that Michael had gone up to see a dealer and was moving towards a bedroom with a girl when Andy appeared.

From where I was sitting I could see Michael swallow a handful of 'Es' before taking to the wheel again and I kept my eyes tightly shut. On the way home Michael announced he was going to take a short cut, which should have been a relief but by now I was just praying to God that we would survive. He lunged the four-wheel-drive through the shrubbery on the central reservation. He charged up kerbs, over flowerbeds and across corners, within inches of trees and parked cars. I was convinced the jeep was going to roll on the bends, sure we would die as he tore up the pavement towards a brick wall and hand-braked into a sideways drift. The short cut was through a wooded area and Michael slalomed through the trees. By now I was weeping, convinced I would never see my children again. Andy shouted at Michael to slow down, over the other passengers' uncontrollable laughter. When we arrived back at the villa I walked up the drive offering silent thanks that my prayers had been answered.

I slept for most of the next day. The producer sought me out in the afternoon and said what an amazing evening it had been, what a cool guy Michael was, and how Bono had called to ask if they wanted to go out with him in the evening. He told me that Elton's producer had invited him to his villa the next evening and that Michael and Andy were definitely going to come and see his Jimi Hendrix outtakes. He was excited about the latest developments of a holiday he had almost written off. He had finally penetrated the enclave, sure that these people would take him places, and elected to stay around for a few more days to see how things developed.

Later, in the early evening, I began to feel more sprightly and walked out into the garden. Paula asked me how the evening had gone and I skirted the truth. Michael bounded over, looking as if nothing had happened; he said he had spent the afternoon exercising. I looked him in the eye, hoping for some hint of contrition for the previous night's events, or an explanation for his demonic driving if he wouldn't discuss the other stuff in front of Paula. But none came – it was as if it had all been erased from his memory. The couple looked again like happy and doting parents as they strolled across the lawn, Paula holding Tiger, and Michael with his arm around her shoulder. A casual observer would never have believed Michael was the same person who had been our guide through Hades the night before. If someone didn't do something to wake him up to the truth of what he'd become, the truth inside his world, the truth of what had been told to him, he would kill himself.

I felt an impulse to speak to someone and the nearest person was the film producer, sitting on his own. 'We could have died last night,' I told him. 'I think you're over-reacting,' he said. 'It was just a bit of fun.' At first he maintained a detached amusement, regarding me as some over-zealous Good Samaritan, who couldn't grasp the code of rock'n'roll. But I persevered, escalating the force of my conviction. As I described my fears for the two of them, a road map to disaster seemed to unfold before me.

As the implications sank in, his smugness turned into a sullen silence. He looked at me with irritated disdain as I insisted both Paula and Michael needed help and only their close friends could make an impact. I told him that if Michael didn't end up in a clinic, he would end up dead. I could see this so clearly I felt I could almost name the time and place. Someone is going to die, I kept repeating. And a few weeks later my premonition was in print.

12 everything I knew was wrong

WITHIN DAYS OF RETURNING FROM FRANCE, Paula called to remind me that she and Michael were off for a few weeks in Australia. I was waiting for something to tip the balance and force me into a decision. I now knew that Paula had woven a web of lies around us all. I suspected she'd been abusing drugs on an horrific scale. I knew that her relationship was a rollercoaster with a buckled rail, and the company she was keeping threatened to put her in hospital. As if this weren't enough, I just knew that more was sure to emerge. I began to make serious enquiries. With my premonition of death I could hardly just walk away.

In the meantime, I maintained my duties with the press. But instead of my usual morning round of calling the numbers in my address book, I left the phone until it rang. But it would only be a matter of time before questions were asked. I was known for my reliable contact and sprightly enthusiasm, and I was painfully aware that I was beginning to sound flat.

———— ◆ ————

By the time I had spoken to all my contacts and mutual friends, I had gathered a number of alarming and shocking facts. Many things now began to fall into place.

I learned that Michael had sometimes been irritable with the girls during their holiday at the villa; the three-day mood cycle that he was locked into marred the children's enjoyment of their summer holiday with their mother and their newborn sister. On day one he would be high, all smooth and loving. The children were in favour and he frolicked with them in the pool. For the next two days they had to keep away. He'd be coming down, hitting morose lows by day three, with intense irritability and temper fits. Paula complained about the children's noise, saying that Michael wanted peace and quiet and so they had to stay out of the way as much as possible.

It seemed too that Paula had exaggerated her problems with Bob. Perhaps he had been dictatorial during their marriage, but maybe his domineering ways were in fact better for Paula than the careless abandon that Michael promoted, for himself and those around him. I wondered whether Bob would ever get custody of the girls. The children were so settled when they stayed with him. He was still strict but much more loving. He was totally devoted to them, helping with their homework, playing, doing puzzles and baking atrocious cakes. On the other hand Paula, who had always been so independent, had become so totally dependent on Michael that in the end she wasn't even capable of looking after herself let alone the children.

Paula was right, she *had* given up everything for Michael: her career, her responsibilities, her children and now herself. Where was the Paula we used to know? From my press contacts I learned that Paula had engineered the initial 'discovery' of their relationship to separate Michael from Helena. She had played the press from the start. She had called the showbiz desks with a handkerchief over the phone and told them that Paula Yates was having an affair with Robbie Williams.

Apparently Paula was determined to be caught with Michael in order to bring his relationship with Helena to an end, but Michael might not have been big enough news. For Robbie, the *News of the World* devoted the manpower, expecting a big scoop. They had tailed her twenty-four hours a day, until she and Michael were discovered in the Halkin Hotel. Paula had been certain that Helena would leave him then, but she hadn't reckoned on the bond of their three-year relationship, which adverse publicity would only reinforce. But by this time the story had escalated into a high-octane tabloid love-triangle, with Bob's 'sainthood' as the crucial flash point.

Paula had to engineer a second scoop and she let the press know they were checking in to Chilston Park. Suddenly Michael Hutchence was bigger news than Robbie could ever hope to be. This time Paula hit the jackpot when she tipped off the press but with a nasty spin-off. She had always been determined to have Michael; she pursued him relentlessly, she was there at every gig, she would turn up at the hotels he was staying in and demand that he come down to see her, regardless of whether he had company.

I had always thought he was unhappy with Helena, as that is what Paula had maintained – that he was going to leave Helena anyway. Of course, Michael could never really end his relationships, neither with Helena nor any other woman. He was still emotionally attached to Kylie whom he would call from his mobile. But I *had* seen with my own eyes that Michael was passionately in love with Paula. However, it seemed obvious that if Michael had really wanted to leave Helena he had had the perfect get-out clause the first time, caught as he had been in a hotel with Paula, but *he* had persuaded Helena that the story was all lies, and encouraged Paula to give her marriage one more chance. The fact was the humiliation of the Chilston Park Hotel had resulted in Helena finally closing the door on him. And it was not only Helena who was a victim of Paula's machinations – it was heartbreaking to see Bob so devastated also.

I had believed that Bob had hit Paula. I couldn't give him any sympathy after that, but now I knew that Paula had made the whole thing up. She had wanted Michael's attention – he hadn't called her and she knew the bait that would lure him back. He would have felt guilty for sending her back to Bob and been very angry with the perpetrator. Michael came straight back to comfort her and threatened to accost Bob, and of course the affair restarted.

I began to feel very sorry for Michael. He had no idea what was really going on, having been told so many lies. Paula's obsession, her flattery, her twisting of facts, and her willingness for him to lose himself, seemed to have made him a victim of his delusions. The drugs would have exacerbated his state of confusion. Paula had been so determined to keep him that she was prepared to try anything. It became clear to me that Paula's drug-taking had escalated from the start, with her trying to prove she could be everything he wanted and needed.

As they settled down in the house in Clapham and Michael began to enjoy the home comforts of his one-woman harem, Paula was starting to panic about the effects of her lifestyle on her unborn baby and suggested that they rein in their hedonism to get their lives back on track. She tried to exert a little pressure, but Michael had said, 'You're no fun any more,' and with all the pressure crushing in from outside, he bolted. When he ventured back, Paula knew there was only one place for her to go – wilder, to show him things he didn't know about himself.

Of course they had been under a lot of pressure at the time but Michael could not confront his problems; he hated confrontation, he would either run or take drugs, and Paula would follow wherever she could. But it had been the drugs that had tipped them into the abyss.

Paula's housekeeper had to clear away all the leftovers in the morning: the cocaine and Ecstasy tablets left out on the counters and coffee tables. Anita had warned the children not to pick up any tablets or anything off the tables – the white powder that might look like sugar. She couldn't even lie in bed in the morning, or afford to risk the children roaming around the house unsupervised.

And then it dawned on me why Paula and Michael wanted to get rid of Anita. She was too close to Bob, the one person who could blow their secret world apart. But were they stupid enough to think that they were capable of looking after four children without Anita? It's hard enough looking after one child when you're straight, let alone four when you're loaded, and Paula had never done it on her own before. How could she get up at 7am every morning to get them to school if she wasn't going to bed till five?

I considered Michael's maniacal obsession with Bob and the extraordinary story of Paula's poor accountant. It was blatantly ridiculous to think that he would swindle Paula; he had always been so transparently honest and kind. Besides, she never had millions anyway. It had all been a neat ruse to impress Michael, to explain her penury and accentuate her apparent helplessness. Michael's girlfriends had all been in another league financially and Paula, who had once been content to shop at Miss Selfridges, was suddenly buying clothes from supermodel, super-pricey shops like Gucci, Valentino, Versace and Prada. Her accountant had done everything he could to stop her spending.

Paula had made it quite clear that she didn't need the house in Redburn Street, convinced as she was that Michael would provide for her. It was only when Michael didn't buy her a home that she was left with no choice but to get her house back.

Michael and Paula had turned on Anita in their rampant paranoia. They were suspicious of her contact with Bob. They accused her of spying and ransacked her bedroom when she was out. There would be no resolution until Paula was off drugs. Maybe Michael will leave her, maybe she will get back to work, I thought.

But I knew it would take more than that now. I had spent enough time in group rooms with alcoholics and drug abusers to know that it was not merely a simple case of putting down the stuff – it was a lifetime of commitment, 'one day at a time'. In truth, though Paula had been straight for most of her life, her vulnerability to addiction – the so-called 'addictive personality' – had lain dormant all the while, waiting for a habit to take hold. It had been so strong that she had been aware of it herself and avoided anything more stimulating than tea. She had tiptoed round it for twenty years, and it would take more than words to make her give it up now that she was addicted. In such cases, it usually took a catastrophe.

I was seriously concerned about Tiger. I knew that Paula wanted the very best for all her girls, but in her present state she might not have realized that Tiger could be at risk from the mixture of prescription drugs she was taking, let alone any other illicit substances. I had recently had confirmation that when Paula was six months' pregnant, she'd slipped in LA and knocked out two front teeth – she had been on Ecstasy at the time.

Paula and Michael had returned from the Riviera and entrusted Tiger to Anita (the girl they had wanted nowhere near their child), while they slept off the excesses of their last few nights in the villa. At least Tiger would be safe with Anita. This bad dream was turning into a waking nightmare. My prescience of death became ever more emphatic.

When I resolved to tell Paula that I could no longer support her unless she cleaned up completely, I called Anita, who begged me not to confront her. She was certain that Paula would sack her and was concerned that with both of us gone there would be no one to safeguard the children.

When I got home Paula had left a message on my phone. Her voice was slurred and she was telling me how much she missed me and loved me, and my resolve weakened. I thought, if only I could sit her down and force her to see sense.

Anita and I met in Battersea Park the next morning. She was driving the Jeep Cherokee that Michael had bought for the family. Tiger was asleep in a baby seat in the back as we discussed my deliberations. Together we explored our options: the solution lay in helping Paula to save herself, while minimizing the risk of tipping her deeper into a denial that might culminate in the children's exposure to a still greater danger. The stakes went far beyond the friendship I had once held so dear. Paula and Michael had resumed their nocturnal lifestyle, drugs arriving by courier in manila envelopes that matched in description the many I had taken at the door myself. On one occasion someone had visited the house to take delivery of one of the packets when Paula and Michael were at the Reading festival. Michael had called to ask for the contents to be checked. Inside was a large bag of yellow-brown powder and another bag of white. The envelope was addressed to Mr Kipper.

Paula's literary agent had called when we were all in the South of France, with a catalogue of complaints. Paula had not delivered a single word for two books for which she had been commissioned, and the publishers were demanding their advances back. Apparently she was now dropping Paula too. She had been both her agent and a good friend for many years. I knew that things had to be extremely serious for her to take such drastic action. Maybe a few sharp shocks like that would do the trick. I wondered whether if I also resigned, citing all that I had witnessed independently, then maybe the message would hit home.

Who was I kidding? Knowing all the stages that the addict passes through, I was aware that it would take a lot more to get Paula to straighten out. Drugs were not that easy to kick – they were integral to a lifestyle that revolved around the man Paula was with, the people they knew, the places they went. I put my ultimate decision on hold, mindful that I was probably better placed to support Anita and keep an eye on the children if I carried on pretending that I was working for Paula. But being chummy with Paula would be extremely difficult to pull off knowing what she had been up to and the lies she had told to both Michael and myself.

When Paula called me two days later she sounded bubbly and positive. She was looking forward to Australia and she assured me she was going to sort out my percentage for the *Sun* contract and Michael, apparently, was going to get his office to contribute towards the expenses we had discussed. Paula said that when she was back from Australia she would want to talk about work again. Then she outlined her plans to get rid of

Anita when she returned, complaining of untidiness and her obsession with the girls, and my heart sank further. 'She won't even go away for the weekend,' Paula said indignantly. 'Michael can't stand her being around any more. All we need is someone during the day, who leaves us alone at night. And listen,' said Paula, in her most coquettish voice, 'if any reporters call you to make a comment on our marriage plans – don't deny it this time.'

The next day I saw Bob taking the girls to school and he smiled at me. How much did he really know? How could I look him in the eye, knowing what I knew and doing nothing about it? His easy charm with the other parents was obvious, his concern that the children had handed in their prep, the bear hugs he gave them, and his laughter when Peaches told him to 'naff off' were touching. I was feeling guilty now about my gleeful role in blackening Bob's name, even though I had been acting on misinformation.

I felt that Anita, the housekeeper and I had all been enabling them to live this drugged-up fantasy. Their vigilant cleaner was leaving to go back to Australia the following week. No more backstop, less protection. I was beginning to hate everything we had become: frightened, controlling, manipulative, scheming, lying. Paula and Michael had a posse of enablers clearing up behind them, making excuses for them, looking after their children, making sure they were safe.

A few days later, my daughter Sophie asked to stay over at Redburn Street with the two youngest Geldof girls. Anita agreed but I had to collect her first thing on Sunday morning because Bob was taking his daughters out. When I arrived Anita was standing on the steps outside the house, deep in conversation with Paula's mother. Anita was ashen and Helene tearful; Paula had left instructions that her mother was not to enter the house nor have any contact with the girls. It was an awkward exchange when Bob arrived, my guilt meeting his habitual agitation. Sophie appealed to him to take her out with them. He agreed and set off with the girls for the park, telling Anita that he would give them lunch.

When they had gone Anita collapsed at the kitchen table and explained why she looked so burned out. She had had little sleep the night before. The alarm on Michael's Cherokee had spontaneously come to life and woken half the street. Anita was flustered; she tried every button inside the car but could not disable it. Finally the neighbours called the police. Inside the house she searched for the owner's manual, going through the papers still in Paula's room from the move. She dislodged an A4 manila envelope containing tubes of Smarties, which she thought was rather odd, but it was late and with the alarm still blaring, she left all the paperwork in a mess on the floor and went on with her search.

Next morning she overslept and wandered into Paula's bedroom where the children were sitting on Paula's bed watching television. The brown envelope, addressed to Mr Kipper (a name she recalled Michael using when he travelled) was open on the bed. The children were handling the coloured sweets, while my daughter Sophie was examining a waxy brown stick that looked like a pencil. Suddenly Anita remembered 'Mr Kipper' written on the parcels delivered by courier. Snatching the object from Sophie and collecting up all the Smartie tubes, she asked the children if they had eaten anything. Sophie said that the brown pencils were too hard to bite. We examined the illicit stash. Several other tubes were packed with the brown fingers – they felt like crayon. We were sure it was a drug, but we had no idea what it might be. Bob was due back later, but we were not about to ask him what they were. After the initial shock that my daughter had been handling drugs, I began to feel incredibly angry. Smartie tubes! How bloody stupid, to send the stuff disguised as sweets to a house full of children.

We found handfuls of Polaroids on a shelf in the bathroom. Pin-sharp in the arctic flash, Paula and Michael grappled like divers in an underwater fight for air, in glossy black latex suits with strategically cut holes. She was pictured burying a strap-on dildo deep into his bottom in a bizarre reversal of roles. The zipped-up bodywear and balaclavas, worn for all-over stimulation of the skin, evoked a sinister violence in the pictures. Part of me was fascinated, amused even; it didn't really bother me what people did in the privacy of their own bedrooms, but for this stuff to be within easy reach of the children was beyond any possible realm of acceptability.

We called the national drugs help line from my mobile phone and described the brown pencil drug. The experts thought it sounded like opium, but had little information on the drug in its rawest form. Being bulky it yielded low profit margins and was rare on the streets – they called it the drug of connoisseurs, mostly imported by individuals for their own consumption. Anita said she couldn't live like this anymore and I was still feeling dizzy thinking that my little girl might have been harmed. We agreed that we did have to do something now. But what? We decided to scour the entire house for anything else by which the children might come to harm. Behind the mirror on the mantelpiece in Paula's bedroom were three or four pieces of foil. One contained a yellow powder (probably ketamine). Another looked as if it had been burned with a flame (probably heroin). Another almost certainly had traces of cocaine, and a further still held a sort of white and black charcoal which we never identified.

We searched through the house and found more – a tin of white powder and some tablets. As I started to flush it down the loo, Anita stopped me. Sensibly, she wanted to retain the evidence, but I couldn't think beyond the danger to the children. She pointed out that only radical action would eliminate the danger for good.

We found something else in our search – the deeds to the house, still in Bob's name. This flew in the face of the story I'd been told by Paula that she had won the court case outright. Bondage magazines and more Polaroids were added to the pile with the drugs in a mounting haul that looked like the spoils of a police raid on a brothel. We found pornographic videos amongst the children's Disney flicks and packets of Rohypnol, Prozac and Temazepam. It was a horrifying cache. What had happened to Paula? How had she gone so far?

We vacillated between blaming it on Michael and blaming her. In an escalating dance of desperate seduction, Paula had done anything to keep Michael with her. Perhaps Paula took Rohypnol before these acts of eccentric sex to numb the rising tide of self-disgust. The drug line told us that Rohypnol was often abused with other substances, to smooth the high of coke, to hide the effects of alcohol in a breath test and particularly to heighten sexual response. I began to feel sorry for Paula and suggested to Anita that we give her one last chance. We decided to call her in Australia. When we finally got through, a barely recognizable voice clearly indicated that she was in no fit state for a chat, let alone a deep-and-meaningful discussion about her lifestyle. We decided to wait another day and call her again.

Anita dreaded Paula and Michael's return. There would have to be an explanation why their paraphernalia had been removed. Paula left a message on my answering machine. In a little-girly voice, she asked if I would take over as her new literary agent, as she had received a fax from her current agent, terminating their arrangement. Paula didn't say why, but she was spitting, calling her agent a bitch. I rang her back but missed the window of her lucidity, instead getting an incoherent stream of garbled words. It was time to get an expert opinion.

Without naming names, I described the dilemma to my family doctor. He talked of all the visits he had made to private homes and hospitals for children who had taken their parents' drugs by mistake. He said it was a very real concern, not to be taken lightly and impressed upon me the possibility for any one of the children to end up dead. He then said that it was, without doubt, a responsibility of mine to inform their father of the facts and pointed out how dreadful it would be to live with the guilt if anything happened and I had not tried to do something about it.

I made an appointment to see my former therapist who specialized in addictions, working closely with a number of well-known addiction centres including PROMIS, the famed chain of UK clinics. She really put everything into perspective. The children must come first. She pointed out that, by protecting them, I had helped Paula and Michael to live as they had for far too long. I was no better than any of their other friends, whom I had been denouncing. I explained my fears that in acting I might end up making matters worse.

'It can't get much worse,' she said emphatically. 'You can't make Paula and Michael stop taking drugs, but you can stop making it easier for them to carry on. You've got yourself into this mess; you're going to have to face the consequences. From today you must focus on what has to be done rather than how it may affect you. Your friendship with Paula was over a long time ago. There is no Paula, there is no Michael – they've chosen their path. The only help you can give that poor girl now is to detach completely and salvage what is left. You could walk away and leave it to Anita, but that would be unfinished business, wouldn't it?'

So I took on board everything that had been said to me. I didn't feel as optimistic as she did about the outcome for Paula. I had lost my wonderful friend forever to something that was stronger than our friendship or anything I had to offer – her addiction to Michael, the obsession to do anything to keep him. As long as he wanted to ply himself with drugs, so would she. I remembered the day she walked into my life, the beautiful girl who bridged the future and the past, bringing unlimited potential into the present. She was not like anyone I had ever met before.

13 busted

MICHAEL AND PAULA WOULD SOON be back from Australia so we had to act quickly. We agreed that we needed allies – well-meaning and high-powered people who could bring pressure to bear on Paula to seek help in a clinic. We divided up the list and set about our recruiting drive.

We spoke to a girl at Michael's office. She was concerned herself, along with the rest of the staff – they all recognized that Michael had changed. She had seen the mood swings, she said, it was hell if he came into the office on a down day. She knew all of Michael's friends and associates, but she could think of no single person whom we could approach, who might be willing to talk Michael into cleaning up. We could sense that she was sympathetic and we took her out for lunch, to discuss it further.

Michael's staff had known for a long time that Paula had been pulling Michael's strings – she would call in and instruct them to arrange her flights to LA or Dublin, and then tell Michael that the *Sun* had paid. The girl mentioned Michael's consuming hatred for Bob, that it spilled out into nearly every conversation, and I told her that the adverse press had been a deliberate exaggeration and that Michael was driven by an overburdening sense of injustice relating to the false information Paula had fed him. She said that she guessed as much, but the rest of the office still viewed Bob as Satan's right-hand man.

Ironically, the see-saw of public opinion between Bob and Paula had tipped the other way. Now Bob was clearly seen as the villain, and as hard as it had been for people to see Paula in a positive light, it now seemed impossible to shift their views on Bob.

Michael's assistant needed to understand that this was no rock'n'roll dalliance with recreational drugs; if something wasn't done then Michael was going to die. The poor woman was horrified, but she had neither the resources nor the authority to organize anything effective enough to make Michael listen. I didn't have to think too hard to guess at her boss's response. It would be something about drug stories being good for record sales. This was the music industry, everyone's on something, who's going to break cover and tell him what to do with his life? But Michael didn't have his usage under control; he was delusional, imagining that he had set the FBI on to Bob. She said that the people around him would be too scared of losing their jobs to challenge Michael about his lifestyle. I spoke to everyone that Paula, Michael and I knew in common; the telephone must have been red hot, but no one seemed to care.

The friends that we could contact had mostly drifted away or stuck with Bob. They had no inclination to stick their necks out for one of their many friends who had gone astray and it was doubtful how much influence they could bring to bear on Paula, now she had a new inner circle. We were back where we started, facing each other across the kitchen table, wondering what to do. Finally we agreed, 'We're going to have to talk to Bob'. We tossed the responsibility for telling him back and forth. I blinked first. With all the stories of Bob's ferocity and my own experiences of him swirling around in my head, I agreed to go and tell him that his children were in mortal danger.

———— ◆ ————

Bob had been busy in the kitchen, finishing off the food for Pixie's seventh birthday party. He was attempting all the right frills, with balloons everywhere and party bags neatly folded at one end of the room. It was faintly amusing that the man who launched the biggest aid festival in history was clearly struggling with a kiddies' tea party.

'Hi, come on in,' said Bob warmly. I was surprised by his easy manner, as Anita had primed him about what I was coming over to discuss. He obviously knew the nature of my professional relationship with Paula, so I expected a much frostier reception. 'I'm a bit worried about the jelly,' was the second thing he said, peering into the fridge. I began to relax a little, not having met the wall of fury I had been expecting. 'I followed the instructions and the fucking stuff won't set,' he said, asking me to see what I thought. I picked one up, hoping he wouldn't notice my hand trembling and examined the watery substance. 'The little tyke will kill me if I don't get it right.' His chuckle was full of affection, unexpected from a man whom Paula still described as an overbearing father who never put the children's needs before his own. There was flour all over the work surfaces and pots and pans piled in the sink. I apologized for encroaching on his busy schedule.

'No matter,' Bob replied in a more blunt Geldof manner, as if to remind me why I was there. 'What would you like to drink? I've got every tea that's going; a jolly jaunt with Jeanne to Covent Garden last weekend ended up like a tour of China's finest tea houses.' It was odd to hear him use the word 'jolly'. That was a Paula word, a word she used a lot. Metal ducting snaked across the ceiling in a bizarre tubular sculpture that dominated the architecture of the house. As we sat down, Bob complained about the lack of space, and the awkward features that Michael had spent so much money on installing. 'Minimalism is fine if that's your vibe, but this piece of shite is a disgrace. Who in their right mind would deliberately endorse something so grotesque?' Bob asked. He pointed to the Mulberry fabrics he had bought to give the place some warmth and said he'd draped some in his bedroom to alleviate the feeling that he was sleeping in a boiler room. He kept firing questions at me, apparently interested in my opinion on the décor, but never quite gave me the time to answer before launching into another barrage of criticism of the designer. It was strange, he was talking to me as if we were intimate friends, and all along I was waiting for the grilling of my life over my part in damaging his reputation. I got more tea and digestives before Bob finally invited me to speak.

I swallowed hard, took a deep breath and explained that this was very difficult for me. I was feeling disloyal, but Anita and I had tried every other avenue. Bob said he had worked out bits and pieces, but he had not really joined all the dots. He had felt powerless to act for fear of jeopardizing his visiting rights. I told him of my premonition, my gut fears for them both and how frustrating it had been, failing to raise support from any of Paula's friends. As my tale unfolded I felt a rise of latent nerves that made me shudder as if the room were cold, and Bob's emotions took him back through the hurt, the frustration, the anger, the loss and his complete incomprehension of what had gone wrong.

'How did she get herself in this mess, what's fucking happened to her?' Bob's head was in his hands, he began to pace the floor and a more strained look replaced the carefree demeanour that had greeted me at the door. Again and again he revisited his overriding question: was the old Paula, the Paula with whom he had spent eighteen years, a scam, an act, a figment of her own invention, one with which he had willingly colluded? Or was the Paula that had emerged with Michael the real Paula? 'Why, why?' he kept repeating, 'why did she have to go and leave me?' I hadn't been expecting this. Had Bob not assimilated any of the reasons? He told me that he knew about her damning accusations that he was thoughtless, controlling, arrogant, and neglectful. He asserted his commitment to Paula – he had always been more reliable than Michael, to whom he kept referring as 'the part-time boyfriend'.

During the year leading up to her sudden departure, Bob said he began to suspect that she was in fact mentally unwell, and that he had tried his best to help her though those dark periods: 'I would lie in bed with her and hold her until she stopped shaking with fear. I assured her that she was fine and that I loved her.' I was amazed by his outpouring of grief: his vulnerability, the expression of how deeply he still cared for this woman he described as the greatest love of his life, and how even now he could not think of a single woman in the world who could match her uniqueness. 'When you're that in love you don't leave; if she was going mad I would have coped, I would have loved her with all the madness,' said Bob. He mentioned her ongoing bulimia and pointed to the state of her teeth in more recent years, ravaged by the constant vomiting. They would lie in bed and he would pick the tartar from her teeth, and encourage her to improve her eating habits. These were not the acts of an oblivious partner. 'When you're in love with someone, you put up with it "in sickness and in health".'

He remembered many romantic gestures: the amethyst rings he gave her for each girl's birth, presents from New York, putting up with her 'Take That' phase and how irritating it was to find all his mugs replaced with 'fucking Gary Barlow'. And how worried he was when their normal alarm clock was swapped for 'Take That' merchandise. I suspected she had deliberately played on her teeny-bopper phase just to goad him. It did amuse her to wind people up without letting them in on the secret. Perhaps the teenage pop groupie thing started as a wind-up. Intentional or not, it had irritated the hell out of Bob.

Bob told me he had felt like a fool after apologizing to Michael for suspecting him and Paula of having an affair. He told me he had taken so long to propose to Paula because he regarded the responsibilities of marriage so gravely, and then he added his shocked bewilderment of how lightly she had taken her own marriage vows. In his own mind he was without doubt the injured party, convinced that no blame lay at his door. Desperate for answers and concerned by Paula's obvious decline, Bob had gone to visit an eminent psychologist. Bob told me the prognosis had been that Paula had undergone a form of mental breakdown, probably brought on by the death of her father. Memories of her childhood, unexplored while Jess was still alive, surfaced in a tidal wave of hurt, confusion, loss and anger. Unable to contain the intensity of this experience, she subconsciously regarded death as her only escape. Courting danger as she was, showed her determination to avoid the pain. Paula had new friends, an entirely new way of living, so far removed from the way she had lived before that it indicated a fundamental shift in the way she viewed herself. Following the patterns that would unfold in such a case, the psychologist was emphatic that if she didn't die by misadventure, she would eventually commit suicide.

'Why has she done this to herself? She knew the vibe. She knew this stuff would chew her up and spit her out. Why did she want to go and be a rock chick all over again? Not grow up,' he said. He blamed her 'part-time boyfriend', but also said they were both as bad as each other. He called Michael an immature twat and described his own experimenting with drugs as a thing of his youth, not a pastime that he would indulge in at his age and with the responsibility of having children.

We discussed the possibilities of getting Paula to a clinic and trying to make her see sense. Bob was as concerned as we were that Paula planned to sack Anita. Paula had called him a few weeks earlier to warn him of her intention and he had tried to persuade her to re-think. 'It doesn't make sense, why would she get rid of the one person who makes her life easy?' Bob wanted the children away from the danger but was adamant that they would return to their mother when Paula got better. 'I know only too well what it's like to be without your mother,' he said.

Then he talked of his relationship with Jeanne, how he valued her and was beginning to feel deeply for her. He worried that she might find it difficult to have three children suddenly thrust upon her. She was an aspiring young actress with a great career ahead of her and she might bolt from the prospect. But he would put the children first if there were no alternative but for them to come and live with him.

He was articulate about his emotions, but his voice remained calm and rational. He did seem relieved that he no longer felt alone. He explained the terrible frustration of knowing, and the 'waves of fear' that would turn into consuming terror every time he dropped the children back at Paula's house. He hadn't realized the extent of the drug abuse and repeatedly confirmed what we both knew already: if he moved in to take the children away, the courts would view it as a confirmation of his need to control. He cited the court's decision and the newspaper coverage that found in her favour and not in his.

With one arched eyebrow and a smirk he said wryly: ''Coz Agar, that finely tuned PR master-plan of yours certainly had us on the run.' He was amused but I squirmed. As we sat on the small sofa, an item Bob had brought with him, he told me of the time he had returned from Ireland where he had been doing a gig to find that his wife and three children had left. 'All that was left was a note on the mantelpiece: "I've left and taken the kids". I was mad with pain,' Bob told me. He described that evening, sitting in the house desperate to hear his children's voices and how he went up to their bedrooms to smell their pillows for some kind of relief from his agony.

Then he had called the housekeeper, as he couldn't reach Anita as she too had been sworn to secrecy and she had kept her word. But Bob had been beside himself, crying and pleading for her to tell him where they were. Eventually the housekeeper told him the area, just to get him off the phone. He walked out into the streets at two o'clock in the morning, crying out for the children one by one.

The memory of that night still affected him deeply, his voice cracked with emotion and he told me of his weeks of indescribable torture, facing life without Paula. His desire had been to end it all, he said, and he would have done, but for the intervention of his best friend who stayed with him on a suicide watch for months. He told me of his utter despair and inability even to get out of bed in the morning. But his friend nursed him through, sleeping on the floor beside his bed.

Jerry Hall had also come to his aid, but he remained disappointed and confused at how many of his friends knew the trip that Paula and Michael were on, and chose to 'protect' him from the truth. Although he was dismayed by my part in the spin for the papers, he was grateful that at last someone had had the courage and decency to approach him with the truth and to offer support. 'Too many people want to play it safe, sit on the fence, I suppose,' he said.

I asked him if he was still in love with Paula and he told me that he still missed her and her humour, her quick wit and supreme intelligence. Bob covered his face with his hands. 'Oh, shite, this is bad, this is fucking bad, isn't it, what am I going to do?'

We recognized the unlikelihood that Paula would willingly embrace treatment. Certainly not while she was still with Michael. Bob acknowledged her obsession with Michael and the improbability that Michael would find the lucidity from within that was required for change to occur. We concluded that we had to come up with something decisive and time was not on our side. Bob needed to think it through but for now his thoughts had to return to his daughter's birthday. We agreed to meet the next day.

Bob, Anita and I met at Paula's house; the children were at school. He paced up and down the sitting-room floorboards, combing his fingers through his hair. 'Okay, what the fuck am I going to do?' His attitude was quite different that day, fluctuating from frustration and anger to sadness and despair: 'The courts in this country don't give a toss about the fathers.' He told me about the Families Need Fathers charity. He had become involved around the time of his divorce and had become quite active in the movement. Bob said he had known from the start that something would go wrong and he wanted the best understanding of his options. He cited many cases similar to his own, where the father lost in court. The courts seemed always to rule in the mother's favour. 'If I seek custody, which could take months, I'll lose in the end, anyway,' he said, negatively. These were hardly the words of a man who thought he could influence judges, as Michael was convinced. This was a man unequivocally certain that he stood no chance of getting custody of the children, no matter what evidence was presented or how damning it would be of Paula and her lover.

Bob explained that, in order for a judge to take a speedy decision overturning the existing custody order, there needed to be concrete evidence that the children were in immediate danger. That would be the only circumstance to warrant an order to re-house them with their father. Drugs in the house were not enough, even if Anita, the cleaner and I all supported the claim. Welfare officers are always brought in, a lot of investigations made – all this took time, and time was what the children did not have.

I insisted that he had to do something and pointed out that if he could organize Live Aid to rescue Africa then he had to be able to rescue his own children. The wide-ranging conversation covered all the implications of action. Suffice it to say that we were clear that something had to be done. We had to get the girls out of that house, by any means possible that were legally binding. But how?

Anita suggested going to the papers.

Bob speculated that if the news of the drugs made it on to the front cover of all the papers, the judges would be forced to act in full view of the public and that might unsettle their adherence to the standard form. But Bob said that it was pure speculation. How would one engineer such a thing? The imponderables were too many, the chances of success too few. We had to try, though, whatever it took. And therefore it became the seed of the plan that we hatched together.

It was a complicated scheme that depended for its success on the pressure that the papers would exert on the sentiments of the judge. Therefore the court hearing had to coincide as closely as possible with the media exposé and there would have to be time for the story to be published before a hearing date was set. This was no mean challenge, for we would have no control over the date that the courts would give for the emergency hearing. Certainly the police would have to raid Paula's house for the drugs, and this was perhaps the most volatile component, because we could hardly influence their date and time of arrival, and there would be no warning. If the custody hearing went in Bob's favour, he could move the girls to safety and hold on to them. We only had a short time before Michael and Paula returned.

Bob told me that from now on I must tape all my calls. He told me where to get the kit and offered to hook it up for me.

He remained pessimistic about the success of this rickety plan, however. My contribution would be contact with the papers – the ultimate PR assignment, from which there would be no return. I could feel that this campaign would be my last, but that was fine by me.

In our plotting we imagined that we would get a date for the hearing and exactly two days before we would make a call to the drugs squad and inform the papers that this action had been taken. The police would turn up thereafter and the papers would be waiting to pounce. Thus the story would be run on the day that Bob marched into the High Court. Anita offered to make the trigger call that would set all this in motion. Bob's part was to get the court booked for a hearing, which in turn would set the date for Anita's call to the police. Bob went to see his solicitor.

———— ◆ ————

Matthew Wright knew this was too big for him as show business editor. He referred me to the editor. Two hours later I was in a blacked-out limousine on the way to the Isle of Dogs. In a private meeting our whole strategy was revealed. If the *Mirror* would help, they could have an absolute exclusive. The editor was grave, less fired-up by the potential of the story than he was sad at the outcome. He lamented that Paula had done this to herself, recalling her former brilliance in print and on the box. Though he was sceptical that the sensitive timing and coordination could be achieved, he was concerned enough for the children's sake and willing to help out where he could. He wasn't optimistic but he said if anything could shake Paula out of her oblivion, this would do the trick. I repeated that if something didn't change, they were going to die.

He called later and told me that they were bringing in an independent co-ordinator (a freelance journalist) to run the operation, but he remained unsure if it could be made to work.

Next day the freelancer called on behalf of the *Daily Mirror*. He understood that the deal was time-sensitive and asked if we could meet at my house? Two hours later he was sitting on my sofa. The interview lasted minutes and he gave no details. There would be no problem getting the drugs squad to turn up, but someone must willingly let them into the house. He said: 'If this doesn't get her off the drugs I don't know what will.' But he had no stake in Paula's life except a juicy scoop. The condition was that it remained a strict exclusive to the *Mirror*, no other paper was to be contacted or the deal was off. The unspoken rider was that he would have unlimited access to every facet of the story. It would run for days and I dreaded to think how long we would be in his debt...his only question was, 'When do we start?'

This meeting left me strangely shaken. I informed Bob of the progress and we both took a deep breath. The plan was on a stronger footing and now he could go forward with the legal arrangements. But I was nervous – our action to involve a national newspaper felt illegal. Bob reassured me by saying: 'All you've done is to talk to a good friend in the media. How was that illegal, compared to the corruption in which Paula and Michael have involved themselves? It didn't matter how it happened, the children must be saved.'

Bob's legal team had only days to prepare. We all had to make a trip to his solicitors to give our affidavits – Anita and her brother, the housekeeper and her boyfriend and myself. They had the Polaroids and Anita's deposition stretched to many pages, going back years. In the barrister's view, with the material danger the children had been in, it was the worst case of its kind he had ever seen.

The gravity of the meeting seemed to crystallize Bob's mood. He moved away from feeling sad and became angry that the case was so severe, and that his children were caught in the middle. He said that the legal action was going to cost him a mint, but he was not prepared to scrimp; he would spare no expense. And he didn't even hold out much hope that he was going to win, but if at best this action would frighten Paula into a clinic, it would be worth the money.

Bob's solicitor applied for the emergency temporary custody hearing, citing the evidence that the children were in mortal danger. And we all waited by the phone for the call that would set the court date. Without the hearing, within a window of opportunity that was rapidly closing, it would all be for nought.

The call came. I was liaising with the freelance journalist and, in turn, it appeared that he was liaising with the drugs squad. The 'drugs raid' would be a low-key affair, so as not to attract any outside attention, particularly from other papers. There would be two plain-clothes officers, dressed as if for a meeting. A time was arranged for the raid to occur. Anita requested that it happen when the children were not in the house. As I remember it was planned for about four o'clock in the afternoon, but the time kept changing at our end, working round the logistics of picking up our children from school, and Anita's availability to open the door to the police. The journalist complied and meanwhile built his back-story, asking how Bob was feeling and other emotive questions.

In spite of the importance of the scheme, we did appreciate that there were wider implications than the task at hand. There was a distribution network using sweet wrappers to disguise harmful narcotics possibly delivering to other households with children. I spoke to the journalist, encouraging him to expose the drug ring and its supporters. He said we'd left it a little late for such an operation; they would have to establish surveillance and follow the couriers, and the time for that had passed.

Bob collected all the children and took them home with him while the raid occurred. He had decided to drive the children to the Kent house in the dark later in the day, to have them clear of danger even before the hearing. Anita was at the house ready for the police to turn up. I was at home just in case any other paper spied the officers arriving at the house and called for a comment, to which I would have to say that they were there to check the gas meter. Anita called and said, 'The eagle has landed'. Even though she knew they were coming she found their physical presence so much of a shock that she hardly had to act her part. The police were polite and respectful, and searched the house while a WPC sat with Anita to calm her shaken nerves. Having easily found the stash, the policemen made a cursory search of the rest of the house and left.

Leaving a comfortable time buffer, I drove round to Bob's, all the way checking on the mobile with him that there would be no press outside his house, and no one following me. His sister and Jeanne were there helping with the children. There was an air of tense expectancy, like the calm before a storm – after all, the raid was merely the first step to rescuing the children, not an end in itself.

What took me by surprise was the sight of Pixie and Peaches cuddled up to Jeanne. Jeanne was exquisitely beautiful and very calm, gentle and loving, not exactly sure about what was going on but aware that her job was to reassure the children. They had clearly formed a close bond with her.

Bob's sister was angry, she said it had all been terrible for Bob, and recounted being at the house in Chelsea when Paula arrived to pick up anything she had left behind. She had pleaded with Paula not to take everything, at least to leave some pictures of the girls but Paula had been extraordinarily cold, and she had taken everything. She wanted the old Paula back – we all did.

We sat discussing the current action and were convinced that Paula could be railroaded into a clinic. It was not an attempt to get her into trouble nor take away her children forever, only until she got herself straightened out. Bob was adamant about this. Once Paula was in a good clinic she would thank us all – I'd seen that happen countless times, it was a natural by-product of the experience. The old Paula would have been in full support of what we were doing; she knew true friendship would engender this tough love approach.

That night Anita went with Bob and the children to Davington Priory. I left for my house with Tom and Sophie, assuring Bob that we had done the right thing. Anita stayed with the children while Bob returned to London and we kept in hourly contact, awaiting the morning papers, to see if the story had hit the front pages as promised.

At 1am a panic-stricken Anita called. Somehow she'd seen the *Mirror* – perhaps on a late-night current affairs show on TV or had bought it from an all-night petrol station – and we had not made the front page. Without the coverage, the hearing would be hit or miss. I called the freelance journalist and he said, coldly and calmly, 'I suggest you wait for the morning edition.' It was in print but they couldn't release it in the first edition because the other papers would have time to steal the story. Then he added ominously, 'I'll be speaking to you tomorrow.' Because, of course, having delivered his end of the bargain, he now owned everything we thought and felt thereafter.

———— ◆ ————

Meanwhile, on the other side of the world, Paula, Michael and Tiger were being lauded as 'Australia's royal family'. As in London, their every sneeze was public property and reason enough for a mention in the papers. Paula was outraging the locals by breast-feeding Tiger in restaurants – so much so that a couple of columnists consulted Debrett's and found that: 'It is bad manners to expel any liquid from any orifice in public, and breast-feeding is no different.' Though one of them did go on to say: 'This is from a journal representing a society where the aristocracy's idea of expressing affection is to suck each other's toes.'

Michael was there primarily to start the publicity machine for the forthcoming INXS album. This was an eagerly awaited event all over the world, and nowhere more so than in Australia. When asked about his lengthy absence from the rock scene, Michael said: 'We all have our wilderness years, whether it's drugs, alcohol, lack of fame, whatever.' He said his experience of fame had been 'horrifying'. 'You lose control of the perception of one's self – you become a cartoon,' he said. 'In fact what happens is you are no longer a human being.'

Michael's paranoia concerning Bob pervaded his conversation. At supper with the only girl he had ever told his mother he would marry, his business advisor and others, Michael became animated in his damnation of his nemesis. He was still fixated in his belief that in British society Bob's knighthood and sainthood made him unassailable, and afforded him influence over the press and the law.

On that visit Michael's mother Patricia Glassop recalls in her book a party at the house of the INXS publicist. She was sitting with Paula on a sofa and Paula quietly announced to her that Michael had asked her to marry him. Patricia was taken aback to hear the news in such an unofficial manner, but she went into the next room to congratulate her son. Michael just laughed, and said, 'That's silly, she's just having you on. We're not getting married.' Far from throwing himself into domestic life, Michael sent Paula back to the hotel with his mother, while he partied on.

On the night of the drugs bust, they'd been out at the opening of Sydney's first Imax cinema. When Anita called Paula to tell her about all the drama that was happening, she caught them after the function. Paula said vaguely, 'Oh, that's nice...' and Michael came on the phone, saying, 'We love you Anita...' – the Ecstasy response to everything. When we saw the pictures that reached the British press a day or so later, Paula and Michael were walking up a red carpet, Tiger's head was covered in a leopard-print chiffon veil (the couple were still aware of the value of baby photos), and the couple looked loaded.

Bob was sombre. Though it was not his child and, one could say, a bit of a sore point for him, he felt the pathos of Tiger's life. His kids were safe, he said, and they had a large family with Anita and Anita's family (who were fond of the Geldof girls) as well but Tiger had nobody. Except, he thought, Michael's family, but Bob was confused: did Michael's family know what was going on, did they know that Michael was deeply into drugs and that Tiger would be in danger. I asked Bob right then if by some miracle Tiger's parents were both admitted to a clinic, would he look after her, and he said yes, as if it were the most natural thing in the world.

On the morning of Thursday 26 September, the front pages of the

Mirror carried the whole story, revealing for the first time the extent of Paula and Michael's involvement with drugs. Of course, the amount that was found at the house far exceeded what would normally be deemed as personal consumption, so the charge could be harsh.

The story dominated morning TV, the news and the radio as I took the children to school. My phones had been ringing non-stop since 6am, but I was returning no calls. When I arrived at the children's school, it was under siege by the press hoping to catch Bob with the children. When I got home the house was being door-stepped by about five reporters.

When news of the drugs bust broke in Australia, Paula and Michael maintained a stoical front and professed to have no idea what was going on. Mandy, Rhett's wife, observed that Michael seemed extremely stressed by the news. Paula was adamant that this was Bob seeking leverage to take Tiger away from them. Patricia remembered suggesting that she could see the case for his own children, but Bob would surely have no claim on Tiger. But Michael could not see this logic; his neurosis about Bob fuelled his conviction that Tiger was within easy reach of the long arm of Geldof.

Paula and Michael immediately issued a statement through their solicitor, saying: 'The news has come as a complete surprise to them both. Paula and Michael have received no contact of any kind from the police and they wish to make no further comment.'

In articles carried by most of the papers, Bob said: 'I've just learned about the raid. I don't know anything about it. I'm trying to find out more. I have nothing to say.'

And Miss Yates's manager, Gerry Agar, said: 'I'm aware of the situation and will be speaking to Paula as soon as I can.'

Paula's solicitor called Bob and it was arranged that as soon as Paula returned she would be able to visit the children. Paula announced that she was coming back to London, and constantly complained about having to leave Tiger behind as she was still breastfeeding. We learned later that Paula and Michael were scared that Tiger would be taken into care if she returned to Britain with her mother.

That night INXS presented their new single, 'Searching', at the ARIA awards. It could have been a fitting metaphor for the band's search for a new sound, and it certainly held portentous undertones for the situation back in London, but the lyrics seemed to have more in common with Michael's search for happiness with Paula: *If you could face the pain and I could do the same, it would be clear tomorrow, but would it start, but will it start, again?*

About ten hours later in London, Bob was at the High Court and he obtained the temporary custody order we had hoped for.

———— ◆ ————

Shortly after the drugs bust a surprise call came from my PR friend. He asked me a very curious question: was I being motivated by a desire to be vindictive? 'Vindictive about what?' I asked. 'Because Paula let you down with the work that you lined up for her,' he replied.

The turn of the conversation had me on my guard so I switched on my recording device. In the last conversation we'd had he had been scathing about Paula and Michael, even stating that he would never take a child of his own to their house. I said that planting drugs in Paula's house would be pretty extreme revenge for her lack of enthusiasm, and that Paula and Michael's attempts to lay the blame elsewhere were typical of addicts when cornered.

Then I had a conversation on the phone with the film producer, but his angle was slightly different. 'How do you know that Anita might not have a vendetta against Paula?' he posited. He was well aware of the circumstances of the drugs discovery because I had called him to ask if he knew what opium looked like. 'We're hardly going to be planting a drug that we have never seen, let alone one that's expensive and almost impossible to get hold of,' I replied, but he was not convinced.

Bob's reaction was to say, 'These people are just another bunch of Paula's fucking sycophants, Gerry.' He'd seen them before, he said; for years he'd seen these clusters rise around her and he'd tried to warn her before of these 'Rasputins' in her midst.

Next day, the drugs squad came to take a statement. I was questioned by an officer with chiselled good looks, an all-year tan and the classic undercover cop uniform of leather jacket and jeans, prompting Bob's nickname for him – 'the film extra'.

Our police officer told me that his team had clearly shaken Anita and he'd felt sorry for her. His companion, a young WPC who was taking notes, said that she had sat with Anita to calm her nerves while the house was searched. But it had not been the enormous stash of opium and the S & M snaps of Paula and Michael that had shocked the police the most – it was the state of Anita's living conditions. Both officers looked appalled as they described a damp basement box room, with threadbare carpet, and peeling wallpaper, a camp bed and all Anita's clothes in carrier-bags, while the rest of the house displayed 'sheikh chic', as Paula had described it.

'You wouldn't treat your dog like that,' the film extra said to me, 'let alone the person you've employed to look after your kids. What kind of people would let someone live like that in their house? And with all their money?' But the officer was as excited as a policeman ever gets. He said that they'd always known there was a drugs racket that supplied the showbiz world, but they could never get anyone to talk. This would be the first time anyone had come forward and offered to work with the police to get a conviction. But he wasn't over-optimistic. He said, unlike 'the man on the street' who couldn't afford proper representation, celebrities have the funds to hire the best possible team, and it was probable that Michael and Paula would get off. But he did feel it would scare them into rethinking the way that they had been conducting their lives, and that, for us, would be a result.

My contacts in the press were all sympathetic, particularly as I rammed home the danger to the children. The prevailing sentiment seemed to be: it's not our business. Even the most cynical and resistant among them began to get my point, but something else of import was emerging. Rumours round the desks had been intensifying, and in their opinion the story had been only days from being bust wide open by the papers anyway. That opinion was substantiated by other sources too.

My house was still under siege and the phones ringing constantly. On Friday 27 September I made a formal statement to the press: 'I wish to make it plain that with immediate effect I have terminated my business relationship with Paula Yates.' More than anything, the announcement was to give them the message that I had nothing further to say or do on the subject, so they would leave me alone.

Though our mission had been a success, it was far from over. The emergency custody decision had been granted as routine in a thirty-minute hearing. There would be a full custody action in a few days' time, for which Paula was coming back from Australia. Meanwhile life was far from returning to normal. I had the faint impression I was being watched; lenses poked out of cars, photographers took snaps while I chatted in the playground and I arrived home to find someone going through my bins.

On Sunday 29 September a tabloid carried a front cover story that claimed I had been with Paula in a nightclub and witnessed a drug transaction between her and Steve Strange. It featured an 'interview' with me that had been cobbled together from a previous phone call when I had told them what I knew about the drugs. I'd never met Steve Strange.

Later, I happened to discuss it with a close media contact and she said she had read it and it didn't stand up, particularly the line that read: 'Such are her feelings on the issue that she did not request and nor did we offer payment for her heartbreaking insights into the scandal' – a strangely honest statement, which I could only surmise carried a legal rider.

In hindsight the article did me a very particular favour. Within it I was quoted verbatim, saying of Paula: 'The awful, awful thing is that she doesn't realize that she is going to kill herself.' That statement could have been devalued by the surrounding inventions, but the message was picked up by other papers, and repeated in subsequent interviews. *Hello!* agreed to print the truth: that I witnessed no drugs deals with Paula and Michael. I waived my fee, missing out on thousands of pounds.

Subsequently, Steve Strange took the paper to court and won the case –

his lawyer obtained a transcript of my conversation with them, proving I had never made those claims.

On Monday 30 September, Paula was on TV striding through Heathrow's Terminal 2. It was the new sleek, chic, bobbed, supermodel, Prada Paula – she looked stunning and very together. She said that Tiger wasn't feeling very well and had remained in Australia with Michael's mother. But before she was whisked away by a solicitor, two minders and a chauffeur, she slammed the allegations against her and Michael saying: 'We've had Live Aid, now we are getting Lie Aid.'

Back in Redburn Street, Paula had apparently mislaid her keys, but claimed that Bob had left her with none. Locksmiths broke into the house and changed the locks, no doubt to bar Anita and Bob from further access. Her solicitor said: 'When we were in there we discovered that the back door had been left open and we wanted to check whether anything had been added or taken away from the premises.' Why would anything have been added to the premises?

Paula went straight to Kent to visit the children. I was in contact with the household through Bob, who told me that when Paula arrived, she looked distraught. The removal of the girls from her house and the forthcoming custody hearing had her almost breaking down with the fear that she was losing her children. Bob's heart went out to her and he extended every care that she would accept. Seeing Paula that day Bob was convinced that the exercise had already been a success and he told me he was sure that, after this shock, she would sort herself out. Nevertheless, he was determined to stand by the spirit of our action and give Paula an ultimatum that if she didn't heed the warnings to get professional help, he would continue to do his damnedest to ensure the children's safety.

I was on the M4 when Paula called me on my mobile. The phone kept cutting out and, consequently, when she managed to get through again she was begging me not to hang up. She was hysterical. I told her that it had been impossible to talk to her about these recent events. She denied that she had received any call from us. Michael had obviously returned to London, as I could hear him in the background shouting that Bob planted the drugs and that his whole life was in ruins – he would not be allowed into America with a drugs conviction. Paula tried to reassure him; she sounded calm and in control when she was talking to Michael, saying 'I'm going to sort this out.' But back on the phone to me she totally lost it, blaming everyone else for the drugs. Paula was not going to let anything affect their relationship, so her icy resolve took control.

Bob told me that he had taken a similar call, except that Paula was blaming Anita and her brother for planting the drugs. Bob told her not to be so stupid; Anita wouldn't know how to obtain drugs if she wanted to, or even know what they looked like.

When Michael called me later, I could feel his desperate tension. 'Why didn't you just put the drugs back?' he asked, direct and clear. 'Put them back where?' I replied, amazed by his obtuse reasoning. Was he saying I should have ignored the opium, hidden it so the children couldn't find it, so we could all carry on with our lives as if nothing was wrong? 'You know I would never harm those children,' he argued. 'Not intentionally,' I replied, 'but what if the girls had tried a tablet?' 'They have never come to harm. Paula loves those kids, you know that, Gerry.' Michael's tone was hardening with each volley and I continued to press him on the dangers: 'They haven't come to harm because you had Anita and Dina (the housekeeper) making damn sure. How would you feel if Tiger was visiting a house where drugs were left in easy reach? Would you take her back there? Would you turn a blind eye?' Michael ignored my questions; instead he continued bemoaning the effect all this was having on Paula. He kept dodging the questions: about Bob's rights to be a concerned father, about the changes to their personalities and about both of them getting professional help. 'Why have you sided with Bob now? What has Paula done to you?' asked Michael, failing to grasp what I was trying to say.

'It's what she's doing to herself, Michael. You know she's not the same person anymore. It's heartbreaking to see what's happened to her.' I was almost at breaking point – a mixture of anger and mourning overwhelming me. 'Why can't you see what you are doing? Why don't you wake up?' I asked him earnestly. Desperately I begged him to look closer at everything that was happening in his life and think – what was true and what was fantasy? 'Come on, Michael, you're a bright guy,' I said, 'None of it adds up.' I remember a pause. He was silent and I became hopeful that a glimmer of clarity had penetrated his paranoia and denial. Eventually he said, 'I can see that there's no point continuing with this conversation.'

I received another call from Paula, but this time I didn't give her a chance to speak. I repeated almost word for word what I had said to Michael. I was angry and I told her, 'You of all people – you would never have knowingly put the girls at risk, what's happened to you?' I reminded her that other children visited the house and I said I thought that they were both very selfish and self-absorbed, and the call had to end because I burst into tears, an outpouring of all the stress that had built up over the last two weeks.

◆

A contact in the press told me of a rumour going round the desks that the drugs in Paula's house had been planted and that I had a grudge against Paula because she had sacked me. It would have been almost amusing had it not had such ominous undertones. Bob, Anita and I were astounded; in all the endless talks about our action, we thought we must have covered every angle, but we never considered for a second that the finger of suspicion might be pointed at us.

Bob said he had already been asked if he had planted them himself. He asked me if I had any idea who might be spreading this rumour. One thing was for sure, Paula must have been close behind whoever it was, keeping her hands well clean. It was pretty clear that she was not going to take our action lying down. Our fear was that with the outward denial of the facts would come an inner denial to herself, thereby making it easy to talk herself out of needing any help. No one seemed to be taking much notice of the yarn, but I knew the story would find its way into print in no time.

Meanwhile my Vauxhall Corsa was being vandalized. First I came out to find my windscreen wipers had been bent back and crossed over. Then the side mirrors were snapped off. Also, someone was calling the house phone and leaving no message. I was picking it up only to hear silence, or perhaps breathing, on the other end of the line. I called Mr PR for help and advice. I was finding all this very stressful now. I needed to hear a friendly voice that had always been a reliable source of comfort and reassurance.

There was a slight harshness, a coldness in his response. I sat in numb silence as he told me that he was extremely disappointed by my behaviour. That he was going to stand by Paula and Michael and he had no sympathy for me whatsoever. I could only reply, 'I don't understand.'

He told me that Michael was a very influential man, that he couldn't afford to have his career wrecked by this scandal and that if he was convicted on a drugs charge he would be unable to visit the States again.

Thereafter, the call did not go the way I expected at all. He denied all knowledge of Michael's drug-taking and became increasingly threatening and abusive. I realized that he had been given the impression that I had mentioned the names of others in my affidavit. I assured him that this was not the case, but he reasserted that I would be ruined and all of Michael and Paula's friends would rally around them and ensure a very bad press for me. I refused to give in to this bullying and withdraw my statement and brought the conversation to a stop. I was also relieved that I had taped it and that my friend Liz, who was with me at the time, had witnessed it too.

Liz put her arms around me and I burst into tears. She called the police straight away. They arrived a couple of hours later to take statements from both her and myself. The rumours of drug planting were building up by the minute. Journalists were leaving messages asking for comments on the new allegations and I was given information about one of the people who were leaving messages on the editors' desks.

Bob consoled me. 'Take no notice,' he said. 'It's all part of the madness; it's laughable and it only matters that your friends know that you wouldn't be involved without good reason; the rest can go to hell.'

A newspaper ran a story hinting that Paula was framed. This was the first time it was actually printed and it was clear that the counter-campaign to destroy our reputations was gaining pace. Had I not maintained my contacts in the press, we would neither know what was happening, nor have any chance of retaliation.

Bob was bullish in his insistence that I refrain from speaking to the press, and he and I had our first clash. I told him that I wouldn't be framed as an accomplice to something so evil and I would protect my reputation and give an interview if necessary. It was imperative, I felt, that we attempt to stop this campaign. I challenged him point blank with my belief that I had every right to answer the allegations against me and that while he had a halo to protect him, there was blood in the water and it was oozing from me. Bob exploded, insisting I comply with his strategy of dignified silence, and I felt the full force of his domineering personality.

I knew the editor of *Now!*, a celebrity and lifestyle magazine, and I offered them a brief interview. On the phone I was careful to limit the information that I gave, implicating no one else. The main drive of my message was that someone was going to end up dead. They asked me if I had seen Paula and Michael taking drugs, but I wouldn't be drawn on the details; I emphasized that my priority was to protect the children.

On 2 October the piece came out, featured on the front cover...
GERRY AGAR SAYS, 'SOMEONE IS GOING TO DIE.'

When I found I had a flat tyre, I thought my run of wretched luck with the car was continuing. But it was only when the tyre was slashed again, and a note was left under my repaired windscreen wiper, saying 'You'll Be Next' in letters cut from a newspaper, that I realized I was being targeted. Following the silences on the other end of my phone, my stalker started to reveal himself. The calls came late at night when my nerves were at their weakest. With grave menace the voice would say, 'You're dead', then ring off. A day later he would say, 'Better watch out', or 'You know what to do to stop all of this'. In no time I was jumping at the ring of the phone, terrified to pick up, scared to retrieve my messages.

As well as reporting the incidents to the police, I told all my contacts in the press about the threats. I became nervous of going home and, while Bob had his country house in which to hide if he were feeling under pressure, I took to calling in on friends in the area. The next instalment of Paula and Michael's claims was so outrageous that I confessed to Bob that I had nearly wet my knickers when I heard it: Anita and I were having a lesbian affair. I took Bob's advice and called his solicitor.

'Bob's very concerned for you,' he told me. 'What's being going on?' I told him that the tyres on my car had been slashed five times, the paintwork had been scratched with a key from front to back several times, and I had a note through my door that read, 'You're dead, Agar'. For some reason the use of my name made it even more terrifying and immediate. Then I had come out of my house one morning to take Tom and Sophie to school, and sitting on my bonnet was a papier-mâché Satan-head the size of a football. It had devil horns, ugly black markings, and it seemed to embody pure evil. With it was a note that just said 'Bitch'. 'This is disgraceful,' Bob's solicitor said. 'Bob's told me that he knew there'd be risks involved, but he's been really appalled by what's been happening to you. Nobody could have predicted this – I'm really sorry.' His advice was to keep the evidence and inform the police of each incident. He repeated that I could call on him whenever I needed to.

Finally I had to face my ex-husband with the news of Sophie handling the opium. 'I hope they lock them up and throw away the key,' he said. He told me that the children should not be exposed to my problems and he was right. I knew that I would have reacted in exactly the same way if I had known that he was living my life, but I didn't want Sophie to be sent away to boarding school as a result. 'I'll talk to him,' Bob offered. 'I'm really sorry about all of this, Gerry.'

14 'will we regret this?'

A PRELIMINARY HEARING FOR THE official custody battle for the Geldof girls would start on 3 October. Bob again made it clear to Paula that if she were to get help for her drug problem, the children would be waiting for her at home. But she was in deep denial, refusing to concede that she had any problem; instead she asserted that this was a conspiracy to ruin her and Michael. She was defiant: it would never succeed and she would prove it in court.

When Paula arrived at the High Court, she was weeping into her dark glasses. A mob of press blocked the entrance, forcing Paula's bodyguard to manhandle her into the building and she wandered away, comforted by her legal team. Bob found a back entrance and the two faced up in the courtroom, avoiding one another's gaze. Almost immediately the judge, Mrs Justice Hale, imposed an injunction on the case, preventing publication of any detail about the proceedings.

Bob called me saying that he had heard worrying rumours. 'What's all this about you taking 'Es'?' I assured him that I had only ever smoked weed and I suggested that he offer the court my willingness to take a drug test. His lawyers booked hospital appointments for Bob, Anita, Dina and me to take the test.

Paula maintained to anyone who would listen that Anita and I had planted the drugs. Our motivation, she said, was that Anita was about to be sacked, I was owed expenses and Dina was going out with Anita's brother's best friend. She showed people the *Now!* magazine interview I had just given, and pointed to the picture of me taken in my home, in which I perched on a sofa draped in an Indian fabric she had given me when she was moving from Clapham. Paula claimed that the fabric had been draped on her bed when I had planted the drugs and that I had stolen it at the same time!

By the end of five days in court everyone was understandably exhausted. The case had not gone well for Bob: the worst though, he told us, was seeing Paula so distressed; she cried continuously and pleaded with him not to take her children away from her. Our hearts went out to her and Anita said that she would go back to Paula immediately if Paula asked her to.

The case closed on 10 October with a complicated compromise in which the custody of the children was shared, mediated by welfare officers.

'Why has she done this to herself, why, why?' Bob kept repeating. He told Anita and me that he was convinced Paula would never take drugs again and spoke of how wretched he felt at having to force such a drastic action. 'Will we regret this?' Bob asked me. 'She hates us now,' I replied, 'but if she really gets herself clean, she'll be clear-headed, enough perhaps to see that we were looking after her best interests.' 'Where's the old Paula gone?' Bob reflected sadly. 'She used to be such a fantastic mum.'

Bob was disappointed, feeling that shared custody was not the result for which we had worked so hard, but his lawyer insisted that the outcome had been excellent, almost legal history in the making. He could have lost, but instead the children were one step away from being wards of court, which meant that if there was cause for further action, it would be a mere formality for him to gain total custody and control. In the end the one who really lost out was Anita. She had been ostracized by Paula, and Bob would not let her stay with him in London. Instead he offered her the opportunity to stay in Davington Priory.

It was October, the beginning of winter, when Anita moved her stuff into Bob's draughty old house out in Kent. She told me that she was broke. Bob said he was moving on, and told her that she must move on too, suggesting that she get herself a job and a new life. But Anita insisted that she had to remain in the house so that the girls would not think that she had abandoned them. 'I promised Peaches and I will never break that promise,' Anita repeated.

In another call Bob told me that Michael's Australian solicitor had flown over and asked for a meeting. Bob was curious as to the purpose of the visit. The solicitor informed him that he needn't worry about Tiger, that she had been ill but all her problems had been sorted out. Why would he jet halfway round the world to tell Bob that? He asked Bob not to seek custody of Tiger, and reiterated that any fears he might have had for the little girl were allayed. This was the final clue that convinced us that Paula had been telling Michael that Bob was seeking custody of Tiger along with the other girls. We could never confirm this, but it fitted the pattern of Paula's fabrications, designed to motivate Michael into action or keep him bound to her.

'But it's all going to be okay now, Paula has told me that she has even come off the Prozac,' Bob told me. 'Really?' I replied, amazed that he was so easily convinced. 'I think calling her an "addict" was a little strong, Gerry. I know she's really sorted out now. She still hates Anita, of course, and your name's mud, but it's the kids that matter,' Bob said. I tried to explain that if she still hated us then she still blamed us; therefore she had not taken responsibility for herself, and without that she could never get clean. I went as far as rubbishing the possibility of Paula coming off everything so quickly without a great deal of help and a complete absence of temptation. 'What about Michael?' I asked. 'Is he clean too?' 'He's going to get his act sorted out as well,' Bob assured me.

After the custody case was settled, a piece appeared in a paper in which Paula tried to clear her name of the drugs charges, insisting that they had been planted by enemies out to destroy her. This followed the news of her arrest and subsequent bail. The drugs squad questioned her for about an hour and the mainstay of her statement was: 'When I went away, they weren't there. Somebody must have planted them.' A source close to Paula said: 'She was quite happy telling her side of the story. She maintains the drugs aren't hers. She has named names and won't take this lying down.'

The senior officer in charge was most spooked by Paula. Bob told me that throughout the proceedings she remained blank and indifferent, apparently ignoring their dialogue, but the moment they made a mistake she pounced on it. It was extraordinary, the film extra told Bob. Her memory for detail and her quickness to jump on the slightest mistake made him realize that she had been listening to every word all along. Bob told the officer that he wasn't at all surprised and even found it amusing. 'Wait till you see her in court,' Bob had said.

Although we agreed that Paula would undoubtedly run circles around the police and their legal team, we had begun to admit to being nervous about the case. Bob told me that Michael was bringing with him an army of the best barristers and that he had been warned that it was highly likely he and Paula would get off with a caution. For Bob the work had been done. He was convinced that they would get their act sorted out. I wondered if he was reconsidering his involvement as a witness.

With the conclusion of the custody case came the inescapable involvement of the welfare officers. These local council social workers were appointed to assess the family's ongoing situation and to mediate any ensuing acrimony until they were convinced that a settled routine had been established, and that the children were safe from excessive trauma.

The girls had been assigned to Paula during the week, and to Bob on Tuesdays and weekends. It was proposed and agreed that the two younger children, Peaches and Pixie, must continue at Newton Prep, because they needed the continuity. Fifi refused to leave Bob, even against Bob's encouragement that she must have a relationship with Paula, and must give her a chance. He told all the girls that they had to see their mother. To him, it seemed that any mother was better than no mother. But the welfare officers decided that it would be more appropriate to send Fifi to the security of boarding school, away from the acrimony and instability. From the moment the court case ended and thereafter, Paula vowed that Anita would have nothing to do with the children ever again.

The welfare officers fully supported Paula's request for more time to adjust to the new situation and told Bob that the children needed to rebuild a relationship with their natural mother, without the interference of any other guardian – namely Anita. But Bob intervened, particularly on Peaches's behalf; he argued that no contact would do more harm than good, so it was agreed that Anita could see the girls one day per month.

Anita spent the whole winter on her own, counting the hours until her monthly day would come, and fretting that Peaches would think she'd been deserted again. Even when she could enjoy the company of the children she had brought up and protected, Bob would not let her stay overnight – she had to sleep on friends' sofas when the girls came to the Priory.

Meanwhile, on that one day every month, Paula would call repeatedly, screaming. If she heard the dog barking in the background (Anita was looking after Flossy because Paula had always hated the dog), she would shout, 'What's that fat bitch doing there?' Bob would remind her that it was part of the agreement, and he would assure her that Anita was not staying the night.

The welfare officers were visiting once a week and would interview the girls separately. They became aware of Peaches's daily letters to Anita, begging to see her and finally realized the effect that not seeing her nanny was having on the little girl. After about three or four months they gave the order for the children to see Anita a further afternoon, every two weeks, at Bob's house for tea.

Michael spent Thanksgiving with his sister Tina and she reports in her book that inevitably his conversation turned to the drugs bust and his perpetual antipathy towards Bob Geldof. Michael continued to maintain that it was Bob who had planted the drugs in an attempt to snatch custody of Tiger, and he claimed to have private investigators staking the house who could prove it.

In London the intense speculation that surrounded the drugs bust burbled along in the press. We awaited the outcome of the forensic tests on the substances found in the house. We had regular contact with the drugs squad and the Crown Prosecution Service, and there was distinct apprehension about their proposed action. But I experienced no relief from the campaign of intimidation that was still being waged against me.

I was cut dead by mutual friends. The phone threats found me at Liz's house every few days and I had been told by my stalker: 'You're dead, your life is going to be a misery', but he said the harassment would stop if I retracted my statement about the drugs. And I was having to park my car a few streets away to avoid the ritual vandalism and pernicious notes.

One day, I called by my house in a hurry to pick up Tom's sweater and get him back to school. I sent him to grab it, telling him to go up and tell Marlin, my *au pair*, that I would not be back that night, but at the last minute I told him not to bother. Twenty-four hours later I was to realize the fortuitousness of that random decision. The next evening I was going to a function and had to dash home to change. The house was dark and quiet. Assuming that Marlin had gone out, I didn't shout up to her room. I was puzzled to find the house untidy and the kitchen sink full of dirty plates. This was most unusual: Marlin was always meticulous with her chores.

I walked into her bedroom and turned on the light. Marlin was lying on the bed naked. Way before I finished saying, 'Are you all right, Marlin?' I realized that she was blue and lying spread-eagled with her mouth open. Then the stench in the room hit me. In a blind pumping panic I ran back down the stairs, falling most of the way. I phoned 999 and screamed at the emergency services to get an ambulance round. The ambulance arrived and I shouted hysterically for them to hurry upstairs before it was too late. When they came back down they told me she was dead, but my mind just wouldn't accept it. In fact she had been dead for two days.

Within minutes the house filled with police and the road was cordoned off. I sat in my living room convulsed by shivers, while the police tried to interview me. The officer in charge was gruff, clearly suspecting I was involved. With delusional insistence I said I was sure she would be revived in hospital.

When Bob heard about Marlin's death, he could not believe what was happening. He was totally spooked, saying, 'This is a head-fuck.' He winced at the thought that my son could have discovered her naked body sprawled over the bed. In the light of the death threats I had received we were all drawing obvious conclusions – perhaps they'd thought Marlin was me. 'The rumour is that I killed her,' I told Bob. 'And I heard it was Paula,' he replied. He asked how on earth I was getting through all this. 'I'm praying!' I replied.

I returned to Liz's house and collapsed completely. In my post-traumatic state I found that I could not countenance the idea of taking off my overcoat. I took myself to bed, refusing any offer of assistance from Liz. There I lay, on top of the bed, with the main light on. My eyes would not close and my brain would not shut off, constantly replaying the sight I had witnessed several hours before – someone I loved who'd been part of our family. Liz and Anita suggested that I should see a doctor.

For three days I did not sleep. I would drop off but instantly wake again in a panic. And I could not remove my overcoat for a week: it seemed to be my final line of defence against this crazy world I was in. Liz took over. She drove my children to school, she liaised with Bob and my ex-husband, organized my PR accounts and took all my threatening phone calls.

Naturally Marlin's death was all over the papers. The police remained baffled by the cause of death and a post mortem was ordered. The news went out on Swedish national TV connected with the Paula and Michael story, and Marlin's parents were forced to make an announcement denying the rumour that she had been killed. The news of Marlin's death seemed to fuel the 'arsenic club' – as I had now come to think of Paula's cronies – with more ammunition. Friends in the press phoned to tell me that they were getting anonymous calls saying that I had killed my nanny to stop her from talking because she knew too much. Neighbours told me that the press were camping outside my house and when I arrived at school they were there in force. As the pack closed in around the car, my daughter said to me, 'Being famous isn't nice, is it, Mummy?'

Any attempt to return to my house was futile; when I broke through the pack I couldn't even turn the key in the lock – my hands began to shake and I felt sheer terror. I was now living permanently at Liz's house and wondering if I would be able to cope with another day.

The police were satisfied that I had not been involved with Marlin's death, but the press were hopeful that it would lead to the next juicy instalment in the Paula and Michael show. The papers ran tentative reports on the death but for legal reasons and, I hoped, for the sake of good taste, there were no speculations about the cause of death. While awaiting the results of the autopsy I had to endure what turned into weeks of insinuation and whispering in the corridors at school, and a friend told me that the gossip was: 'Did you hear, Gerry Agar killed her nanny?' It went on for six weeks. The complicated autopsy finally found that Marlin was suffering from a rare heart condition, of which she had not even been aware.

When Bob had not heard from me for a week, he called Liz.

'Gerry's mother died. She's just come back from officially identifying her body,' my friend informed him, while I sat on the sofa unable to speak. In the space of a couple of weeks I had identified two dead bodies, and I was fighting for my sanity. 'I can't believe all of this,' Bob said. 'I'm really sorry, call me if there's anything I can do.' Anita offered to move in with us. Bob agreed that we could probably do with the help. My doctor suggested anti-depressants and I finally gave in to a course of Prozac. Within a week I could report similar feelings to those Paula might have experienced and that the drug did have side effects.

The Prozac caused me to wake up in a bed soaked in sweat, so that I had to wrap myself in large towels before I lay down. After ten days the drug kicked in, but it left me feeling numb. It was as if it had blocked off all my feelings, and I experienced panic and depression if I mixed the wonder drug with drink. I decided to come off the Prozac a few months later, when I discovered that I was pregnant. It wasn't easy and I vowed never to use the drug again. On 23 November the police forensic tests were completed on the substances Anita had found at the house in Redburn Street, confirming it was opium.

That December Michael was with INXS out in the desert near LA, shooting the video for the album's first single with the celebrated director Walter Stern. Michael had just spent a gruelling couple of months in LA promoting *Elegantly Wasted*, amid the band's fears that their re-emergence was not exciting the kind of interest that they had been used to.

It was clear from the interviews Michael gave that he was concerned with the band's direction. 'I don't know where we fit in now,' he said in one interview. With the general insecurity surrounding the album, the record company Polygram decided that the release should be postponed until March to avoid the inevitable competition at Christmas with higher profile acts. The band opted to use the intervening period for an intensive global publicity drive. Michael and his band brothers had never before been told that their album would have to wait to be released, so this was a testing time for all of their egos. Though most of the band members had been musically dormant for the three years since their last album, they were all keen to hit the road again. Their credibility was at stake and so was their future together.

Paula, Michael and the three younger girls were spending Christmas in Australia. While the couple complained to the Australian press about their persecution in London, professing their delight in the Australian welcome, Bob told me he was taking a rest, but was nervous of their return.

'You know, she never gave one present to Fifi at Christmas,' Bob told me. 'The two little ones had loads; it really hurt Fifi, but I made it up to her as far as I could.'

I could only wonder at such a drastic transformation in my former friend that she would punish her daughter's rebellion in such a hurtful way. The girls had been allowed to see Anita for a day before they had left for Australia, and Anita was both overjoyed to snatch a few hours with them and sad to see them go.

'The girls have told me that Paula and Michael are getting married out there; what do you think? They've even packed their bridesmaids' dresses, but they've been sworn to secrecy,' Anita told me.

15 in excess

WHILE MICHAEL WAS ON HIS publicity tour in early 1997, Paula tried unsuccessfully to cope on her own with a baby and two children, the ongoing legal dispute with Bob, her still disastrous finances, the impending drugs charge, the perpetual absence of her lover, and the constant intrusion of the welfare officers. It was to this maelstrom that Michael would have to return, if he wanted to see Tiger. Otherwise, he was globetrotting through a stream of radio interviews, TV appearances and numerous showcase performances trying to garner interest in the new album. Michael told the press of his joy with fatherhood, how much he loved Paula and how difficult it was to be away from his family. In one revealing interview Michael was asked if the pressure over the past two years could have had serious implications on his emotional well-being. He said:

> Yes, it could, but, you know, I guess I'm stronger than I realized. I've got important people to take care of here. People and children. I've got to make sure that everyone's OK. When you're very young, in your teens and 20s, you're basically useless to society. It's just, 'Heads down, let's go!' But eventually you start to raise your head above the horizon a bit and other things start to come into view and you realize that there are other things in life apart from yourself.

Paula's hysteria continued and the welfare officers reported that she was threatening suicide. I felt sure that she had never stopped taking drugs. There were sightings of the children on the street on their own after dark. Stories of hysterics abounded. The teachers at school reported that the children were turning up with dirty uniforms, homework not done and matted hair.

The rumours began to circulate that Michael was going to leave Paula. Bob was convinced that he never would: 'They're too alike,' he said, 'peas in a pod, twins.' But for a while we were hopeful – if Michael left, Paula would have lost the person she obsessed about; perhaps then she could be coerced into a clinic. All the redeemed alcoholics and drug addicts at the twelve-step meetings described hitting rock-bottom. This was a final event that somehow punctured their pride and signalled to their brain that they were sorely in need of help. It might be a failed suicide attempt, or a failed business, a failed marriage or bankruptcy. More often it was the final collapse of every support system in their lives, but in their recovery, they

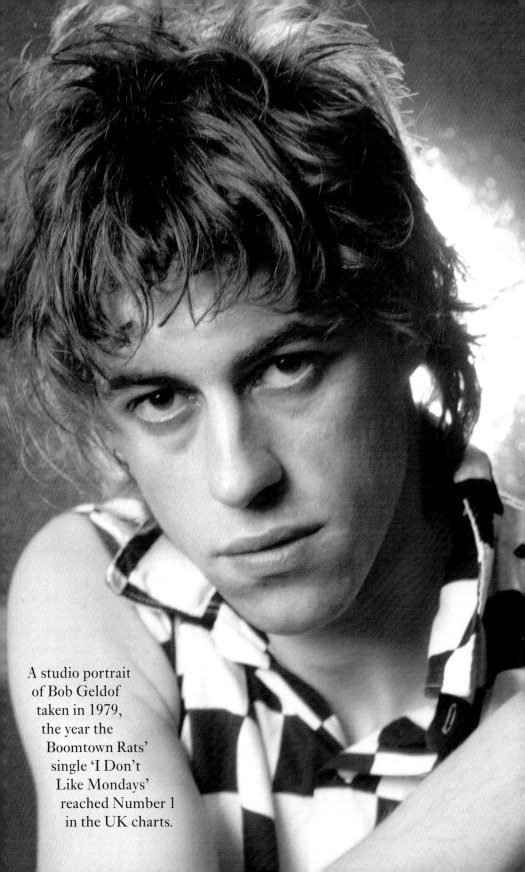

A studio portrait
of Bob Geldof
taken in 1979,
the year the
Boomtown Rats'
single 'I Don't
Like Mondays'
reached Number 1
in the UK charts.

The Prince and Princess of Wales joined Bob, Paula and Fifi at the London Live Aid concert at Wembley Stadium on 13 July 1985.

The live concerts in London and Philadelphia were linked by satellite and beamed around the world to millions of viewers.

Bob worked tirelessly behind the scenes to ensure Live Aid went as smoothly as possible.

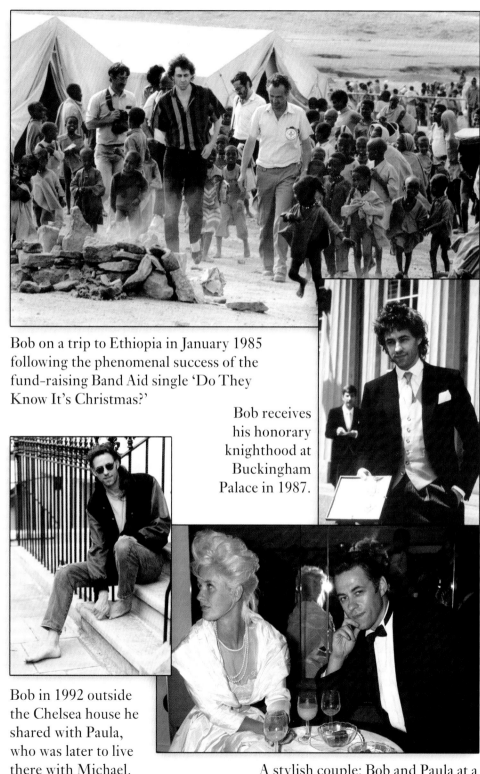

Bob on a trip to Ethiopia in January 1985 following the phenomenal success of the fund-raising Band Aid single 'Do They Know It's Christmas?'

Bob receives his honorary knighthood at Buckingham Palace in 1987.

Bob in 1992 outside the Chelsea house he shared with Paula, who was later to live there with Michael.

A stylish couple: Bob and Paula at a function in September 1989.

Paula, with hair extensions, arrives at the High Court for the divorce hearing.

12/6/96

- After 3 days of complete bloody nightmare in the High Courts of Justice Bob + Paula have with collective sighs of relief arrived amicably at a happy decent solution to their housing arrangements.

Paula + the kids will move into the house in Chelsea.

Bob will move into Michaels house down the road.

Thanks very much.

Bob   Paula

P.S. Neither of us will talk about this any further so please don't doorstep us. Thanks

A note signed by Paula and Bob announcing the 'house swap' with Michael that settled the bitter legal row over housing arrangements.

Looking relaxed and relieved, Bob and Paula leave the court on 12 June 1996.

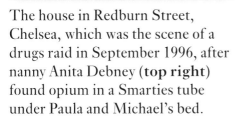

The house in Redburn Street, Chelsea, which was the scene of a drugs raid in September 1996, after nanny Anita Debney (**top right**) found opium in a Smarties tube under Paula and Michael's bed.

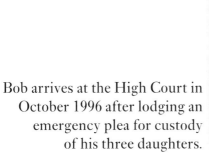

Bob arrives at the High Court in October 1996 after lodging an emergency plea for custody of his three daughters.

Bob and long-term partner, actress Jeanne Marine, at the première of *Evita* in December 1996.

Bob at the Big Top Festival in Middlesbrough in September 2000. On his latest album, *Sex, Age and Death*, he vocalizes his pain at Paula's desertion of him and her death.

Sandy River, Kruger Park, South Africa - May 2001: Nelson Mandela with Bob and his children. From left: Peaches, Tiger, Pixie and Fifi.

came to bless this moment of meltdown as their ultimate saviour. So far Paula doggedly eluded her own rock-bottom; Michael dangled her just short, often flying back from his tour to pluck her back from the edge, and the friends in whom she was trusting now protected her from the logical conclusions that were begging to be made. We all lived in hope that we would one day be able to take her in hand.

Once into the new year, I was starting to feel a little more capable. Liz had been an incredible support for weeks and I never felt the slightest bit unwelcome, but I began to hanker for my own space, so I ventured back to my house. It was eerie returning, and I never felt entirely secure there again. It seemed that the harassment was abating but it never disappeared completely. One morning I went downstairs to find my front door wide open – it was 18 February. I remember the date because it was the day before Sophie's birthday, and my bag had been in the hall with £100 cash in it to pay for her party, which was now gone. It may have been an unconnected burglary, but so many bizarre things had happened that I just didn't think so somehow. This latest incident prompted me to put the house on the market.

A few weeks later I had a frightening encounter on the school premises. This time the culprit was in full sight of several parents and teachers. I was waiting in the reception area when an old adversary of mine bustled in and shouted across the space at me: 'You better watch out, Agar, you're in a lot of trouble' before she marched off into the building. Stunned and speechless, I clutched Sophie's hand and guided her to her classroom, hoping that this woman had left by another door. She hadn't, and as we walked up the long corridor I could see her bearing down on me. Her expression was menacing and I had two choices, turn around and flee or face her head-on. I looked down at my daughter and assured her that everything would be all right. As the woman approached I could tell that she was about to unleash another tirade, so I decided to look her straight in the eye, with the best show of strength I could muster. As she walked past me she threw herself to the floor, shouting, 'You fucking bitch!' Teachers came flying out of their classes and I looked down at the extraordinary sight of this woman faking being a mugging victim, shouting, 'Help me! Help! She just attacked me!'

'I didn't do anything,' I said to Sophie's teacher, who told me that she had seen the whole thing from her window. The drama queen was led whimpering to see the headmaster and I left the school immediately.

The headmaster never called me for my side of the story and chose to believe the other woman; I was barred from the premises. I never found out what she had told him but it was clear he was taken in by this parent sobbing in his office. Later, other parents confirmed to me that they had seen what had happened and it began to filter through that this woman and Paula and a small band of parents whom she had coerced had been spreading pernicious rumours about me for months. Bob was astounded; he talked to fellow parents and made an appointment with the headmaster to challenge him about my suspension. 'It's no good, Gerry,' Bob told me. 'The headmaster believes her; apparently he said that you were swearing at the top of your voice.' He was baffled but conceded that this was yet another circle Paula had gathered.

I thanked Bob for all his support and thought privately how little I had understood about him. He had stuck his neck out to help me, even though he knew that I had contributed to a vicious campaign to discredit him. Later we heard that both Michael and Paula were using my suspension as proof to family and friends that I was not to be trusted.

On 4 March, Paula was back in court for a final showdown with Bob over the house. She was dressed in a tight white mini-dress, leopard-skin jacket, shades and black high heels. Though she'd told us all that she'd been awarded the house back in 1996, we knew that it had been only temporary residency, but now she was after more than just Redburn Street. Bob had always pleaded that he was only on a salary from Planet 24 and he had no other liquid assets, so now Paula wanted half of the Kent house. Bob did not turn up at the hearing, but he had agreed to hand over the deeds to Redburn Street if Paula would relinquish any claim to the Priory. So finally she had full ownership of the house she had bought with the proceeds of her work on *The Tube*.

A few days later, a furious row erupted at the house in Chelsea. It was Friday, and Bob had arrived to collect the children for the weekend. Michael was appearing on Chris Evans's *TFI Friday* that evening and rushed back afterwards to find the incident had blown over. Paula had been insisting that Peaches stay behind in London because she was unwell. Bob told me that there was manifestly nothing wrong with Peaches and the children were begging their mother to let her go. But Paula alleged that Bob had hit her.

Reporters claimed that they saw scratches and bruises on her arm as she left the house for the airport, to go away for a few days with Michael. When I spoke to Bob he was distraught, insisting that he'd never hit her. I was adamant that he make a statement to the press, but he was totally resistant. He said he had nothing to prove, no one who knew him could think that of him, it was Michael who hit photographers; he didn't give a shit what they thought of him. I suggested that he should, because I knew the rumours of his violence were already out there; it might take a little event like this to re-awaken the interest in the stories that no one would write before. It might count against him in future court action, that people might wonder why he wasn't denying it – when does a dignified silence become a silent cover-up?

Bob issued a press release to the effect that, 'I have never raised a hand to Paula in my life. I am not known as a violent or uncontrolled person.' Eventually the police decreed that the case would end up before a court, but this was after the papers had published details of Paula's statement to them, claiming that Bob had gripped his wife by the face, lifting her up and forcing her back against a wall. Paula had told detectives: 'His thumb and fingers were digging into my cheeks. It was very painful.'

Meanwhile, the argument raged over the prosecution of Paula and Michael for possession of illegal substances. The CPS were nervous that they might be attacked for not following through with the action after the public outcry that ensued following a recent arrest and subsequent caution of a celebrity.

The problem was that their star witnesses had been backing away since the custody hearing. After the joint custody ruling and the involvement of the welfare officers, Bob felt disillusioned by the law. He was aware of the army of lawyers that Michael was amassing to fight his corner and it was no secret that the smart money was on him winning anyway. Moreover, Bob was averse to perpetuating the effects that the ongoing media interest and stress on Paula would have on the children. They had suffered enough, so he withdrew.

Anita, too, was nursing her own disappointments. With her contact with the children significantly reduced, she feared antagonizing Paula any further and losing that precious time altogether. So Anita pulled out. I wanted to see it through; I could see that the scare had not been sufficient to change Paula, and the children were still manifestly in danger. However, the threats continued and after repeated pleas to the police for help, even giving them names to follow up, they chose to do nothing. I told the police that they had not instilled any confidence in me, and that as the children's father and nanny no longer wanted to give evidence, I was left too exposed. So I too had to decline to appear.

The CPS met several times to discuss the case. They tried to put pressure on us, saying that we could be subpoenaed, but in the end they felt that the case was going nowhere.

In late March 1997, the police and the CPS issued a statement that Paula and Michael would not be charged for possession of illegal substances because of 'insufficient evidence'. The police said they felt used, then discarded. We had got what we were after, they claimed, but now that they wanted their prosecution we were nowhere to be seen.

It must have been some consolation to Michael that he started the Elegantly Wasted tour finally clear of the drug charges. INXS knew they could not fill the stadia they had in their heyday, so they billed it as a 'back to basics' tour, going back to their roots in intimate venues.

The band spent April playing venues scattered widely across the

States, as a final sales drive in their largest market before the album officially hit the stores. They would be back for a concentrated assault on America in August, but before 'the rest of the world' they had two weeks off, and Michael took Paula to Bali.

It was early in May, and while Paula and Michael soaked up the coconut oil, Hughie Green, the entertainer and host of the TV show *Opportunity Knocks*, died of cancer, aged seventy-seven. At his funeral, Hughie's closest friend, Noel Botham, took to the pulpit to say his last farewell. At the end of his speech and to the shock of the congregation, Botham claimed that Hughie made him promise to reveal that Hughie had a secret love child: one of Britain's best-known female television personalities. He gained no friends in the family with the timing of this revelation, but the press was rife with speculation. Botham remained a model of discretion, saying: 'I haven't given the name to anyone and I have no intention of doing so.' Botham later said Hughie had fallen in love with Heller Toren before she married Jess Yates, and that Hughie had told him that when Heller gave birth to Paula, she said to him, 'This is your daughter.' Botham said: 'Paula will have no idea about this, but it was his wish that after he died I should tell the world. As Hughie said, "I will throw the cat among the pigeons."'

Paula's mother, now Helene Thornton Bosment, angrily denied the allegations, saying she had not even met Hughie when her daughter was conceived. In a strangely inconclusive statement, she said,

> *It is well known in our family that Paula was conceived a month after my marriage to Jess Yates. We wanted a child and she was born the following year in peace and harmony. Any innuendos contradicting these known and proven facts are gravely offensive to me and to my family. It's an absolute lie – and a very hurtful one.*

It was soon categorically refuted by Jess Yates's former lover, the show-girl whose affair with the *Stars On Sunday* presenter had ended his TV career twenty-three years previously. She said Hughie had made up the story as a final dig at Paula's real father, his bitter enemy Jess Yates.

Even Hughie's known children said: 'We believe we are the victims of a well-orchestrated set-up. This has caused so much pain to so many people. A DNA test is the only way to do this.'

When Paula returned from Bali, she was reported as saying: 'My immediate reaction is to say it's all rubbish. DNA testing's been mentioned but I can't make a decision until I know the legal position.' In private, she found it distasteful but laughable. To her mind, there was no way that her mother, the beautiful screen siren, would have had an affair with a toad such as Hughie Green; after all, her father hated him, and she had been brought up to revile the man. Paula had always imagined Helene having affairs with the likes of Sean Connery or Tom Jones.

However, for the first time in years Paula did phone her mother, and Helene promised her that the rumour was not true.

Two weeks after the Bali trip Michael was having a fling with a stunning young model. The girl's story was published in a tabloid. Michael had met twenty-three-year-old Carolina Rorch on the South African leg of the band's tour. She described in graphic detail the nights she spent with Michael in the Peninsula Hotel in Cape Town, drinking champagne, taking cocaine and making passionate love. She said Michael was 'one hell of a stud' and that he was 'very adventurous and unselfish in bed'. He told her about Paula and Tiger, and appeared worried when Carolina said she would be in London the following week, warning her to 'be careful what you say in bars and stuff there'. She never heard from him again. For Paula this must have been familiar territory – a perfect snapshot of what must have been countless other trysts for Michael.

The Bali trip seemed not to have made any lasting impact on Paula's ability to manage her life. Michael's mother Patricia recalled in her book that in late June Michael called her from Vienna before he went on stage. Patricia said that, for the first time, she could feel his depression. Michael said to her: 'I can't take it any more, I don't want to finish this tour, I'm so unhappy.' He was feeling trapped by his love for Tiger in an unending cycle of responsibility for Paula. He said he wanted to leave her, but she had convinced him that her problems were down to him, since she had cast herself adrift from the protection of Bob to be with him. Michael told his mother that Paula had been threatening him: he would never see Tiger again, or she would sell a story to bring in money, or she would harm herself and the baby. These threats were similar to other threats she had made to Bob. But Patricia's fears were allayed when she joined Michael in LA in early July at the beginning of his west-coast tour of the States. He looked happier than she had seen him for ages.

It was then that Michael introduced his family to an attractive woman he claimed was a journalist with *Rolling Stone* magazine, but Patricia immediately knew the truth. In deference to this deep and sensitive spirit whom Tina and Patricia came to love, they would not reveal her real name, referring to her in their book by the pseudonym of 'Blair'.

Blair was undemanding and brought out Michael's romantic and playful sides. According to his sister Tina, Michael continued to see Blair even after Paula arrived in Los Angeles for a short visit. Patricia wrote that Michael was particularly excited about seeing Tiger as Paula had told him that his baby daughter had not only taken her first step, but that she was running now. After hugging and kissing his little girl, Michael placed her on the floor of the hotel lobby, in eager anticipation. Patricia described her own sadness when she witnessed her son's embarrassment and disappointment when Tiger made it clear she would not be walking for some time.

Paula jealously guarded Tiger from Michael's family from the moment she arrived, insisting that the child needed rest or feeding as an excuse for removing her from their company. She stayed in her room when Michael was not about and was openly hostile at the slightest provocation. Patricia remembers talking to Michael on the phone in the hotel about Tiger's fever. When she suggested a product that might help, she heard Paula shouting: 'I've got four fucking children, I've written fourteen fucking books on child care', so angry was she that he was conferring with his mother. Next morning Tina called the suite to arrange a family breakfast and Paula answered complaining that Michael had been out all night.

The affair with Blair followed the pattern of Michael's romantic history. He seemed stuck in a three-year cycle, with someone literally in the wings before he finished with his present girl. Even without the tribulations that were part of the Paula package, his internal alarm was ringing, but this time the stakes were higher than ever before.

Paula told Patricia on this visit that she and Michael were to be married on a South Sea island. Michael again assured his mother that marriage was not on the agenda. Though Michael said he was unhappy with Paula, he was tied to her through his love for his daughter and imagined the only solution would be to move her and Tiger out to Australia where she would be surrounded by a supportive family. But he seemed unable to address the fundamental flaw in his plan – Bob's inevitable unwillingness to let his children go. His mother could see that the equation did not compute and later wrote to him, with a gentle dissection of the situation. When Michael died, this letter was found in his hotel room.

Patricia chronicled Paula's extraordinary behaviour at the end of their stay in LA. As Patricia and her husband Ross were packing, Paula appeared at the door of their hotel room clutching Tiger. She screamed, using many expletives, that she never ever wanted to talk to Patricia again. It would seem that Paula then tried to discredit Patricia in Michael's eyes. She stage-managed an extraordinary scene designed to give Michael the impression that Patricia was trying to abduct Tiger and take her back to Australia with her.

Michael had not believed Paula; his mother would know that she could not take a child on a plane without a passport.

Patricia wrote that she was 'devastated by the incident'. She didn't want to lose Michael's love and trust. She didn't want to worry him – he had enough on his mind. That painful and upsetting incident at the hotel was the last time Michael's mother and sister saw him alive.

Paula had always been acutely aware that when Michael was out of contact for more than a few hours, there was every likelihood that he would be in someone else's bed. His nocturnal absences in LA can have left her in no doubt that he was playing away. After Paula's return from the States, she was found on the floor of the bathroom with an empty bottle of pills beside her. Bob was playing a gig in Dublin and he called Jeanne to handle the fall-out. Michael took a flight back in a momentary gap between shows. Meanwhile Jeanne was heroic in her response to the emergency on Redburn Street and while the ambulance men revived Paula, Jeanne distracted the girls and made them tea, constantly assuring them that their mother would be okay. The event only served to increase the burden of duty on Michael and he reverted to his untenable catch-all solution to move them all out to Australia. When Bob visited Paula, she asked him, 'Why did you leave me?' – a pathetic snapshot of her failing grip on reality.

As INXS continued their tour of the US, Michael gave Blair his itinerary. He called her from every city, and paid for her flights so that she could join him wherever he was.

On 31 August Michael was in St Louis when the news broke of Princess Diana's death. He was heartbroken and vociferously condemned the press for their aggressive tactics. That night he gave one of the worst performances of his career.

In between INXS gigs, he and Blair read books together or watched TV. Michael was also working hard on his acting technique, having landed a cameo role in a small independent film called *Limp*, to be shot in Canada. He was to play a jaded record producer who lauds Kurt Cobain's suicide because it increased record sales. He invited Blair to go with him to Vancouver but she declined. The members of the band were well aware of the issues troubling their frontman. He had complained to several of his 'brothers', as he considered them, about his ailing finances and the constant pressure from London.

Early November 1997: INXS were in New York, and Paula and Tiger paid a flying visit. Michael had whipped up the crowd to a frenzy at the Beacon Theatre, New York. Six songs in, his tailored three-piece suit had been peeled off in layers in a trademark strip guaranteed to raise the temperature to boiling point. In a tank top, black baggys and bare feet, Michael stalked the stage like a caged panther. He strutted his way through every rock god pose as if he'd written the book, and the crowd were on their feet, stretching forwards to absorb every last ion of sexual energy oozing from him. At the end of one number, he stopped, the magical craze of lighting abated and he stepped off-stage, to reappear a moment later holding Tiger Lily.

There was a moment of reverential awe, then the fans exploded ecstatically and Michael handed Tiger back to Paula waiting in the wings. Michael perched himself on a stool and signalled for calm. The next song was 'Searching' and he dedicated it to Paula: 'We've all been through a lot of shit and we are good people, and I love her very much.'

The applause rose in deafening appreciation of everything he was, whether or not they fully understood what 'the shit' was.

That day he'd given one of his last interviews and, without realizing the significance the piece would one day hold, reporter Sharon Krum from Adelaide's *Sunday Mail* managed to capture his depth and intelligence, and his hurt. In his now well-practised declamation of the British press, he spoke of their harassment of himself and Paula.

It was worse for Paula than me, and it hasn't stopped. I think the equation is very simple and sad... the press, especially in England, makes a construct of a human, and then they either do two things with that person. They make them beyond human, or they dehumanize them. Bob was taken beyond human to sainthood, and if you left him, that leaves one choice. You are bad, you are wrong, it's as simple as that... The situation is quite opposite, if you only knew. It's all lies. People don't know the truth, and I can't talk about it now.

You see the destruction of the person you love in front of your eyes, the attempted destruction, and to fight it is to be violated all over again. The question I have is, where are the human beings in all this?

The stuff that has happened to us, it could make you lose your faith in human nature.

The reporter asked him how he kept his sanity through all this. 'I am barely doing it,' said Michael.

But when he spoke of Paula, he said he'd never been happier and the reporter wrote that he looked it too. 'She is a mother of four, a really good mother, like the best mother you have ever seen, she's extraordinary,' he said proudly. 'I'm the luckiest man alive.'

Then Michael digressed into the cult of celebrity. He brought up Princess Diana's death and how it challenged our passive encouragement of press intrusion.

See, it's against the law to destroy Jews, blacks, people for religious causes. The law and Parliament have stopped discrimination like that. All we have left is celebrity, and every society has to kick a dog, it's a fact. Someone to raise and someone to burn. It's human nature. Celebrities are the last bastion, and it's not against the law... They say you asked for it. That's bullshit, I am not a cynical manipulator of the media, I never have been. I think there should be limits... People have forgotten that celebrities are human beings... This is why the Princess Diana episode has made everybody take a breath. I remember once she pulled up in the car and pulled Paula in and said: 'Between you and me, I'm so happy when you're on the cover, it gives me a day off'.

Michael said that he had been shattered by Diana and Dodi's deaths. 'This has to be a wake-up call for people,' he said pointedly. 'Your appetite for celebrity has led to this. Your vicarious pleasure for 25p has cost the life of magic.' The reporter commented on how remarkably calm Michael appeared. He attributed his sanity to fatherhood...and Paula.

Paula was planning her Christmas trip to Australia with the girls. She was desperate to see Michael, not least because she felt that Tiger no longer glued him to her. He talked of settling her in Sydney, yet she knew he was four months into an affair. What were his intentions? She had to be near him to insure the outcome. But she could not be open about the exact details of the trip because she planned to fly out some time before the children's term had finished.

Bob had agreed to the trip in principle. Despite his knowledge of Paula's tumultuous relationship with Michael, he championed the children's time with their mother. But as the trip drew closer he began to suspect that there was a hidden agenda. The rumours that Paula was to settle in Sydney had been running for twelve months, but were never taken seriously. Now the rumours intensified and Bob knew that offers of work were materializing out there. The word from the children was that Mummy was looking for a house with Michael, but he always imagined that she would spend more time in Australia, while the children were at school and staying with him.

Paula already had the tickets but she withheld the details of her departure as long as she could. When she told Bob of her plans, she was offhand with the information, as if it were a mere formality, but Bob was not happy that the girls would miss the last three weeks of term; in this he was backed strongly by Anita. Paula was instantly defensive, panicking at this last-minute obstacle. She could not risk leaving without Peaches and Pixie. She was already on shaky ground, one procedure away from losing them completely. She knew she was going for a while, and how it would look to welfare officers and the courts if she disappeared and abandoned her children, quite apart from her own need to have them near. Something in her insistence stirred Bob's dormant fears that Paula planned to take the girls and not come back for a long while.

This was certainly not okay with him. It was enough that he had agreed to what he thought would be a few weeks' Christmas holiday, enough that he had agreed to entrust his precious children to Paula and Michael, but he had never sanctioned them going on the road with Michael, knowing only too well the chaotic environment of such a trip. He had imagined a family affair, with the worst of Paula and Michael's chemical duelling tempered by the influence of Michael's relatives. Now it seemed to him that they were taking the piss. But Paula was defiant and seemed to be saying that there was nothing Bob could do; the plans were set, the tickets bought, she would go regardless. Bob had to act fast. I remember his panic as he rushed to implement legal proceedings against her. And this was where the previous custody action paid dividends. Bob was well within his rights to challenge Paula's plans, morally and legally. Where usually one parent would get full custody and control, he had equal rights, and could expect to get full support in court for his wishes.

After five days in New York, Michael flew to LA to continue work on his solo album. But he was restless; he chose a hotel for its proximity to the night scene. His old friend Nick Conroy, with whom Michael had lived on the eve of his INXS success, observed that Michael appeared to be avoiding his usual companions, attracting around him an entourage of known drug abusers. The effect of determined drug use is to isolate the user from anyone who is not high. Nick could sense that Michael was beyond reason, but he offered his help if Michael needed him, even suggesting he stay with him in his apartment. Michael declined the offer but said he would be in touch.

Even Blair could not get through to Michael.

16 'I've had enough'

ON TUESDAY 18 NOVEMBER, Michael booked into the Ritz Carlton, Sydney under the name of Murray River, the name of a well-known Australian landmark. The hotel telephone system, which only recorded outgoing calls, showed that he had spoken at length to Blair the next morning and twice the day after. He did not call Paula until the Friday morning.

Michael spent Wednesday 19 November with INXS's Sydney publicist, looking at an apartment for Paula and the girls to use when they arrived. On the next two days he rehearsed with the rest of the band at the Australian Broadcasting Corporation's studios. The final rehearsal before their Australian tour was planned for the Saturday, but the Friday session was to be the last time INXS would ever play together.

The band said that at the rehearsals Michael was on great form and betrayed no sign of his inner turmoil. A TV crew had been allowed into the ABC studios to video the rehearsals for a current affairs show. The anchor, Richard Wilkins, said:

I've looked back at that tape quite a few times, but honestly there's nothing there that would suggest that he was unhappy or depressed or anything. He's winking, flirting with the camera – and just very confident and self-assured. He looked happy with what he was doing and, you know, really charged-up about the tour.

He was drinking, but he definitely wasn't wasted. Michael could be pretty excessive, but there's a difference between slightly tipsy and smashed – and he definitely wasn't smashed. If anything, he seemed so happy that it made me wonder whether he had already made his decision.

Newspaper reports documented Michael's final few hours. He had dinner with his father and stepmother at an Indian restaurant near the hotel. Kell knew that Michael was preoccupied by the pending court case and remembers that his son seemed 'a little uptight' but Michael assured him that he'd 'never felt better' and generally appeared to be in good spirits.

Kell and Sue dropped Michael back at the Ritz Carlton at 10.30pm and he went to the hotel bar. When Kym Wilson, an actress and ex-girlfriend of Michael's, turned up, as arranged, with her boyfriend Andrew Rayment, they found Michael enjoying the company of two young female fans.

Michael told Kym and Andrew that he was expecting a call about the outcome of the court case with Bob, so invited them up to his room. They drank beer, vodka, champagne and cocktails. Kym said that Michael talked about how desperately he wanted the girls with him and how he was longing to see Tiger. He also spoke disparagingly of Bob. While they were with him, Michael received a call from his agent in New York, Martha Troup, who told him of potential film projects. He was upbeat and excited when he relayed this news to his guests. The couple stayed with Michael until dawn on Saturday. By this time Andrew was falling asleep and Kym was struggling to keep awake, so Michael told them to go home. His long-time friend Richard Lowenstein said:

> *Michael always had a problem being left alone at the end of the night – especially if it was a couple leaving together. I've been doing all-nighters with Michael and I've seen it happen when couples leave together and his face would just fall. That was the time when he'd reach for the phone and make the call to Helena or Paula or Michele.*

At about 5.30am Michael took a call from Paula. She told him that the hearing had been adjourned until 17 December, so she would not be coming to Australia with the children. She described him as sounding 'desperate' on hearing this news. Paula's friend, Belinda Brewin, who was with her, also spoke to Michael during this call. Michael rang Bob and begged him to let the girls come out for the holidays. Bob described his tone as being 'hectoring, and abusive and threatening'. Gail Coward, a guest staying in the adjoining room, heard Michael shouting abuse down the phone; the coroner was satisfied that this abuse was directed at Bob. Bob and I conversed at length about the whole affair. He told me that Michael was not making any sense and was so delirious that Bob could not get through to him with the facts. But it was clear that Michael was convinced that there had been a final and complete ban on the girls travelling – which was not the case. The hearing had indeed been adjourned until 17 December; there would indeed be a delay in their departure so that the girls could complete their term, but there was no other finality to the arrangements for their holiday in Australia. Anita said that in court Paula had repeated over and over that she had the tickets and that they were expensive, clearly hoping that this fact would sway proceedings, but the judge was rightly sympathetic to Bob's cause and adjourned the proceedings until school was out.

Back in Sydney, Michael, by now in a distraught state, turned to two women he trusted implicitly. First, he called his ex-girlfriend Michele Bennett, but got her answer-machine. He left a message in which he sounded 'drunk'. He then tried Martha Troup at about 9.40am and spoke to her voice-mail: 'Martha,' he said, 'Michael here. I fuckin' had enough.' When she picked up the message a few minutes later, Martha rang the hotel room but got no answer. Michael tried another number for Martha at 9.50am; he left a message which, Martha said, 'sounded as if he was affected by something. It was slow and deep.' Martha was so worried on hearing this that she called John Martin, the tour manager.

At 9.54am Michael tried Michele again and this time she picked up. Michael started to cry and Michele promised to go round to the hotel straightaway. She got no answer when she knocked on Michael's door nor when she rang his room. She left a note for him at reception.

Michael had left a note for John Martin, saying that he would not be going to rehearsals on Saturday, so he left him to sleep in. Just before midday a maid let herself into room 524 and, finding the door obstructed, pushed it open with all her strength. Michael's naked body was kneeling on the floor facing the door. He had tied a belt round his neck, and attached the buckle to the door handle. The buckle had broken away and he had slumped to the floor. The room was in disarray and there were pills scattered around.

Michael was pronounced dead and all hell broke loose.

———— ◆ ————

Most of Michael's family and friends learned of his death from reporters calling for comment. In London it was 4am, ten hours since Belinda Brewin had spoken to him on the phone, but she had just taken a call from Martha Troup and now she was banging on Paula's front door. Eventually a bleary-eyed Paula opened up; the phone was ringing at the same time. Knowing what the call would bring, Belinda yelled, 'Don't pick it up' and in her haste to intercept Paula, she blurted out her tragic news. Paula punched her in the face.

Once the truth had registered, Paula screamed and screamed: 'My baby, my baby, Bob's killed him.' Her anguish was such that it woke the street. When anger overtook the grief she called Bob in Kent and shouted down the line: 'You've murdered Michael as surely as if you'd strangled him yourself.' From then on Belinda took over.

When I started hearing rumours about Paula's new 'best friend', I vaguely remembered her mentioning Belinda, back when Paula was sane. They'd struck up an acquaintance at the '1 o'clock Club' for mothers and children. Belinda appealed to Paula to write her a character reference in a custody battle, suggesting that her celebrity status and being a writer of baby books would count for something in court. Paula said she complied out of compassion.

That evening, Belinda and Paula flew British Airways business class to Sydney, with Tiger and Andrew Young (Michael's lawyer and Belinda's then boyfriend). To board the plane, Paula had to be sedated by a doctor, so overwhelming was her grief, but despite this and the champagne they were drinking, she wailed, 'My baby's dead, Bob's killed my Michael' throughout the flight. Meanwhile, a dozen red roses had arrived at the house, with a note attached: 'To all my girls, lots of love, Michael.'

In Bangkok, during a refuelling stop, Paula told a reporter on the same flight that she would dye black the wedding dress in which she was to have wed Michael and wear it to his funeral. Then her anguish overcame her again and she started shouting: 'Bob Geldof murdered Michael Hutchence. That bastard killed Michael. He is called Saint Bob. That makes me sick. He killed my baby. We have had three years of this.' She asked for a buggy to take her and Tiger from the VIP lounge back on board, but the attendant could not comply. Paula lost her temper, threw a glass of champagne in his face and kicked him. When the Thai police arrived, they refused her permission to re-board the plane until Andrew Young stepped in and explained her trauma.

They touched down in Sydney at 6.30am and were picked up on the apron by police in an unmarked sedan, keen to slip her past the press. They were whisked straight to the New South Wales Institute of Forensic Medicine complex in Glebe, where they were met by the INXS tour manager.

Michael's body was arranged in a viewing room, which was decorated with heavy curtains like a funeral home – used for families to identify bodies and designed to help the grieving feel more comfortable. Paula was encouraged to spend as long with Michael as she needed. Comforted by her companions, Paula left after twenty minutes, still sobbing.

The whole world mourned with her: his family, his friends, the band, the fans, the music industry, and the entire population of Australia. The news was carried on every front page, every TV channel, the radio and the Internet, and through the grief ran a universal incomprehension. After a moment of stunned reverence, the media buzzed with speculation. At first the cause of death was in question: Were there others present when he died? Was it foul play? Was it a sexual game that had gone horribly wrong?

As a matter of routine, Michael's room was treated as a crime scene. The local detectives established that there were no signs of forced entry, and no trauma to his body that might suggest a struggle. His bedroom was in disarray – signs of a fit of anger. His bedclothes were on the floor and other indications suggested he had at least tried to sleep. Suitcases were open and various medications scattered throughout, including a Becloforte ventolin inhaler for his asthma, Nurofen, Zovirax, two containers of unidentified pills, an open packet of Prozac, and nicotine patches.

While the world waited for the autopsy and coroner's report, the theories multiplied. Some said he had expressed an interest in auto-erotic asphyxiation, the practice of self-strangulation while masturbating, which heightens the intensity of orgasm. There were rumours that he had bite marks on his bottom and that there may have been other people in the room, but these were dispelled during the investigation.

In September 1997, during a break in the tour, Michael had returned to London. He had been irretrievably low, and trying to chase the gloom away with drugs was clearly no longer working, so he was referred to a consultant psychiatrist at the famed Priory clinic in Roehampton. This specialist was asked for a statement after Michael's death. The doctor said that he had seen Michael twice (once with Paula) and concluded that, although Michael had concerns over his career and the dispute with Bob, he was 'committed to and happy with' his relationship and loved Paula and their daughter. The doctor went on to state that Michael showed no signs of drug dependence or suicidal thoughts.

It is true that Michael was not hooked on any one substance in the classic sense. To most, the image of the 'drug addict' is the hopeless, homeless heroin user, but Michael was always elegantly wasted, and he had an inbuilt self-control that arrested most of the outward symptoms of intoxication. But owing to the regularity with which he banished his troubles with a cocktail of substances, he was most certainly addicted to chemical escape.

Though rock historian Glenn A. Baker said Michael was the industry's least likely suicidal character, there was a growing realization that suicide would be the verdict. Baker said:

Of all the rock stars I've interviewed I would have picked a dozen others as being potential candidates for this act... Michael was the consummate rock star, he took upon the role of a rock star so comfortably, he floated above the pressures. Why he would choose this moment to throw in the towel I think will always remain a mystery.

But there were those who knew he was depressed and that became the focus of the commentary.

Another close friend of Michael's, Greg Perano, who has admitted to suffering from depression and being close to suicide himself, said:

I believe that there were just a few minutes in which Michael wanted this to happen. A few minutes later he might not have wanted it. It may sound horrible but I think it's what he wanted. He was at his peak. He was still charismatic. He hadn't grown fat, bald or old. People still thought of him as young.

After Michael's death, Bono wrote a song addressing his friend's dilemma, 'Stuck In A Moment You Can't Get Out Of'. In an interview a few years later, Bono told the reporter:

I have no doubt in my mind that Michael killed himself. He felt that he was in a corner. He thought that he couldn't be a good enough father, or couldn't get into a position where he might be. That's what the song is about. As far as Michael was concerned he was stuck. From the outside, you could see that this wasn't always going to be the case, but that night he couldn't see a way out of the situation.

The band were pretty clear that Michael had been under immense pressure and acknowledged that he was perfectly capable of taking his own life. 'He would flirt with everything and everybody... you know, danger was just one of them,' said Andrew Farriss. But in the end they felt that he had not let them see the totality of his hopelessness.

'When someone keeps reassuring you how positive and good they are feeling, now I'm starting to realize that they're people to be worried about, you know,' said Tim Farriss. Tim took pains to issue a warning about the growing evidence that the mix of prescription anti-depressants and alcohol can make a person suicidal.

With the evidence in and the autopsy complete, the state coroner Derrick Hand said that he was satisfied that cause of death was suicide by hanging. He discounted the possibility of auto-eroticism, stating that there was no forensic or other evidence to substantiate this suggestion. For him the evidence pointed squarely at suicide and he listed the statements by friends and family that collectively corroborated evidence of Michael's distressed state of mind and noted that he had a quantity of Prozac, alcohol, cocaine and other prescription drugs in his blood stream. In conclusion Mr Hand stated:

I am satisfied that the deceased was in a severe depressed state on the morning of 22 November 1997, due to a number of factors, including: the relationship with Paula Yates and the pressure of the on-going dispute with Sir Robert Geldof, combined with the effects of the substances that he had ingested at the time. I am satisfied that the deceased intended and did take his own life.

So with the publication of the coroner's report, all the rumour and innuendo died away, but that still left everyone asking: why?

As recently as 2002, Andrew Farriss gave an interview in which he said: 'What's really frustrating for me is that I've got just about as many questions as his friends and family and the public do. The awful thing is I was quite close to him and I don't know why he really killed himself.'

Michael's overriding concern on that night was whether Paula would be able to bring the girls to Australia. Michael believed from Paula's call that they were not coming at all, not that there had been a delay. This belief obviously drove him to desperation. Paula did not make her phone records available to the police. We know that she called Michael at around 5.30am Sydney time to give him the news. His response was to 'beg' Bob to change his mind. Surely the couple would have been in contact following this conversation to discuss Bob's reaction? The hotel records show that Michael made no further calls to Paula, and he did not have a mobile.

Incoming calls were not logged. In Belinda's statement she recalled that she had asked Paula when she had last spoken to Michael, and Paula had said around 7 or 8pm London time (6 or 7am in Sydney. This points to a second call to Michael from Paula – a call that is missing from her memory and missing from her statement. If there was a final call from Paula, what did she say?

She had a history of making threats to Michael – did she do so in this final call? Michael had been imbibing recreational narcotics since his teenage days. I have no idea how regularly he took Ecstasy, though his whole persona seemed at times to be defined by the drug. I'd seen him take a handful, and he'd been doing that for ten years or more – his manager Chris Murphy recalled a show in Paris in 1988, where Michael popped several as he walked on stage in front of 25,000 people. That could have been augmented by cocaine, a drug so prevalent in the music industry that it had the easy availability of cigarettes.

Meanwhile, had Michael developed a taste for opium and heroin? While all illegal drugs have the tendency to promote depression and paranoia soon after come down, heroin can induce symptoms of schizophrenia. When you go down the list of tell-tale signs of drug abuse, it reads like a description of Paula and Michael's last years:

Depression or feelings of hopelessness and/or helplessness.

Different degrees of hostility or ambivalence.

Tunnel vision: narrow attitude on problems and solutions.

Inability to request or accept help.

Different degrees of nervousness or anxiety.

Withdrawn or rebellious behaviour.

Unwillingness to communicate.

Sudden general personality changes.

Paranoia, which can include a feeling of persecution or hostility towards others.

Exaggerated feelings of self-confidence with growing underlying feelings of inferiority.

Increased hang-ups in close relationships, especially with parents or those of the opposite sex.

Greater impulsiveness, acting without thinking it through.

Total denial that drugs might be harmful.

Sudden mood changes.

Breaks promises; lies frequently.

Power-playing and manipulation of family, friends or co-workers.

Priorities change.

Changing attitude toward straight (non-using) friends, family and rules.

Blames others for his/her own irresponsible actions.

Suicidal ideation.

After Michael banged his head in Copenhagen in 1992, friends said his personality became more volatile, he suffered his first bouts of depression and the symptoms persisted for months, prompting him to take up a course of Prozac. More recently Paula had put him on four tablets a day; he had been jetting to multiple locations so his intake could never been monitored by a doctor. One friend observed that leading up to his death Michael was popping the pills like candy. Chemists don't even fully understand how Prozac works, or even why it takes ten days to start acting. There is an even vaguer understanding of the effects of mixing drugs, where often the combined effect exceeds the sum of the parts. A combination of anti-depressants and alcohol alone is now known to be dangerous: it is seen to catalyze confusion, sudden deep depression and occasionally suicide. Prozac and Ecstasy have very similar chemical structures; though there is no wide evidence of danger in combination, it is suspected that together they could lead to Seratonin Syndrome, an emerging complication of which little is understood, but of itself can kill.

Paula's devastation at Michael's death incapacitated her from the start, and Belinda engaged as an intermediary between her tormented charge and the world at large, liaising with family, the authorities and the media. When the funeral was over, and Paula and Belinda were back in London, Belinda's involvement increased. Paula had been 'out of it' for days and Belinda was soon speaking on her behalf to every stakeholder of Paula's life. In fact, Belinda filled the void that I had left. She tended her grieving buddy, looked after the girls and protected Paula from anything that might upset her sedated fragility.

17 'I've lost my future and my past'

AFTER MICHAEL'S DEATH, the years in Michael's shadow were over for his brother Rhett. He was in evidence wearing a Hawaiian shirt, making regular trips to the Ritz Carlton to view room 524 and the makeshift memorial outside the hotel. Meanwhile Paula was installed in a hotel room in Quay West on the harbour. Belinda was quoted as saying:

> I am so worried about Paula's health. She is stretched way past her limit. I hardly dare leave her alone. I think she is on the verge of a complete breakdown. She is always crying – at times hysterically – and I can't get her to eat. She has been drinking too much and the only things that calm her down are sedatives. When I do get her to sleep, she wakes up screaming because of nightmares.

Paula was unable to leave the hotel room. Neither was she capable of being involved with the funeral preparations, which were even then testing the cohesiveness of Michael's family. Through their tears and grief, the Hutchence women grappled ably with every detail of the ceremony. Kell, it seemed, was in contact with Michael's business manager, Colin Diamond, who was the main executor of the will, along with his brother and an accountant in Hong Kong. Once they had finally met, Kell returned to the rest of the family with the news that Michael had stated in his will that he wished to be cremated. This came as quite a shock to everybody concerned, but in their grief they didn't question this decision.

It was Kell who suggested that Harry Miller, a top PR consultant, should be hired to control the media frenzy that spiralled out of control the moment Michael's body was discovered. Patricia and Tina liaised with the funeral director, the Dean of the church, the band and well wishers, while Kell's focus was on the media. Arrangements for the funeral were made even more fraught by increasing friction between the family members. Their grief was exacerbated by ancient wounds and was turning to mistrust, the pressure of which was not relieved by the arrival of Paula. Subconsciously they may have blamed her for Michael's death, and an air of hostility flared up when Kell went to visit her. In his own account, relayed by Michael's mother, Paula lashed out at him physically when he told her that he was assigning her a bodyguard and warned her: 'If you make one wrong move you'll be bodily picked up and carried out of the cathedral and dumped in the gutter where you belong.' Just as Serena had suffered at Paula's hands when she wanted to attend Jess's funeral and remain in the house they'd shared, now Paula was to experience the same treatment.

As the motorcade snaked from the hotels, mourners lined the streets and stood at windows and on balconies in quiet respect. Thousands of people thronged outside St Andrew's cathedral, fans and press gathering to watch the parade of famous faces and to express their grief. The church had been chosen for its size, as the family wanted to allow the greatest number of close fans to attend. With Harry Miller's help they had allowed only one TV crew inside so that the widest possible congregation could pay their respects, a deal for which no money changed hands. The cathedral was already filled to capacity and, outside, the service would be conveyed to the overflow by a PA system. By the numbers that gathered for the funeral it was clear that Australia felt it had lost a royal prince.

Paula and her entourage were organized to travel in the fifth limousine of the procession, behind the family, the band and crew, their wives and girlfriends. Patricia and Tina said that they had taken directions on this from the funeral director and that no slight was intended, but it only added insult to Paula's deep injury. While the papers reported the tragic dignity with which Paula conducted herself at the service, and that she and Helena had hugged on the steps and given comfort to one another, Patricia and Tina recalled a different scene. As they got out of the cars at the cathedral, the priest greeted them at the door. While they conversed briefly, they became aware of running and were barged several times by people entering behind them. When they went to take their seats they found to their horror, that the right-hand front row, reserved for immediate family, had been hijacked by Paula, her entourage and bodyguard. The funeral director had not been sufficiently alert to stop them and, opting to avoid a scene, Michael's family were forced to sit on the left, with their view of proceedings obscured by a large display of flowers from Bono.

The papers said Paula sobbed throughout Rhett's eulogy. Wearing a loud striped suit given to him by his brother, he spoke of the agony and ecstasy of being the brother of a rock star. The newspapers reported his words. Choking back tears, he said:

From the very beginning all the signs were there that Michael was destined to live an extraordinary life. I have an early lyric book of Michael's from when he first started writing. It has a list of ten things he wanted to achieve. The first one was 'Conquer the world'. I can't remember what the other nine were but I am sure he achieved them too. My heart goes out to Paula and beautiful darling girl Tiger, and the other girls, to the band, his fans and all the people who knew Michael and have lost a tremendous friend. I went and spent some time at his room in the Ritz to see if it had any answers. It seemed a sad room. It definitely wasn't Michael. And if Michael, who loved Oscar Wilde, would have identified with the famous poet's last words – 'Either this wallpaper goes or I do' – then I would understand. These words might have some meaning for us all – to mourn too long for those we love is self-indulgent. But to honour their memory with a promise to live a little better for having known them gives purpose to their life and some reason for their death.

Michael's coffin was borne out by the remaining INXS members and Rhett, and as they slid it into the hearse a deafening peal of thunder broke directly over the cathedral and it rained for the first time in months.

Michael's will was eventually faxed to Patricia and Tina from Hong Kong and the management's Gold Coast office, only after the women had employed an attorney. The will bequeathed US$500,000 to Greenpeace and to Amnesty International; of the remainder, 50 per cent went to Tiger, and the rest was to be divided equally between Kell, Rhett, Tina, Paula and Patricia. Ultimately, they found that Michael formally owned nothing of worth in his estate: no property, no vehicles, and no rights to his music, not even to the solo album, which he had funded himself.

Patricia and Tina received a global media mauling for employing an attorney – an act, it was assumed, that had signalled their selfish challenge to the will. Their intention was quite the opposite. They had no challenge to the substance of the will, only its execution. Instead of an estate attorney Kell had employed an entertainment lawyer, and within days of the funeral had brokered a deal with Channel 7 for an exclusive interview, for the reported sum of AUS$175,000. In the ensuing months he was to sell interviews widely. He was portrayed as the kind and grief-stricken father, with pictures in *Hello!*, sitting on a rock, looking wistfully out over Sydney harbour. In direct contrast Patricia and Tina refused all offers to talk, and their self-funded efforts to investigate the administration of Michael's estate were the subject of continuing derogatory media speculation. Michael's business manager had given instructions for Michael's ashes to be split three ways between Patricia, Kell and Paula. In an interview Kell said it had been his decision to divide the ashes. But even by Christmas, for reasons that were never communicated, the release of the ashes had not been authorized. It was not until three weeks later that Michael's mother was allowed to retrieve her share of her son's mortal remains.

The breaking of Paula's heart released a torrent of tears. She wept for days after the funeral; she sobbed through the twenty-two-hour flight back from Australia and was still crying as she was helped into a car at Heathrow.

Hardly able to form the words, she said: 'Michael was the love of my life. I will never get over his death.' She accepted that Michael had been loaded when he took his life, but said: 'Nobody will ever know for sure how Michael died.'

Belinda looked after Tiger while Paula booked into a clinic for grief counselling. When she came out there was more torture awaiting her stricken nerves – bailiffs were under instruction from the estate agents who had sold her Clapham house. They were still waiting after eighteen months to collect their fee. The only consolation, perhaps, was that, more than ever before, she had highly valuable thoughts inside her head. Within days of touching down in London she had a deal with *OK!* on the table, reputedly worth £200,000, but before she could give an interview about her devastation over Michael's death, the landscape changed dramatically.

In her desperation to raise funds, Paula put her house on the market, and arranged to take the DNA test required to disprove the rumours that Hughie Green was her biological father so that she could sue the *News of the World*. She supplied a sample to a top genetic laboratory, secure in her belief that the truth was on her side. It was compared with samples from Hughie's two legitimate children and there was a positive match.

It is said that there is almost no pain worse than finding out that you are not who you thought you were. Paula was in a unique position to confirm this; she already had an eternity before her to ponder the message that Michael had left her in his unexplained death. She said: 'In the space of a week I've lost my future and my past. It obliterated everything that I thought had been me.' As if her troubled parentage was not already enough of a burden; as if recent events were not enough of a punishment, in the flick of a test tube she had again lost her beloved father.

Paula's mother had to concede that the scientific tests were all but infallible and said: 'When I first heard about the tests I thought they were a good idea, but I can't believe the results. I just feel stunned. If a person is married and they conceive three weeks afterwards it is natural to think the person they married is the father. I still believe Paula is Jess's daughter.'

'She obviously doesn't understand that a DNA test is not like some paternity suit in the old days. It is a fact,' Paula replied. 'I'm horrified; I thought I was at the darkest point in my life, now this. I loved him. I never wanted anyone else to be my father. To learn your real father is a man you have always despised is beyond comprehension. Hughie Green is nothing to me. Jess, Michael and my children are everything.'

Paula continued, 'The thing I keep asking myself is why didn't my mother tell me? Why didn't she tell me after the allegation was made? Why did she let me go through the humiliation of a DNA test when she must at least have known there was a good chance of it being true? If she had warned me, I wouldn't have taken the test.'

Paula was said to be close to total breakdown. She was seen walking the streets barefoot, clasping her little Tiger Lily to her side.

Helene was adamant, despite the evidence, that Green could not be Paula's father; however, when pressed she did suggest a bizarre theory in print to account for Paula's paternity. She surmised that Jess must have drugged her and 'given' her to Green shortly after their marriage. The awful truth about her parentage cast a bitter irony over Paula's three-year battle for ownership of Jess Yates's house. Serena was still living there, despite Paula's efforts to evict her, which had cost her a fortune in legal fees. Now, Paula had no greater right to the property than Jess's last girlfriend.

During this period, a third of Michael's ashes were being cast into Sydney harbour in a touching ceremony organized by Kell and Rhett. Patricia and Tina had originally imagined a family rite to say their final farewells together, but with the ensuing divisions it seemed that Michael's remains would find three separate resting places. Patricia and Tina were not invited to attend the ceremony with their urn, but Paula was, though in her present state she would not return to Australia for several weeks.

On 6 February 1998 the coroner's report on Michael's death was released. It did nothing to explain his fatal reasoning, but it was a final rubber stamp on the verdict of suicide, discounting any other speculation. This official ruling rekindled interest in the singer's death and, though Paula had made various statements with differing opinions over the weeks, she now only begged for her lover to be allowed 'dignity in death', and declined to comment further. Kell had been giving interviews almost every week since that fateful day in November, denying that Michael was depressed, choosing instead to suggest that he'd died from a drug and alcohol binge and he promoted the view that Michael was deeply devoted to Paula at the time. So Tina finally broke her silence with a press release and an interview, in which she stated that Michael had never planned to marry Paula: 'He had been trying to get out of the relationship,' Tina said in an Australian magazine. 'He felt trapped and boxed in. Michael was very unhappy with Paula at the time of his death.'

Tina recalls in her book *Just A Man* that at 3am, she was awoken by a call from Belinda. She was polite but said that they had some 'damage control' to do after Tina's comments had been twisted by the papers. In the morning, Paula called and said: 'Tina, I have fifty journos outside my house. You have not attempted to get hold of me and Tiger, I suggest you ring Belinda. It's literally a circus out here because of what you said out there. We have to do damage control. It's your responsibility from tonight on.'

When Paula's *OK!* magazine interview came out, it was a massive twenty pages with pictures of her and Tiger at the house she had bought in Hastings on England's south coast. She spoke of the awful night she heard that Michael was dead, how she cried and cried and how she broke the news to Peaches and Pixie: 'For as long as I live I will never forget how Pixie cried. Like someone had ripped her heart out.'

When she was asked what she thought had really happened in room 524, she said: 'I think he was beside himself with anger and a loss of hope and pain and desperately missing the girls. I think he was drunk. He spoke to Bob and then…whatever happened, happened. I don't know. I think it was a lot of things meeting head-on. I don't think he meant to die. And nor does anyone who knew him…'

When asked about the rumours that Michael was involved in some kind of sex game that went wrong, she said: 'I don't think there's anything on earth Michael wouldn't do. I don't know what was happening. Maybe we'll never know. I still don't think it was a deliberate act.'

She continued: 'Everyone knows I blame Bob. We won't be speaking again. Ever. I left the court, turned to my barrister and said, "This will kill Michael".' He died a few hours later. Paula revealed that she had considered suicide and that worried friends had refused to leave her alone, even at night. She said: 'It crossed my mind every five minutes. It still does. But it's not an alternative because I have the girls.' And Paula vowed she'd never have another man. She said: 'I waited a long, long time to be with Michael and now I'll wait a long time to be with him again.'

She said she didn't have a relationship with her mother. The interviewer then said: 'Gerry Agar has claimed that it's not for want of trying on your mother's part.' And Paula retorted:

I can state absolutely that my mother has not tried to contact me except to send me a note of condolence that said she won't be missing Michael because, of course, she never met him. So please don't ever quote Gerry Agar at me. The woman is quite simply a middle-aged mum that I happened to meet on the school run who has made a great deal of money out of my family and caused us a great deal of pain.

---- ◆ ----

In March, Paula was back in Sydney with Belinda and her bodyguard, guests of Australian TV Channel 9 for a reported $60,000 plus expenses. She was to record an interview for current affairs programme *60 Minutes*. She had collected her portion of Michael's ashes and held a ten-minute vigil in the room in which he died. When she left she was in a state of renewed anguish and she spied a photographer training his lens on her. She marched up, grabbed the man by the throat and pushed him back across the bonnet of a car shouting: 'Leave me alone – my husband died here!' When the police interviewed her she claimed that he had punched her, an accusation he strenuously denied.

The Australian press lapped up everything she had to say, and provided her with a platform from which to reassert her claim, in the strongest terms to date, that she could not accept the coroner's verdict. In fact she stated that she was taking advice and planned to mount a legal challenge against the verdict of suicide.

In a radical reversal of her original statement to the world that Bob killed Michael, she said:

> I will be making it abundantly clear that because of information that I and only I could know about Michael, I cannot accept the verdict. The coroner didn't meet him or know him and he would not have left his baby – never, never, never, never, never! Michael thought suicide was the most awful thing in the world, the most cowardly act, just a cop-out. He was too much of a gentleman, too much of an old-fashioned protector to have left me the way I've been left. He would not have left our baby. Never, never, never, never, never.

While she and Belinda were in Sydney they planned a secret christening for Tiger and sold the rights to OK! magazine in the UK for a rumoured £100,000, though Belinda dismissed rumours that the event was about to take place as 'complete bollocks'. That week Paula called Patricia; she was still seething about Tina's comments in the press and berated Michael's mother for failing to phone her during the week of the funeral. Patricia reminded her that in LA Paula had been emphatic that she never wanted to hear from Patricia again. Paula denied she'd ever said that but her mood suddenly switched to syrupy sweet, as she explained that she wanted Tiger to have a relationship with her grandmother. But in no time the demon erupted again, she sounded drunk and was back on the offensive about Tina's betrayal. When Patricia stood by her daughter's statements, she recalled that Paula said: 'Oh please, Patricia, let's not talk about anything else when Michael's ended up hanging on a doorknob.'

In a series of subsequent calls Paula's tirade meandered across well-trodden ground – she continually insisted that Michael would never have left her, and that therefore he had not committed suicide. Patricia's patience was waning and she encouraged Paula to accept it so that she could move on, but Paula retorted that she was just jealous because she'd never got to sleep with Michael! Between these offensive conversations, Belinda was calling to arrange for Patricia to attend the christening, which Paula had omitted to mention. It is unclear whether they were sharing the same space, but Belinda seemed unaware that Paula was in rapid decline. She was making no sense, and finally threatened Patricia that she was about to harm herself and Tiger and the blame would lie at her feet. Tina's answering machine was recording similar harassing calls and when Paula could not get through, she phoned Tina's work and said words to the effect that she had a famous human rights lawyer and five attorneys with her and they were in agreement that Tina and her mother were violating Tiger's human rights, and she'd better call back if she ever wanted to see her niece again.

Patricia engaged her lawyer to make formal requests for these threatening calls to end, but they persisted and she claimed that she could hear Tiger crying in the background. Finally Patricia phoned the police and impressed upon them the sensitivity of the situation with regard to the press. When the police called at Paula's hotel three hours later, Paula was asleep and Tiger seemed to be in good hands. Two days later, an article ran in the press that the police had been notified over Michael's mother harassing Paula about his will. Paula was quoted as saying: 'For Patricia to suggest that I would neglect my child is disgraceful, especially when one of her sons hung himself.'

Belinda said Patricia had phoned about the christening and told Paula she was reluctant to attend because: 'The problem is, Paula, you are a pig.' Paula told the paper that Michael sometimes displayed anger about his mother, and Belinda added: 'He used to call her the witch or the bitch.' Even at the extremes of his emotions, Michael did not have it in him to describe any female in such a derogatory way, especially not his mother, of whom I heard him speak in nothing but glowing terms.

By all accounts, the ceremony was a rushed affair lasting only twenty minutes. There were no hymns, no adoring speeches by the family and Michael's name was never mentioned. Somehow, when everyone left, the christening certificate was left behind on a pew. In the restaurant booked for the post-ceremony party, the guests were asked to wait while Paula and Tiger attended the crucial *OK!* photo call. She appeared two hours later, but the child was over-tired so she made her excuses and left. Later Paula claimed to the press that Patricia had snubbed an invitation to attend the christening. 'All of Michael's family came – except for his mother and sister, who I must hasten to say, were invited,' she said. 'I rang Michael's mother three times and begged her to come. She said to me that Michael never loved me . . . this was a monumental moment for Tiger and to reject Tiger – that's nothing to do with a family feud.'

From the discarded certificate the papers were able to publish the line-up of Tiger's godparents: Belinda Brewin, Martha Troup, Josephine Fairley, Catherine Mayer, Andrew Young, Colin Diamond and Nick Cave.

Back in the UK Paula had to check back into Clouds again. She was apparently suffering from 'something close to a nervous breakdown', and one of her close friends, quoted as a 'spokesman for Ms Yates' told the papers:

> After unceasing pressures from Patricia Glassop and Tina Shorr, amounting to worldwide writs against Tiger Hutchence's inheritance and against the wishes of her father Michael Hutchence, Paula Yates has been forced to return to a [rehab] clinic for further grief counselling and stress-related treatment.

Another friend said:

> Paula is ill but not that ill. It's been one thing after another since Michael's death and she just had to go away for some counselling and

full-time care. She'll be fine eventually, but I've watched her being bludgeoned day after day.

First it was the suicide verdict, which none of us believe because Michael adored her and Tiger Lily so much, then the news that Jess Yates wasn't her father and Hughie Green – a man she never knew – was, and now the wrangling over Michael's money.

Frankly, it was better that she go away now for some help rather than risk topping herself.

She said Paula would remain in the clinic until she felt more 'balanced so that she can then come home and be a fantastic mother again to the girls'.

Belinda, who was looking after Tiger, told the press: 'I don't think Paula is in any fit state to think about anything. She is barely able to survive the next five minutes at the moment and it upsets me greatly to talk about it. She really is not in a good way. She is just getting through the therapy.' Belinda criticized the timing of the legal challenge, saying correctly that it revolved around assets that the family claimed were not included in Hutchence's will. Though Paula had nothing to do with these proceedings, she said:

I am at a complete loss as to why they've decided to take this course of action, irrelevant of anybody's feelings. Tiger Lily is Michael's only child – she's twenty months old and has no father. There must be some compassion somewhere, and you would think that whatever their feelings for anybody, they would bury them and make sure that Tiger is well looked after.

At no time did any of Paula's friends mention her substance addictions, the prescription drugs and the alcohol. There is no doubt that Paula was in more emotional pain than anyone should bear in a lifetime, but at the clinic they would be tackling her addictions as a necessary precursor to addressing the underlying causes – in fact the clinic she was in, Clouds House in Wiltshire, specialized in drug and alcohol detoxification with a programme based on the AA twelve steps. Her friends were always specific in their insistence that Paula was there for grief counselling and stress, citing the ongoing problems with Bob and now Michael's family's legal wrangles.

——— ◆ ———

Around the time that Paula was taking her DNA test, my baby daughter, Millie Loveday, was born in a remote farmhouse near Glastonbury in Somerset. I had moved there in April 1997 when I discovered that I was pregnant, as I could no longer take the continued acrimony of life in London. Anita came to stay a couple of weeks before I was due to give birth. The following day, she had to leave. I was sad to see her go, but relaxed into my solitude with my beautiful baby daughter.

My peace was shattered, however, by a ten-page article which appeared in the *Sunday Times* magazine some weeks later. I had agreed to an interview at my home with an investigative reporter called Tim Rayment about Michael's death. During the discussion I had explained that I believed Michael's drug abuse had contributed to an inability to separate fact from fiction, which had been exacerbated by Paula's fabrications about the custody battles, Bob's power and her finances. This condition had, in my view, deepened into paranoid delusion, which together with pressures in his own career had led to suicide. Rayment seemed to agree.

When it appeared in print, however, I was staggered by the 'spin' the story had taken. Just as Paula had persuaded me to create a PR myth to discredit Bob, she and her 'inner circle' were now doing the same thing to me. The crux of the article was that Michael's mental decline could be tracked to the drugs bust from which he had never recovered and that I was therefore responsible for his death. It was implied throughout that I had planted the drugs, and publicized the find from motives of vengeance, believing I was owed money for PR work it was claimed I had never done. 'She was never more than a mother from the school run,' Paula said of me. The 'inner circle' also repeated the lie that I may have killed my nanny because she knew too much. Rayment quoted Paula's friends' insistence that she was teetotal and had never been seen taking drugs.

It was evident that the intelligent man who had interviewed me had also been drawn in by Paula: spun around, flattered and cajoled until he didn't know which way was up. Just as her friends were. Just as we all had been. Especially Michael. What went through Tim Rayment's mind when Paula died of an overdose can only be imagined.

18 decline and fall

PAULA SPENT HER BIRTHDAY in the clinic. Once she was out she moved into a rented house in Courtnell Street, Notting Hill, having sold Redburn Street for around £800,000. Two weeks later there was an ambulance outside. Paula had suffered a 'health scare' and a friend said she'd been found in a 'distressed state'.

She had been shooting a travel show with Channel 4 in Sri Lanka. It was her first paid job for many months and she must have hoped that sunshine and work would distract her, but the storm clouds hung on the horizon. A friend who was with her on the trip said he'd never seen her so unhappy and at night she joined the crew as they relaxed, drinking with them under the stars.

In London her friends expressed surprise: Paula was not known as a drinker; in fact, they said, she had always declared that she did not like alcohol. She was only back at home for a day when Belinda let herself into the house and found Paula unconscious, hanging from a door. One friend was quoted, saying: 'We all noticed that she wasn't herself and was taking things badly. But none of us thought it would come to this and we're in shock at the news.'

Another said: 'I've dreaded a call to tell me Paula has tried to take her life in the same way that Michael died. I always knew that she would try to copy him. It's something she's done all her life – copied those she loves.'

Among her unnamed friends, one of them seemed to have the measure of the situation: 'Paula's sick. She needs a lot of help. She isn't thinking straight but knows she must come to terms with Michael's death. One minute she'll talk about getting her life back on track and the next about killing herself. She's become unhealthily obsessed about being with Michael again.'

Beneath all my anger at the treatment I had received from Paula's new crowd, I grieved for my lost friend as if she had taken her own life over a year ago. Paula had been trying to escape her pain with drugs and drink for almost as long as she had known Michael; now she was very ill and she wanted to push the eject button. Her illness had been out of control for months and only sustained professional help would lead her towards recovery. But this was the original catch-22: she would not get that help unless she asked for it, but in her state she couldn't accept that she needed it. Her only hope was the co-ordinated efforts of the people around her. If they acted together she still had a chance, and so did the children, but I had already said goodbye. I had moved beyond hope and fear; for me it seemed that only a miracle could avert the inevitable.

So Paula was back in the Priory, a hospital for severe psychiatric disorders, and from there she was referred back to Clouds for detoxification. Paula's now regular trips to these establishments were sparking increased media interest in the role of detox clinics, spawning spin-off stories in the papers. Once again, she was at the vanguard of a movement now well established in the public awareness.

In Australia, Patricia was making concerned noises about the latest development in Tiger's home life and there were renewed rumours of a custody bid. She would make no definite comment but one of her closest friends said: 'There have been no serious legal moves yet but we have always taken the threat very seriously. Patricia got the police around to the hotel when Paula was in Australia. The threat is to prove that Paula is unfit. What happened this week obviously makes it easier.' But this may have been a legal bid too far for them at the time, as their action against the executors of Michael's will had been underway for some weeks and in a surprise development, Colin Diamond had resigned from his role. Michael had been declared technically bankrupt but it was said that up to AUS$40 million was located in property deeds and offshore trusts stretching from Hong Kong to the British Virgin Islands. Several of the trusts were believed to be in tax havens in the South Pacific, including Vanuatu and the Cook Islands. These assets were effectively owned and controlled by the appointed trustees, and had been structured in this way to avoid tax liabilities. Under the terms of such trusts, beneficiaries of a will are not entitled to inspect the trust accounts.

Patricia and Tina were suing the executors of the will to include the trusts in Michael's estate, which would not affect the percentages specified but would increase the pot from nothing to the rumoured AUS$40 million. They repeatedly asserted that this was to ensure that all the beneficiaries received what Michael had intended, especially Tiger Lily.

In an interview she gave later in the year Paula said that the final trigger for her term at Clouds was severe flu. She vehemently denied that she had tried to emulate Michael's suicide and blamed the ambulance crew for the leak to the papers, hinting that they had spawned the lurid story. Clouds, she said, had been 'quite fun in a kind of boarding school way' and had helped her to stop blaming herself for Michael's death. She said she had checked herself in and spent a month there.

At Clouds House, the basic treatment is said to take forty-two days, with increased treatment plans, depending on individual cases. They say that the chances of relapse are dramatically reduced if the course is completed. Paula was out within a week and seen shopping in Knightsbridge on the arm of her new love, twenty-six-year-old Kingsley O'Keke.

A friend said: 'She has had a tortuous time since Michael died and there were days when she felt she could not go on. But her time in the clinic has turned things around for her, not least because she has met Kingsley. Paula is smiling again and it has a lot to do with Kingsley. They are getting on very well.'

Others claimed that, despite the age gap, Paula and Kingsley were instantly attracted to each other as they clung together for support and had since become inseparable. They said he'd been a 'tower of strength' as she battled to recover after her suicide bid.

They had met in the rehab clinic and were ejected together. The tabloids had them 'at it like rabbits' in the wooded grounds of Clouds House and sneaking into one another's rooms for sex. In truth they could easily have been discharged for much less. One of the central edicts at the clinic is that patients put their treatment first. There are no distractions allowed: no TV, no books or magazines, no stereos, no mobiles and no exclusive relationships. The treatment encourages patients to examine with each other their most intimate feelings and memories, in a safe and caring environment. Though the contact between patients often prompts the breakthroughs that underpin recovery, the atmosphere is fertile ground for exciting courtships to flourish. But these relationships are inevitably based on dysfunctions that complement one another (opposites attract) or shared traumatic experiences ('we had so much in common'). The clinics forbid such liaisons because the thrill of a new relationship is just another drug and a fundamental objective of the treatment is to teach the patients to form bonds with healthy people. Paula said they were expelled for hanging out with the same people too much and that might well have been the case, but regardless of the rules she put the relationship before her recovery.

Back in London, the couple redefined the term 'whirlwind romance'. Paula was looking happier than she had in months and rumour had it that they were setting up home together. Kingsley's age prompted predictable 'toy boy' references. He was ruggedly handsome with a dark mop of shoulder-length hair and intense eyes. With his casual manner and penchant for chinos he could have walked straight out of a red-brick university, but a three-inch scar that stretched from his mouth to his ear spoke of a darker history; a story that the papers took seconds to uncover.

The boy who observers said was helping Paula rebuild her shattered life was a heroin addict, and the press was full of his alleged past in crime and drugs. O'Keke grew up on a council estate in west London with his mother, who was only four years older than Paula.

When the news of Paula's new relationship broke in Australia, Kell was furious. Since the funeral he had been at pains to forge ties with Paula for the sake of his contact with Tiger and he had become her staunchest defender. But he must have been outraged for his son's memory when he said: 'I don't mind her having an affair if it helps her get back on her feet. But there is such a thing as good taste,' and O'Keke's background convinced him that Paula was no longer a suitable mother; in fact he even went so far as to say that he had never considered her a suitable mother.

At the time, Belinda was in Australia with Tiger. They had been there for six weeks, giving Paula space for her treatment, which was supposed to run for that period. The trip was to afford Michael's family time with Tiger and they had stayed regularly with both Kell and Patricia. Such recent contact with their granddaughter made the danger to her seem even more immediate.

Kell launched a custody bid in the Australian courts, part of which included an alert at points of departure for Belinda and Tiger to be detained while police contacted Kell. Belinda told Paula about Kell's action and Paula told her to return immediately, but when she turned up at the airport the police moved in. On the phone they gave Kell a split-second decision whether to hold Belinda and Tiger or let them go on their way. He relented and allowed them to leave. During her time in Australia, Belinda had allegedly been telling Michael's family the truth of what was going on in London. She said she had been looking after Tiger for the best part of a year. Belinda said Paula was impossible; she'd had enough of her, and would have walked away had it not been for the fact that Tiger needed her.

Kell was recovering from a bypass operation and began to question his own strength and resolve to engage in a trans-global fight through the British courts. (He died, aged seventy-eight, of lung cancer in December 2002.) Ultimately he dropped the lawsuit, but not before it served at least a minor purpose. Paula dumped O'Keke, officially stating that his presence would jeopardize the custody suit being brought against her for Tiger.

O'Keke turned his ten-week fling into a retirement fund by selling his story to the tabloids. His lurid account was serialized over two days, but of all the tragic details, it was not the bizarre bedroom antics that caught the public imagination. O'Keke confirmed what had so far only been rumoured – that Paula slept with Michael's ashes sewn into a sequinned pillow.

——— ◆ ———

My understanding of Paula's life came more and more from the press and was presented as a series of contradictory façades. In her seasonal appearance in *OK!* she presented a hyper-real version of herself, circumspect and philosophical, missing Michael but moving on and staying strong for the girls. She occasionally ventured out to a fashion show or function with Tiger on her hip and in the omnipresent company of Belinda Brewin. Rumours emerged of potential TV projects that hinted at her tentative efforts to relaunch her career, but she spent her days at home in virtual isolation, desperately trying to negotiate the practicalities of domestic life.

Geraldine Bedell published an insightful article for the *Express on Sunday* magazine in January 1999. Bedell's feature took the front cover with the strapline: *PAULA YATES: IS THERE LIFE AFTER MICHAEL?* She observed:

Many of those who know Paula, people who were on dinner party terms, haven't seen her for at least a year. She has relied more heavily than ever on a small coterie of close friends. These include the journalists Josephine Fairley, and Catherine Mayer. Jo Fairley has said: 'All Paula's friends feel the same. We don't want to dwell on the past, but to focus on the future.' There is a sense of closing ranks, a fierce protectiveness around her.

In a sense, Belinda Brewin has stepped into the shoes of Gerry Agar, Paula's former publicist, who was involved in the drugs raid at her home in September 1996 – the moment, it is fair to say, when things started to go wrong. It was also the moment at which Gerry was dropped and Belinda moved in to help...

Paula claims that Belinda has brought organization into her life, but judging from our conversations, it's more hysteria, upset, with no sense of proportion and little coherence. There's also no doubt in Belinda's mind of her right to speak for Paula – 'We're not interested in what Kell's got to say!' With friends like this, perhaps Paula doesn't need to do anything ditzy herself.

Though Bedell did find voices who praised Paula's wit and wished to see her flourish, she surmised that Paula would only find her feet 'in calm stability rather than the ersatz high drama that has been heaped on the genuine tragedy of her recent life.'

While Paula's not-so-carefully orchestrated public image struggled to portray a dignified widow, her personal appearances often told a more accurate story. She had already passed up a five-figure fee with a last-minute cancellation of her appearance on Sarah Ferguson, the Duchess of York's debut TV talk show *Surviving Life*. And her appearance in the Channel 4 travel show shot in Sri Lanka, which was supposed to be the first of a series, could not be screened after her suicide attempt. But someone at cable channel UK Living, with the steady hand of a seasoned gambler, decided to hire her to host an audience with chat-show king Jerry Springer in front of a celebrity crowd.

Paula was shaky from the start. She flopped on to the couch, seemed unable to sit upright and was constantly chewing at her lips. Her questions were barely audible and she had difficulty following the script. All of this was aggravated by a string of technical failures. None of the microphones appeared to be functioning properly and a UK Living poster peeled off the balcony and fell into the audience. Paula and Springer were eventually given hand mics, but Paula continued the interview without holding hers to her mouth and at one point she dropped it with an amplified crash.

Paula mumbled and sniffed through a series of obscure questions, asking Springer if he favoured guests called 'Kitten', and did all his guests wear maternity bras? Then she broke off, saying, 'My nose is really runny. I hate that when it happens on TV.' Springer appealed to the audience for a hankie and Melanie Blatt of pop-soul girl band All Saints left her seat to hand him one. While Paula blew her nose, Springer quipped: 'I don't like cocaine – I just like the way it smells,' which brought knowing guffaws from the celebrity audience. One onlooker said Paula was in a terrible state and her guest humiliated. Springer tried to rescue the show by taking over and appealing to the audience for questions. Paula snapped: 'Don't ignore me,' and threw her clipboard away.

It was a bizarre parody of Jerry Springer's own show: a fight broke out in the audience and celebrity guests continued to heckle, while they consumed the free drinks and talked into their mobiles. Springer said: 'This is great television... let me take this opportunity to apologize.'

At the end of what must have been the worst TV experience of Jerry Springer's entire career, he was coerced to join a country and western singer in a number, but when Paula's mic broke down, he had to take over the song. In a desperate aside, he pleaded: 'I'm dying out here, just dying – please forget you were ever here!' Paula had already left the stage and afterwards she was hopping mad. Belinda publicly blamed the staff of UK Living for their incompetence and she was furious at Springer for mentioning cocaine on stage. She said: 'Paula has flu. It's nonsense to suggest she was on drugs. She's never taken cocaine in her life.'

Cocaine is a tricky drug. A gram costs around £60; it is usually supplied in a small square slip of paper cut from a magazine and folded into a rectangular 'wrap'. For occasional users, a single wrap can be an evening of fun for two, cheaper than a couple of curries and a few rounds of drinks. But the body builds a rapid tolerance to its effects and increasing amounts are needed to reach the required high. Technically, users can never reach the euphoria that they experienced with their first line and it has been said that all cocaine users are on a mission to replay their very first experience of the drug. For this reason, when cocaine use goes wrong, it goes very wrong and it gets very expensive.

Of course, while the brain gains increasing immunity to cocaine, the nose does not. And neither does the wallet. Whether Paula had taken cocaine before or not, something was eating a rapid hole in her finances.

Even with the sale of Redburn Street and the fees she had been receiving for interviews and photo-shoots (some of them six-figure sums) she had repeatedly fallen behind on her rent, and was reduced to taking out bank loans to finance her lifestyle while the battle raged over Michael's will. Since she hardly ever went out, it is reasonable to ask: where was all the money going?

Through her lawyers, Paula put in a bid to the Australian court for access to some of Michael's funds. The latest news was that she was to inherit £1 million from the will and a friend of hers was quoted saying, 'Once the money comes in it will change things for good.' However, the money would still be tied up in the legal wrangles for months and Paula was looking for a loan for the down-payment on a house she wanted.

Meanwhile, Paula continued to confound the efforts of her friends to deny her substance abuse. Matthew Wright at the *Mirror* reported that Paula had been seen cruising the streets in her jeep, Belinda at the wheel and Paula dangling her legs out of the window. When they spied a photographer taking pictures of them from his car, they left their vehicle. Belinda verbally attacked the man and Paula leaned in through his window, grappled with him and punched him twice. He said she reeked of alcohol. Then the two assailants retreated, 'cackling', to their car leaving the man in shock, with a scratched face and a broken camera lens.

In June, Paula had started seeing twenty-four-year-old Scottish reggae star Finley Quaye. From his red open-top Porsche, Finley had spotted Paula walking down a Kensington street and had stopped to introduce himself. A month later they were doing the rounds of celebrity functions together and smooching at the after-show party at the première of Ewan McGregor's film *Rogue Trader*. Paula said, 'We are together and we are good for each other. It is a great feeling after all we have both been through.'

Paula and Finley had a couple of months to enjoy each other without the pressure of scandal, then Finley was spotted with an unnamed female friend in a West End bar. An observer recounted: 'They were touching, kissing and cuddling non-stop, all night.' And Finley had a hotel room booked next door. It hit the news-stands in the *Mirror* – by-line Matthew Wright – and Paula hit Finley with the rolled-up tabloid until he woke up.

A few days later, Finley was standing in his underpants at the door of Paula's house, denying press rumours that they were to wed. But Paula had a big green Cartier rock on her finger and 'friends said' that she'd told them: 'Finley asked me to marry him. I am not going into details, but it was very romantic and I said "Yes" straight away. I am very happy and I am feeling great.'

They were words of dark comedy and searing agony. They coincided with Prince Charles's Prince's Trust Party in the Park, an open-air pop gig in Hyde Park. Drunk on the free champagne, Paula fell down in the VIP tent, boobs falling out of her dress, and retched into her designer handbag. Two minders carried her out to a limo to save her further embarrassment, but the car only rolled a few feet before the window came down and she was sick again. When she arrived home she fell over twice on the way to her door, and her minders had to take the keys from her as she could not find the lock.

Next day Paula had a triple headache: she was moving to a mews terrace house 300 yards away, and the press were swarming for a comment on the Party in the Park. She said: 'Oh God, I was ill as anything. I had food poisoning. It was oysters. They are still in my fridge actually. I ought to throw them out. They are there as a monument to my illness.'

But Paula and Finley were having problems and Finley was trying to back out of the relationship. Paula took it hard. She'd been in her new house only two weeks before there was an ambulance outside. Ten-year-old Peaches had found her mother sprawled at the bottom of the stairs, unconscious. In a panic, she ran out on to the street in her pyjamas and intercepted a couple returning from a shopping trip. She was crying, 'Please, please help me. My mummy's collapsed. Please come.' They found Paula on the floor in a nightie, and had to cover her up.

The man put a pillow under her head and, as he did so, Paula grabbed Tiger Lily and said: 'I'm so sorry he was taken from us so soon. It was not my fault. We must stick together.' His girlfriend said she had not recognized Paula and she asked her name, to which Paula gave a wan smile and said, 'Paula'.

They said Paula was a mess, pale and soaked in perspiration. When they announced that they would phone for an ambulance, Paula became agitated and begged them not to, but they did anyway. Then they called Bob who was in Spain, and he arranged to fly back immediately. When the ambulance and police arrived, Paula refused to let them take her to hospital and kept begging for them not to take her children away.

Bob phoned the couple to thank them for their assistance. He was told that when Paula came round, she was saying, 'I didn't kill Michael.' Belinda said: 'Bob's got the other kids – I've got Tiger. Paula will be all right after she's slept it off for two or three nights. She didn't have to go to hospital, but there was an ambulance and Bob went off with the children.' When asked what was the matter with Paula, Belinda replied: 'You work it out!'

Next day Paula said to the press gathered outside her house: 'I tripped over a dust sheet and knocked myself out. I've got builders in doing work on the house and there was a dust sheet near the door which I fell over.' When they asked why she had fallen, she replied: 'Ask the fucking builders.' She carried on by saying: 'There's nothing wrong. Aren't my children asleep upstairs? Everything's fine. I'm well. The kids are well.'

Finley admitted the relationship had been so turbulent that he decided to give up girlfriends to concentrate on work and on being a father to his six-year-old son Theo. He said: 'I've been mashed up by too many loose women in the past. My love life is back on the straight and narrow, there'll be no more Casanova.' And Paula was back for a spell in the Priory.

———— ◆ ————

After her Jerry Springer experience, Paula should have been wary of TV appearances but, like a fallen rider, she got back in the saddle. She collaborated closely on a Channel 4 documentary *In Excess: The Death of Michael Hutchence*, which questioned the suicide verdict. Paula was now going public with her conviction that Michael died by accident in an act of auto-erotic asphyxiation (AEA).

I'm doing it for me and Tiger. I desperately want people to see that it wasn't suicide. The truth about what happened to Michael should be known. Michael loved us. He had everything to live for. I know his death could not have been anything but an accident. If any of the people making the decisions had known Michael, they would have known that he loved life too much to want it to end.

She was keen to prove that Michael had not left her and Tiger deliberately, and chose instead to paint his death in the lurid terms of a sexual adventure that went wrong. 'He was a dangerous boy. Dangerous. wild. He could have done anything at any time. The one thing he wouldn't have done is just left us.'

The documentary depended heavily on Paula's opinion and anecdotal evidence. The producers pulled in coroners and academics and as many of Michael's friends who would attest to his lust for danger and excitement. Paula argued: 'The whole scenario of being naked and not leaving a note are two of the things that I find most revealing about all this. Basically I don't agree with a word the coroner said – or how he worded it.'

Paula insisted that if Michael had meant to take his life, he would have done things differently:

He would have dressed. He would have written a note. He would have done it as a ritual. That's if he'd ever thought of killing himself, which I don't believe he'd ever have done. Especially not with his responsibility to me and Tiger, which he took so seriously. So to be found naked and just found like that, he must have been doing something else. Michael would have hated to be found naked, to have lost his dignity. He had lots of dignity, no matter what was happening. So to be just found on the floor naked? No.

Paula recalled Michael's fascination with AEA and said he was keen to try it but was scared that it would kill one of them. It was an unverifiable statement, tailor-made to promote the argument. The interviewer asked:

'Did Michael ever choke you, strangle you or tie you up in bed?' An impish smile dawned, and she whispered to someone off camera from behind her hand. Her face lit up and she replied: 'He did everything.' Paula wanted to undermine the view of this sexual practice as sordid. She took pains to explain that it was not an uncommon act. 'It was no big deal what he did. Lots of people do it. It went wrong. I just want it stopped being made grubby.'

The TV programme on Michael's death turned to Professor Stephen Hucker, one of the world's leading authorities on AEA. His verdict was: 'When the pathologist said there was no evidence, he actually had the strongest evidence – the nudity.'

And Michael's brother Rhett proffered evidence that Michael was already experimenting with AEA: 'From what I'd heard, Michael was in the Chateau Marmont, Los Angeles, in his room with Martha. He looked over and said: "Martha, I'm going to get in trouble." Martha said: "What do you mean?" and Michael pointed to the air-conditioning duct. He had screwed a ring bolt into the duct. At the time she had no idea what it meant.'

Michael's family would dearly love to have believed that Michael's death was accidental. When Geraldine Bedell interviewed Kell in Australia, she said he 'doesn't believe for a moment it was suicide,' and was considering a challenge to the coroner's report. He said, 'There are gaps I'm not happy with.' Several months earlier he had been convinced it was suicide. If nothing else, this showed that even the close family could not move on. Ultimately they would have to make a choice or live in limbo, but none of them could stomach the alternative verdict that Paula was trying to push.

'I don't know what she is on about... in the coroner's report there is no evidence at all of any suggestion of auto-eroticism,' said Kell. 'I don't know why she is discrediting Michael like this... but I'm sure he didn't intend to kill himself.' Kell was manifestly confused. By now there was no love lost between him and Paula, and he was not going to let the world forget that, suicide or accident, there were other theories:

She came out for the funeral and she was in a shocking state, and I said, 'For God's sake, woman, pull yourself together... if it wasn't for you and your ex-husband my son would be alive today.' I feel, quite reluctantly, it's time to reveal that more than once Paula told Michael that unless he married her she would do away with herself and Tiger. Michael told me she said that on at least two occasions. This created a terrible crisis for him. We and the police have often wondered what she said to him in the early hours of November 22, 1997. Michael had become the meat in the sandwich in her fight with Bob Geldof over their children. Paula was exploiting my son and bleeding him dry financially with her massive court costs. She placed him under unbearable pressure and he finally could not take any more. He was trapped with nowhere to go.

Psychologist Oliver James, who worked with Paula on a television series and knew Hutchence, said he believed it probable that the pop star committed suicide, adding: 'I believe they were having problems. He was the average flaky pop star, feeling trapped. Obviously Paula would prefer people to think her partner did not commit suicide because it points to failure and blame. People like her never blame themselves.'

But all these testimonials were predicated on supposition and interpretations of the evidence in room 524, and the programme could draw no definite conclusions. The evidence of the previous eighteen months told a different story. There was no denying that Michael was in a severely depressed state. The conversation with Michele Bennett and the messages on Martha's answer-phone showed a desperately anguished man. Not a state of mind that would promote any feelings of eroticism.

Though much was made of the omissions in the investigation, they amounted to tenuous suppositions that items of little significance were missing from the room. This evidence and similar observations of Michael's sexuality, his penchant for bondage practices, were ably documented by Vince Lovegrove's book, *Michael Hutchence: A Tragic Rock 'N' Roll Story – A Definitive Biography*. He explored similar avenues to the Channel 4 documentary, but could draw no conclusions and focused on the pressure from Paula's chaotic obsessions.

The police and the coroner explored the possibility of AEA and dismissed it. In his report, the coroner was specific that 'there is no forensic or other evidence to substantiate this suggestion.' It has been said that the verdict of suicide is often recorded in cases of AEA, to protect relatives from the indignity of the facts, but would such a smoke-screen have survived the years of scrutiny that have followed Michael's death? The coroner's report was dominated by the evidence that Michael was in a severely depressed and agitated state. The evidence of the singer's state of mind precluded a verdict of AEA and they had the physical evidence from the examination of the body and the means of death. Michael body was kneeling facing the door. He had used a heavy belt, and the buckle had broken away from the force of the body falling into the noose. He would have been unconscious after about ten seconds. Auto-erotic asphyxiation, on the other hand, requires gentle control of the strangulation, gentle pressure in the noose.

In 2000, the New South Wales coroner Derrick Hand was retiring after a decade in the role. He was interviewed about his grizzly career and the controversial cases that had made him a household name in Australia. Top of the list was the Hutchence question that was clearly still torturing the collective psyche of the Aussie population. Hand said:

> *I felt by having a public inquest all it would get is great media coverage and sensationalism. Paula Yates has made lots of claims overseas that she*

is asking the coroner to reopen it; she is asking the Attorney-General to reopen it. Well, she's never asked me to reopen it. She wants her daughter to be told that he died through auto-eroticism, not suicide? Now, I reckon you can explain to your child much better why your father committed suicide because of all the hassles than trying to explain auto-eroticism! There was no evidence of auto-eroticism; the fact that he was naked, that was all. I have no doubt Mr Hutchence killed himself. It was the combination of the drugs, and the combination of the problems he had over the children, and the fact he was not in a great state of mind.

———— ◆ ————

The turning of the new millennium could have been a turning point for Paula. The predictable cycle of her toy-boy affairs and her public humiliations under the influence of alcohol seemed finally to have broken through her low dignity threshold. She admitted her biggest fault had been to put the men in her life first and said she was dumping the boys. She had made so many trips to the Priory, perhaps the programme there was beginning to make an impact too. She said: 'I went to the Priory clinic so much they virtually named a wing after me. But I am much better and I'm dealing with it.'

A string of jobs reintroduced her to the public and raised her profile in the right direction. She had a beauty column in *OK!* magazine and to the derogatory snorts of celebrity pundits, she became an agony aunt for a woman's magazine called *Aura*. A month into the job, Paula was getting glowing reports from her boss, editor of *Aura* magazine: 'She is a very focused, grown-up 40-year-old woman, a reliable professional who never misses a deadline.'

Next up was a one-off for a Channel 4 pop music series called *Top Tens*. On the show for which she was hired, Paula was an inspired, if somewhat ironic, choice as presenter exploring the phenomenon of boy bands. She was in her element chatting to Gary Barlow, Ronan Keating and Mickey Dolenz from The Monkees, and the programme received excellent reviews – the best of the series.

But this was all a brief oasis of calm. Through periodic contact with Anita the previous year, I had been updated with news of the home-lives of the Geldof girls, and Paula by default. Anita had been temping as an itinerant maternity nurse. The night work suited her as it left her free to help Bob and stay in contact with Fifi, Peaches and Pixie. Then Anita was hired through an agency by a top journalist. Anita had the little boy sleeping through the night inside two weeks and her employer was so impressed she asked her to stay on. Anita agreed to stay for six months, but the arrangement lasted beyond this period. Anita was working round the clock, helping Bob whenever he needed her and when she had time off. But her position with her new employers became still more idyllic when her employers made it clear that the Geldof girls were welcome to stay. The arrangement seemed amicable and the girls became part of the family on the frequent occasions when Bob and Jeanne were working out of town. Though he had a demanding and successful career, her employer's partner would often meet Fifi off the bus as she returned for a weekend home from boarding school.

When Paula heard that Anita was working for a journalist she went berserk. It inflamed her paranoia, as she was sure that they were collaborating against her. This was exacerbated further when she discovered that her girls were staying over. Calls began to come through to the house, interrogating Anita, threatening her and accusing her of ruining Paula's life. The calls intensified when the girls were staying and often came late at night.

Ultimately Paula triumphed when Anita's employer, too, became a target of abuse. After a particularly harrowing interchange, the journalist was shaken and decided that it was too dangerous to have the Geldof girls in the house, scared that one of her step-children might inadvertently pick up the phone to a raging caller. With great regret, she told Anita that if the harassment did not subside, Anita would have to leave the household. So once again Anita had lost her precious girls, and her new life that had been going so well was in jeopardy. Luckily the calls diminished significantly once the girls were no longer staying.

In May 2000, the bitter two-year legal battle over Michael's will was brought to an end by an out-of-court settlement. Paula's cut of the settlement was a disappointing come-down from the million she had been expecting, but she claimed she did not want her pay-out, that it should all be going to Tiger. Speaking as Paula's 'agent', Belinda said: 'It is not about the money. It is the fact that this case has been settled without any legal representation for Paula or Tiger. We have repeatedly asked to be represented at the case and now, clearly, they have gone ahead without us. It is outrageous. She'll be speaking to her lawyer very soon.' And this was all the thanks that Patricia and Tina were going to get. They had been co-ordinating the action since Michael's demise. They had repeatedly encouraged Paula and Kell to join forces with them, but received no word from London. Regardless, they had worked tirelessly in their free time for this result and endured constant criticism from the press. They'd sued fourteen people and Patricia had taken the huge risk of funding the suits herself, with legal fees reputedly soaring to AUS$500,000. Now they were vindicated and, as they had always protested would be the case, their action had benefited all those named in Michael's will – particularly Tiger, who was set to inherit a substantial amount on reaching the age of twenty-five.

Since Paula's first suicide bid, her girls had been spending the majority of their time with Bob. But at seventeen, Fifi had spent a year trying to reconnect with her mother and had nursed her following her fall down the stairs.

The danger to the children must have been a constant worry to Bob, however, and perhaps that was why he began to encourage Paula to stay with them at his house. She became a regular visitor and was able to sleep with the girls at night in safety. Anita said she felt for her – she looked dreadfully drawn. There was a positive spin-off from the visits, however: Tiger was able to spend more time with her sisters, and she became fond of Bob.

Paula's visits to Bob's house indicated a new and ever sadder phase of her life. Though she seemed to have a few staunch friends who claimed to watch out for her, in truth she was alone for much of her week and through those periods when Jo and Catherine were working, she could only call on Belinda and she was desperately lonely. Since Michael, her 'boys' had been more of a burden than a support. Her last boyfriend had been twenty-year-old Samuel Robinson-Horley, but he had slipped silently back into obscurity as smoothly as he had appeared.

Although the work front for Paula had seemed to be improving, it started disintegrating only a few months later. She had been hired to present an *Elle* style award, but an hour before the ceremony kicked off Belinda called the organizers to say that Paula had been stung on the mouth by a bee, and couldn't speak. She had been billed to present a one-off millennium edition of *The Tube*, and had even booked Courtney Love as a guest interview, but at the eleventh hour the producers mysteriously changed their minds and hired Donna Air instead. *OK!* passed Paula's £70,000-a-year job as beauty expert to a stunning twenty-two-year-old junior writer, and *Aura* magazine 'folded' after three editions.

In the public eye Paula's stock was still plummeting through the floor. When Belinda pulled Paula out of the *Elle* awards, no doubt she had made the right decision, but when the two of them turned up at the première of *The Next Best Thing*, starring Rupert Everett and Madonna, it seemed that her judgement had failed her. Paula's eyes were half-closed, she wore a smile of mild amusement and was lurching as if on the deck of a boat.

Whatever she had been taking, the effects caught up with her by the time they arrived and she was flying. Inside, she was waving her arms in the air, swaying to her own internal music. She made a scene when she tried to have her picture taken with Rupert and security asked her to leave. But she came back for the after-show party with 'glazed' eyes and looking wrecked. Belinda claimed they had been drinking beforehand at the Ritz.

Later, Paula denied she'd been drinking or taking drugs. She said she was waving her arms about because of the trailing sleeves of her black and lime full-length dress, and she denied being thrown out.

Early in September 2000, Paula gave an interview to *OK!* in which she spoke of new work, a new house in Hastings, escaping London to write and starting to rebuild her life. The cover carried a portrait of her and Tiger that was a virtual duplicate of a cover the magazine had run two years earlier when she had opened her heart for the first time after Michael's passing. The pose was the same but two years of turmoil showed in both their faces. On the cover in February 1998 Paula's face was fresh and unblemished, her expression held a fixed smile that was perhaps slightly unsupported by her eyes, while Tiger grinned with the open unaffectedness and twinkle of a child who had not yet spent two years on earth. Paula 2000 was attempting the same smile but her purple lips would only purse; her light tan could not hide the red blotches that bruised her skin; the lines that had only been a trace two years before were etched as if ten years' deeper, and her eyes were dark and sunken, contorted in a pained half-frown. Tiger's arm hung limply over Paula's shoulder, and she stared through the camera with a look of troubled reserve.

This was the best Paula could do now on her clearest days. Mostly she just existed. She rarely ventured beyond the local shops, but when she did it was often barefoot and alone in a distant narcotic universe. The company she was keeping inhabited the dark sub-culture of Notting Hill that spilled in from adjoining areas and recalled the disaffected ghetto of the Hill's not-so-distant past. One such individual was interviewed by a tabloid:

Paula was barefoot and dressed in one of her pretty frocks when I met her. She seemed stoned. Her eyes were darting around and I thought she was completely out of it. I know all about drugs and I know what people look like when they've taken them. That's what Paula looked like. Paula used to invite me to her house. I would always take her some chrysanthemums. I loved talking to her. She was so kind and would listen to me if I was in trouble. She struck me as being incredibly lonely. Even in her home she always seemed so alone.

Another local character said Paula was sometimes on the street, completely loaded, by 9.30 in the morning, and described how she would frequent a drug den in a council estate off Portobello Road. Paula's dealer allegedly had keys to her house, and on one occasion took Tiger to the park and linked up with other dubious individuals. The shopkeepers around Notting Hill knew her well. One said she was buying about a dozen miniature bottles of vodka every day – sometimes drinking them in the street.

19 the end

LATE IN THE SUMMER OF 2000 I had a holiday booked in Spain. I was looking forward to two weeks in Andalucia, southern Spain. In the chaos of last-minute preparations I picked up a phone message on my mobile from a barely coherent Paula. Since the drugs bust I almost never answered the phone and that is a phobia that still persists today. I'd had very occasional messages from Paula over the years, most of which were vaguely threatening or abusive in tone, but largely unintelligible. This one still had a menacing air but it was tinged with self-pity, and the words were vaguely decipherable.

'You wouldn't talk to me…did Bob give you… Was it the money? You should have shut me in a box…we gave you flowers…' That was all I could lift from the tape. Half-way into the holiday, I awoke with the clear memory that I had dreamed about Paula. It had followed the course of a fantasy that with decreasing regularity had played on my mind since 1996, in which Paula finally understood the action we had all taken when we found the drugs in the house. In the dream Paula said, 'I get it' and I knew with the self-conscious certainty dreams can induce that she was finally at peace.

That morning as we meandered through the holiday rituals of breakfast in the sun and wondering what the day would bring, I grappled with myself whether to mention my dream, nervous that my indulgent partner would think I was becoming obsessed. But I did eventually say it out loud and he just shrugged and said, 'Okay'. Not twenty minutes later, our next-door neighbour in London phoned my partner's mobile to tell us the news that Paula had died in the night.

On Sunday 17 September 2000, Josephine Fairley had called Paula's house and four-year-old Tiger answered the phone, saying 'Mummy's still asleep.' Alarmed, Jo raced round there. Tiger was distraught. She was an early riser, and had been trying to rouse her mother for hours. Paula was on the bed, naked and lying in a pool of vomit. Fairley called 999 and the operator asked her if she could perform the kiss of life. She stammered, 'I can't touch the body.'

Once the police forensic team departed, carrying various boxes sealed in polythene, Paula was removed in a burgundy bodybag and taken to Westminster mortuary for a post-mortem examination and an inquest.

It never became clear how they found out, but soon the police became aware that there had been a girl in the house before Paula died. Naturally the police were keen to trace the young woman.

One of her friends said: 'The girl has latched on to Paula over the last year and Belinda thinks she is a terrible influence. She is badly involved with drugs, especially heroin, and Belinda didn't want Paula near her.'

The friend went on to say: 'Belinda was very angry to discover the girl at Paula's house.'

The girl turned out to be the twenty-one-year-old daughter of a wealthy American. She had met Paula at the Priory, and once the pair became friends she apparently introduced Paula to many of her well-connected circle. She claimed it was she who brought Paula together with Finley Quaye, and she said she had also introduced Paula to her last boyfriend, Sam Robinson-Horley.

Belinda had left her daughter Indiana with Paula that day. Later, when she called to collect her child, she said she found Paula had been drinking and a row flared. 'I was unaware the girl was in the house at the time. She is a silly little girl,' said Belinda. 'Had I known, it would have totally changed the circumstances of the evening. Who knows what would have happened? From my point of view, it would have been a different story and I've told the police that.' Belinda added: 'When I saw that girl at Paula's house eighteen months ago, I told her that if I saw her there again I'd call the police.'

Westminster Coroners Court in central London heard that Paula had 0.3 milligrams of morphine per litre of blood in her body. When heroin is metabolized by the body, it breaks down into morphine. The coroner, Dr Paul Knapman, said that the amount found indicated an intake of heroin that would not have been enough to kill her had she been a seasoned addict – her death was the result of 'an unsophisticated taker of heroin' using the drug: 'The evidence does not point towards this being a deliberate act of suicide. It seems most improbable that she would attempt to kill herself with her daughter in the house. Her behaviour was foolish and incautious at that time.'

The pathologist, Dr Iain West, who carried out the post-mortem, said there were no injection marks and no outward sign that Paula had abused drugs. In her case the drug was enough to interfere with the function of her brain and stop her breathing. Mr West added: 'There was no alcohol in her blood, there was no alcohol in her stomach. There was no alcohol at all.'

Belinda told the inquest how she went to collect her daughter that Saturday evening. Paula had been sick all over the kitchen and could barely walk or talk. 'She was not in a very good state,' said Belinda. 'She was staggering, her eyelids were drooping, she was incoherent. I could tell that she had been taking drugs. I said to her: "What the hell are you doing this for, after this amount of time? This is completely ridiculous".'

Belinda told the inquest that it was the first time Paula had taken any drugs for nearly two years, adding:

She had been drunk on the odd occasion but she hadn't taken any illegal drugs. She said it was the pressure of being back in London. I said that was a rather pathetic excuse. She said she was sorry, she wasn't herself. I suggested she should go for a walk with me. I took her for a walk round the block a few times. I cleared up the mess in her kitchen – she had been quite sick. I put her in the bath and I washed her hair. I said you have to get yourself together. It was her daughter Pixie's birthday the next day. I was quite cross with her really. She said, 'Please don't be cross with me,' and I said, 'I'm not cross. I'm severely disappointed.'

That evening Belinda said she thought about taking Tiger Lily away from the house, but decided against it: 'When I left, Paula was quite coherent, she wasn't in a good state, but she was OK.' Belinda said that Paula had prevented her going into the bedroom, claiming she had been sick in there. But in fact her friend was in there, sleeping off a quarter-bottle of vodka.

Her young friend had arrived at Paula's home at about 2.30pm on Saturday 16 September. Paula was babysitting Tiger Lily, Indiana and a third child. The girl said that they lazed around the house and cooked for the children while Paula, who was terribly lonely, talked about her problems. But she said she did not think Paula was suicidal as she spoke positively about her plans to move to the country.

She said that when she left in a taxi, at about 9.30pm, Paula gave her a kiss goodbye and looked fine. She told the inquest that she knew Paula had taken illegal drugs in the past, including heroin, cocaine, Ecstasy and LSD, and said she had seen Paula snort heroin and cocaine.

She claimed that Paula did not drink any of her vodka and she finished the bottle herself. She had no idea Belinda had visited, as she was upstairs asleep. Asked if Paula had been under the influence of drugs, she said: 'No, I was quite drunk, but I did not see her take anything.'

The coroner asked: 'Did you supply Miss Yates with illegal drugs in the days before her death?' And she was emphatic: 'Absolutely not.'

Josephine Fairley said Paula had been 'a bit stressed' when they had spoken earlier in the week, 'But she was in an extremely positive frame of mind and when I saw her she was very upbeat.' She said when they last spoke at 7.30pm, on the Saturday night before Paula died, she had at first sounded 'a little bit slurred'. 'I said: "Are you OK?", and she said, "Yes, I've just got a house full of kids." But when she went upstairs to talk she was perfectly fine and *compos mentis.*'

Jo said she called three times the next morning but each time the phone was answered by Tiger Lily, who said, 'Mummy's still asleep.' Jo decided to go to the house to try to wake Paula herself to remind her friend to wish her daughter Pixie a happy birthday. But when Jo got to the house, there was no reply to her frantic knocking at the door. She said:

I rang up on my mobile phone and Tiger stood on a chair to let me in. I rushed upstairs expecting to tell Paula to wake up and took one look at her from the doorway and knew she was dead. She was naked, half-in and half-out of the bed, and a very strange colour for a human being.

Jo said by the time Tiger Lily had come up the stairs she had composed herself and stopped the little girl from entering her mother's bedroom. She said as far as she was aware Paula had not taken drugs since going into the Priory: 'I saw her every day and she was in extremely good form.'

A local shopkeeper was one of the last people to see Paula alive. She turned up at his shop at 8.30pm on the Saturday evening. 'She was looking very, very rough,' he said. 'She had no shoes on and she had this strange empty look in her eyes.'

After the inquest, Paula's solicitor gave a statement on behalf of her three closest friends:

An inquest tells you how someone died, and not how they lived. It gives no clue to the fullness and joy of Paula's life. Her friends will always remember her as a loving, warm, affectionate and witty mother, partner, wife and friend.

Who is to be believed: Belinda, who said Paula never took cocaine and had only got drunk occasionally in the last two years, or her 'friend' who said she knew Paula snorted cocaine and heroin? Or Jo Fairley, a respected journalist, who said she saw Paula every day, and as far as she knew Paula had been clean since leaving the Priory, or Kingsley O'Keke, a heroin addict, who said that she had a severe heroin and alcohol dependency?

O'Keke said she was spending £3,000 a week on drugs. Were these the rantings of a deranged mind, mixed up on narcotics and randomly spinning yarns, or were Jo and Belinda the deluded ones? Towards the end of Paula's life, she had relatives helping her out with the bills and bailiffs knocking because of unpaid utilities. A friend said: 'Paula had less than £14 in her bank account when she died.' Although it was widely believed that Paula had inherited £400,000 from Michael, there were reports immediately after her death that she had been sent a legal letter informing her that she and other beneficiaries would not be receiving anything from Michael's estate. If she received this letter in the days before she died, her mental state can well be imagined. She had played every card. There was no more pot of gold, her credit was up to the maximum and she allegedly owed the local pushers. She knew she only had days before it would all be closing in, and there would be no chemical escape without money. On the Friday before she died she must have been near total panic because she called Bob. Paula had wanted to talk to him about money.

Michael's friend Nick Egan said: 'Paula was on a self-destruct course. There was the drink and this thing about heroin. Paula was a British Marilyn Monroe, though much smarter.' The comparison had been made before and Paula may not live on as Marilyn has, an icon that defined an epoch, but like Marilyn she was more than the sum of her parts. You had to meet her to understand fully her compelling energy, but she communicated enough of her unique and inimitable vision of femininity to hold the nation rapt for a decade. In an age where we live vicariously through the faces of beauty caught and perfected by the two-dimensional distortions of a camera lens, so many personalities are disappointingly one-dimensional in the flesh. But her pictures do no justice even to her appearance – Paula was four-dimensional in person.

In death, Diana, Princess of Wales was deified by the patriotic pride of the British people and Paula enjoyed a similar liberation from her mortal fallibility, though obviously not on such a grand scale. Nevertheless, the outpouring of national sentiment, sympathy – grief even – spilled across hundreds of newspaper articles and newsreels, and spawned documentaries and endless debate that still continues even now.

Is it a rule for the writing of modern myths that the death must be shrouded in mystery? Like Marilyn and Diana and Michael, Paula died without explaining herself. With society's obsession for scientific certitude the coroner passed a verdict of 'death by misadventure' but like science he could not answer why. Like Michael's, her death seemed to inhabit the uncharted no-man's land between pre-meditated suicide and random accident. Michael's edged far closer to the suicide extreme and held more mystery but still the papers asked, 'Did she mean to go?'

Paula died when Michael died, but not when he hanged himself. If Paula had a death wish in her final years, Michael had one before they ever met. It has been said that taking drugs is the wish to experience death without finality. When Michael left his body, Paula left her mind. After his death, she said, 'I waited a long, long time to be with Michael and now I'll wait a long time to be with him again.' Well, two years must have felt like an eternity of pain and grief. She had said many times that she had to re-build her life for the sake of the girls, but she never once said she wanted it for herself. And without the fundamental will to live for herself, she was drawn again and again to seek the peace that her soulmate had found.

———— ◆ ————

That Sunday morning Pixie and her sisters had been waiting to go to their mother's to celebrate Pixie's birthday. Anita was there, and she told me that Bob came in looking pale, crying behind his eyes but fighting to hold himself together. With numb solemnity Bob told the children that they wouldn't be going to their mother's that day.

Bob paused before saying the most difficult words he has ever had to utter: 'I'm sorry, Mummy's died.' And then he broke down and cried. Anita, too, felt a rush of love for everything that Paula had once been. The girls were silent as they took in this dreadful news.

Against the odds, Fifi expressed the deepest sadness for her mother's memory. Tearfully, she made a pilgrimage to the house in Notting Hill to lay a bunch of yellow flowers at the steps of the flat. In a symbolic moment of solidarity for Paula, she refused to go inside until the photojournalists camped outside agreed to point their cameras away. They complied and she was free to complete her mission – to feed the cat.

Tiger had been with Jo Fairley in the hours following her mother's death. As the immediate aftermath subsided, it was arranged that Jo's husband would bring Tiger round to be with her sisters. Anita described the scene to me when Bob returned to find the tiny nervous waif sitting quietly on a bean-bag in his sitting room.

Within days Tiger was made a ward of court, compliant with a will that Paula made in the months after Michael's death. Her will stated that she wanted her daughter to grow up in Britain, not Australia, and that Tiger's grandparents were to be denied any contact thereafter: 'I wish that my said daughter Tiger Lily shall have no access to the parents of Michael Hutchence.' In the meantime Patricia spoke out about her concerns for Tiger's future:

We will sit down with Bob and talk it over, that is what we have agreed. As far as bidding for custody goes, so far we haven't ruled anything out. I am glad that she is in a safe place for now. We need to talk about it as a family, but people must not forget that she is Michael's daughter. She is the image of Michael and when I see her little face, it brings back such memories of him. We just want to love her. The situation with Paula was very sad, and now we have a chance to change things.

From her home in Burbank, California, Tina said that she and her mother were consulting lawyers in London: 'This is worth fighting for. I will go as far and as long as it takes to win this battle for Tiger's sake.'

The Geldof girls were distressed at this, terrified they might lose their baby sister. But Bob said, 'Tiger has half a family here at least. That's more than she has elsewhere.'

Patricia feared that Tiger would forget her father's name and nationality. Michael had wanted her to be brought up in Australia, she said, connected with her extended family. And she was concerned that Bob was not at home enough. With his business interests, his album, and his touring, would he have time for Tiger, or would she end up in the care of a nanny? Tina on the other hand would be ideal: she had time, she stayed at home, there were other children in the house and a father figure on tap.

But Tiger's sisters would be devastated to see her go and Bob clearly adored her. Tina was assured that they had no intention of letting Tiger forget who her real father was, nor her mother. They would both be evoked with the greatest respect. Anita planned that her room would be wallpapered with pictures of her family, and encouraged Patricia to send photos of cousins, aunts and uncles.

Anita did the most spectacular collage all over Tiger's room and when Tiger met her Australian family she already knew them by sight. Tiger's successful reunion with her sisters did nothing to rescue Bob. 'We are all so sad,' he said. 'The loss for all the children is insupportable. It doesn't require much imagination to understand the pain.'

When Paula died, her ghost called forth the love Bob had stockpiled for her since she left him. He threw himself into the funeral arrangements, using his grief and longing for Paula to stage-manage for her the perfect closing night.

With infinite tender attention to detail, Bob had Paula's body dressed by Jasper Conran, in a white mink bikini. He convened a congregation of rock-star royalty to unfurl the red carpet and applaud her ascent to showbiz Valhalla. The eighty on the guest list were given a password to grant them entrance to the church. And like every facet of this long kiss goodbye, the password would have been Paula's choice: it was 'Bollocks'.

They arrived in ones and twos, the famous and the family: Dave Stewart and Annie Lennox, Jasper Conran, Jools Holland, Fifi with Belinda, Jo Fairley and her husband, Martin Kemp, Nicky Clarke, Paula's mother, Paul Young and wife Stacey, Bono, Midge Ure, Kevin Godley, Nick Cave, Rupert Everett, Linda Plentl (Paula's half-sister by Hughie Green). It was a perfect autumn day as the Bentleys and Mercedes streamed up the drive to Bob's Davington Priory, for the service was in St Mary Magdalene's Church on the grounds.

The ancient church bell tolled as the cavalcade rolled between the ash trees of the graveyard. When all the dignitaries were seated, enveloped in flowers that seemed to bloom from every crevice of the twelfth-century stone work, Paula arrived. The petite coffin in cream and gold seemed too small to have contained her, whose energy had filled our lives and over-spilled. Bob had brought her home, to the house she had so cherished, to the church in which they had their marriage blessed and to the man who would have sold his soul to have her back alive. In his grief, poignantly manifest at the service, it must have seemed so logical to him. With the lavish decorations, the homage of her esteemed friends and the touching choral tribute by the choir of Canterbury Cathedral, Paula's twilight years were buried in an unmarked grave outside and Bob handed back to her the nation's admiration.

Jools Holland had helped choose the music and with 'Ave Maria', 'Jerusalem' and 'I Vow To Thee My Country', the choir lifted the gathering from their contemplations to a joyous vision of Paula's destination. Family friends read a poem by Keats, and Jools solemnly took his seat at a piano. With his magical hands, Jools transmuted the ringing echo of the choir into the lilting, irreverent tones of 'Blue Skies' while Bono sang. It was a fusion of tradition and idiosyncrasy that seemed infused by the very spirit of Paula Yates, and the ceremony was brought to a close with her own cover of 'These Boots Are Made For Walking'.

The first time Paula left him, Bob had said, 'I guess I will just go on loving her' and he had proved it in an unmistakable way. As the coffin left the church, Bob walked out in front; behind trailed the girls, holding hands. It was the shadow side to the joy and the life, the fêtes and garden parties that Paula had brought to the villagers, and a crowd of them stood silently at the gates, weighing the agony and the ecstasy of their outlandish Lady Geldof.

As the hearse pulled away, about twenty people left in cars for the cremation ceremony. Bob had decreed that this last leg of Paula's journey would be attended by close family only.

Everyone at Paula's funeral agreed that down to the last detail, it was a ceremony of which she would have approved. Bob spared no expense for Paula's funeral. He spent thousands on food and drink for the wake, but it was testament to the deep-running feeling for Paula that most of the guests left after about an hour.

It took little time for Kell to calculate the benefits in Tiger's new life and he revealed: 'We have decided she is best off with her sisters in England... It is the most sensible decision we have made in a long time.'

Rhett echoed his father's declaration, saying: 'The only world Tiger knows now is her sisters and I would hate to take her away from what she knows now, which is her sisters and Bob.' He also spoke of a conversation he'd had with Tiger Lily in which he told her that Paula had gone to heaven to be with her father and she asked him: 'Why didn't she take me?'

It seemed, though, that they did not speak for all the Hutchences and the familial rifts were no closer to healing. Patricia and Tina were touring with the publication of their book *Just A Man: The Real Michael Hutchence*. They were booked for interviews on TV and radio, but their timing was unfortunate. No doubt their schedule was fixed well before Paula died, but their bitter memories of her were entirely out of step with the country's sentiment. While Patricia and Tina fended off the uncharitable reception to their UK tour, they were allowed to spend cherished time with Tiger, no longer subject to the rules laid down by Belinda and Paula. But they had understandable qualms about her future. Tina said:

What happens when Tiger Lily gets to eight or nine and starts asking the

*really tough questions: What was my daddy like? Why was he so
depressed? Why did he kill himself? I have spoken with child
psychologists who told me that Tiger Lily needs to bond with at least one
adult and should have one person who's going to be in her life always. I
would love to look after her.*

*I have a great deal of respect for Bob, but I wouldn't want Tiger to go
to him. How are we supposed to keep communication going with her and
bring her up to know the essence of her father?*

Patricia said: 'It's totally bizarre to think that Bob would want his ex-
wife's child by a man he hated. I just don't understand it.'

But while American and Australian courts put more emphasis on blood
relations, this is not necessarily the way the system works in Britain, and
on consulting a solicitor Patricia and Tina realized that the odds were
stacked against them. In December Bob cruised through a private hearing
at the High Court that commuted his temporary custody of Tiger to
permanent residency with the Geldofs. Kell said from his home in Sydney:

*We are thrilled because it is the best thing for Tiger. This little girl has
never been happier. She has got her sisters and has wonderful extended
family connections.*

*After all the drama we have been through, this decision is just a
great feeling of relief. I talk to Tiger every week now and she is
terrifically happy. She is going to have a lovely Christmas at Bob's
place in Kent.*

And she did.

———◆———

In 2001 Paula's estate underwent its final disintegration. The house in St
Luke's Mews was sold as it stood, with her furniture and Michael
memorabilia included. The Hastings house went, too, and Serena
Daroubakhsh finally inherited Jess Yates's house and contents. The detritus
of Paula's life found its way to auction houses across the country: a doll's
house, paintings, a feather boa, a red ball-pen sketch of dancers she did
when she was eleven. China and a straw bag appeared in the window of a
charity shop in Hastings marked, 'Property of the late Paula Yates'. Her
assets were valued at close to £800,000 but there was pitifully little left
once her debts were cleared.

Paula's dying wish was fulfilled when her ashes were buried with the
pillow containing the remains of her lover.

Bob had poured his sorrow into organizing Paula's funeral and the
wake. Then he had the legal wrangle for Tiger's residency order. But now
he was left without distraction. He couldn't forgive himself, and explored
obsessively the permutations of his ex-wife's death. Was there more he

could have done? He missed her terribly, and his self-reproach weighed heavily on family life.

His redemption was an act of will and grace. When he raised his head he saw his children, the children who were central to Paula's life, and he saw that they remained her greatest testament.

Paula was gone but the best of her lived on, in Bob's heart and in the girls. He had lost Paula but he began to realize that he had not lost anything she had given him. Here were all her gifts aggregated in these small beings, growing, bubbling over with her talent. Then he did a double-take: they had been three, now they were four. Bob realized how much he already loved Tiger Lily. She amused him, she amazed him, he could not hold back his pride and praise. He could not stop saying how proud he was of Tiger.

In a recent interview in Australia, Bob said that Tiger Lily was a 'fantastic kid' and that Fifi, Peaches and Pixie 'adore her'.

'She calls me Dad,' he said. 'We were shopping the other day and they played one of my songs, then one of her dad's. She said, "That's you, Dad." Then, "That's my real Dad." Then she said, "My real Dad's a better singer than you, Dad." I just said, "Sheesh... Thanks".'

INDEX

SUPPORT GROUPS AND ORGANIZATIONS

UK

Alcoholics Anonymous
Support groups for practising and recovering alcoholics
www.alcoholics-anonymous.org.uk
0845 769 7555

Al-Anon/Alateen
Support groups for family and friends of alcoholics
www.al-anonuk.org.uk
020 7403 0888

Molly's Alcoholics Anonymous UK Home Page
Fantastic website, featuring advice, a huge contact list, comments from fellow addicts and a live chat area for sufferers. The site has been used for research by various television programmes. Featured in the Teletext and BBC Online addiction pages.
www.aamolly.org.uk

National Association for Children of Alcoholics (NACOA)
A registered charity that helps children growing up in families where one or both parents suffer from alcoholism or similar addictive problems, including drug abuse
0800 289061

Narcotics Anonymous
Support group for practising and recovering drug addicts
www.ukna.org
020 7730 0009

Co-Dependents Anonymous
020 7376 8191

MIND
MIND is the leading mental health charity in England and Wales
www.mind.org.uk
0845 766 0163

National Association of Alcohol and Drug Abuse Counsellors
www.naadac.org.uk

Turning Point
A variety of schemes and centres countrywide
www.turning-point.co.uk

Recommended Treatment Centres following AA principles and offering help, hope and freedom from alcohol and drug dependency

Ark House, Yorkshire	arkhouse@virgin.net
Broadway Lodge, Somerset	www.broadwaylodge.org.uk
Clouds House, Wiltshire	www.clouds.org.uk
Broadreach House, Devon	www.broadreach-house.org.uk
Castle Craig, Peebleshire, Scotland	www.castlecraig.co.uk

Lazarus Centre, Sunderland   post@lazaruscentre.com

PROMIS, Kent   www.promis.co.uk

Hope House, County Mayo   homepage.tinet.ie/~hopehouse

AUSTRALIA

Alcoholics Anonymous
www.alcoholicsanonymous.org.au
National office: (02) 9599 8866

Al-Anon/Alateen
www.al-anon.alateen.org/australia
National office: (03) 9654 8838

Narcotics Anonymous
www.naoz.org.au
National office: (02) 9565 1453

Alcohol & other Drugs Council of Australia
www.adca.org.au
Family Drug Supportline: (02) 9818 6166 / 1300 368 186

Family Drug Help Line
A 24-hour support service in Victoria
www.familydrughelp.sharc.org.au
1300 660 068

Living Solutions Book Shop
Australia's largest recovery bookshop – alcoholism, drug addiction, substance abuse, twelve step recovery material, eating disorders etc
www.livingsolutionsbookshop.com.au

RECOMMENDED BOOKS

Facing Love Addiction	Pia Mellody R.N.
Facing Codependence	Pia Mellody R.N.
Home Coming: Reclaiming and Championing Your Inner Child	John Bradshaw
Bradshaw On: The Family	John Bradshaw
'My Dad Loves Me, My Dad has a Disease'	Claudia Black
Overcoming Addictions: The Spiritual Solution	Deepak Chopra
Codependents Guide to the Twelve Steps	Melody Beattie
Intervention: How To Help Someone Who Doesn't Want Help: A Step-By-Step Guide For Families and Friends Of Chemically Dependent Persons	Vernon E. Johnson

BIBLIOGRAPHY AND SOURCES

BOOKS

Bob Geldof, *Is That It?*, London, Sidgwick & Jackson, 1986

Tina Hutchence and Patricia Glassop, *Just A Man: The Real Michael Hutchence*, London, Sidgwick & Jackson, 2000

Vincent Lovegrove, *Michael Hutchence: A Tragic Rock'N'Roll Story*, London, Independent Publishing Group, 2000

Ed St John, *Kick: The Life and Times of INXS and Michael Hutchence*, London, Mainstream Publishing, 1998

Paula Yates, *Paula Yates: The Autobiography*, London, HarperCollins, 1995

OTHER SOURCES

The following newspapers and magazines were also consulted:

Daily Express	*Daily Mail*
Daily Mirror	*Daily Telegraph*
GQ	*Hello!*
Mail on Sunday	*News of the World*
Observer	*OK!*
Sun	*Sunday Express*
Sunday Telegraph	*Sunday Times*
Sunday Mail (Adelaide)	*Sydney Morning Herald*
Times	

PICTURE ACKNOWLEDGEMENTS

Corbis: pp. 17 (© Lynn Goldsmith / CORBIS), 19 (centre right, © Hulton-Deutsch Collection / CORBIS)

London Features International: p. 3 (top, © Joe Bangay-BA/LFI)

Ken Lennox: p. 19 (top)

Mirrorpix: pp. 2 (below), 4 (main pic), 5 (centre), 13 (both), 14 (below), 19 (centre left), 20 (top & below), 21 (top right)

PA Photos: pp. 4 (top right, below right), 6 (below), 7 (top), 8 (all), 10 (below), 14 (top), 15, 16 (below), 18 (top), 19 (below), 20 (centre), 21 (top left & below), 22

Redferns Music Picture Library: p. 18 (centre, © Mike Cameron / Redferns)

RetnaUK: pp. 3 (centre, © Tim Bauer), 9 & 10 top (© Michael Putland), 18 (below, © Adrian Boot), 23 (© Mark Henderson)

Rex Features: pp. 2 (top & centre), 3 (below), 5 (below left & right), 6 (main pic), 7 (below), 11 (both), 12 (both), 14 (centre), 16 (top & centre), 24

Topham Picturepoint: p. 1

Picture p. 5 (top) reproduced by kind permission of David Crombie.